Mental Illness and the Economy

Mental Illness and the Economy

M. Harvey Brenner

Harvard University Press   Cambridge, Massachusetts   1973

Library of Congress Catalog Card Number 73–77471

SBN 674–56875–3

Printed in the United States of America

To my mother and the memory of my father

Foreword

The history of science is marked by the perception of relations that exist between two or more phenomena heretofore not recognized as interdependent. When, by the use of methods trusted by scientists, such a relation is perceived and demonstrated to exist under specified conditions, we label the process a "discovery." By these criteria, Harvey Brenner has made a discovery that is likely to be remembered as a milestone in the development of our knowledge regarding the functioning of the economy and the use of mental hospitals during a century and a quarter in New York State.

I admit that I am biased in favor of this research. Dr. Brenner was a doctoral student of mine, and he is now a colleague and friend. However, friendship notwithstanding, I believe that his statistical procedures for measuring the impact of changes in the economy on particular types of sociobiographical groups of persons who were suffering from specified mental disorders are ingenious. His analytical procedures may be difficult to comprehend except by the more statistically sophisticated reader, but they are described carefully and the profuse illustrations of his conclusions with line graphs will be more convincing to many readers than the tables of correlations and explanatory equations.

Dr. Brenner has not been content merely to discover and measure the interrelations between changes in the economy and the responses to them of mentally ill people. He takes the next important step by attempting to explain these relations. Briefly, his analytical explanations of specific findings are derived from social systems theory; the economy, the family, the state, mental institutions, behavior patterns, and so on are all integral parts of the social system. Thus, from a theoretical viewpoint the subject matter of this book is the social system. A social system is made by human beings, and a social system makes human beings. A social system has a culture that is learned, shared, and transmitted from generation to generation by its members. The social system defines how its members are expected to act. Behavior that is different from the norm of definable parts of the social system, such as the family, is viewed as "deviant." Behavior that is a departure from the expectations of the norms of the social groups in which it occurs gives rise to strain in the individual and to stress in the group. The stress-strain relation may be produced by changes in the conditions under which people in a given social system live. In the social system prevailing in New York State during the nineteenth and twentieth centuries, an important factor in the production of stresses in the society and strains in individuals and social groups, particularly in the family, was change in the economy. The particular interest of Dr. Brenner in this study was to trace the responses of people to changes in the economy as measured against their use of mental hospitals. Simultaneously, he has systematically presented an explanation of a particular relation.

The discovery of a relation between changes in the economy and a specified aggregate's response to them, combined with the theoretical explanation, merits careful study. The strong inverse correlations between changes in the economy and the use of mental hospitals found in New York State should be tested in other states and countries, preferably in Western Europe. The theoretical explanations Dr. Brenner presents are likely to be more controversial. They need to be examined carefully. I look for a lively discussion of this study in the literature during future years. The overall findings of this study are a contribution to sociological and psychiatric knowledge.

August B. Hollingshead

Preface

This study describes the inverse relation between the state of the economy and mental illness that is brought to a level of social visibility. The factual basis for the relation involves fluctuations in mental hospitalization levels and rates and fluctuations in the employment index in New York State. Economic instability is found to be one of the most pervasive and continuous sources of stress in industrialized society.

Exploring the general relation further, three phenomena are observed. First, it is clear that instabilities in the national economy have been the single most important source of fluctuation in mental-hospital admissions or admission rates. Second, this relation is so consistent for certain segments of the society that virtually no major factor other than economic instability appears to influence variation in their mental hospitalization rates. Third, the relation has been basically stable for at least 127 years and there is considerable evidence that it has had greater impact in the last two decades.

Since the basic inverse relation between economic change and mental-hospital admission rates has been relatively stable since pre-Civil War times, it has not been measurably affected by any of the major changes in psychiatric practice or in the society as a whole. The important changes in conceptions of mental disorder, the use of tranquilizing drugs, and the organization of community-based treatment, however, may have resulted in a greater proportion of the population being brought to treatment, under conditions of economic stress, since the mid-1950's.

The findings place many of the problems of mental illness clearly within the area of social policy. Decisions affecting the economy at the national, regional, or state levels have profound implications for the management of severe mental disorder. Decisions which lead toward stabilizing economic activity and reducing unemployment tend to stabilize the society and effect a substantive control on the severity of mental disorder. Economic decisions or factors which increase instability and unemployment sharply increase the level and rate of mental hospitalization.

Again, from a practical standpoint, the basic findings can be related to an approach to mental health which emphasizes prevention, or at least control of the extent of mental disorder. This study identifies demographically the single largest population which is at risk for intensive psychiatric treatment. It is the population whose way of life is threatened by temporary or chronic economic instability or insecurity. It is this population, whether middle class or impoverished, well or poorly educated, of majority or minority ethnic background, that is most in need of preventive mental health services.

The major theoretical implication is that, despite our philosophic orientation, the destiny of the individual is to a great extent subject to large-scale changes in the social and economic structure that are in no way under his control. This perspective must eventually affect our understanding of individuality and personal freedom, even in modern times.

After the findings presented in this book were prepared for publication, the data were further updated and, in the most recent analysis, run to 1971. The results show that the basic inverse relation prevails through 1971. Similarly, analysis of state mental-hospital admission rates for the United States as a whole during 1922–1968, in ten-year age groups, and by sex, has recently been completed. The findings, which will be examined in detail in future publications, replicate those for New York State in terms of the inverse relation with economic fluctuations.

The individual chapters of this book are very different in their respective emphases on theoretical orientation, methods of investigation, substantive findings, explanations of patterns of findings in light of previous research and theory, practical implications, and interpretations of causal mechanisms.

Chapters 1 and 2 are introductions to the theoretical and analytical approaches taken in this study. "The Problem and Its Setting" integrates several theoretical perspectives in sociology, psychiatry, and economics. "Methodological Issues and Strategies" discusses the logic of analysis in light of previous attempts, both successful and unsuccessful, to measure the basic relation.

Chapters 3 through 6, respectively, "Mental Illness and the Economy," "Long Term Trends and the Basic Relation," "Stability of the Basic Relation," and "Impact of Economic Change on Mental-Hospital Admissions," present the general statistical foundations of the inverse relation between economic change and mental hospitalization. This relation is seen to be stable for at least 127 years in New York State, which has had the largest population of any state until 1964, and continues to have the largest resident mental-hospital population—more than twice as large as that for Pennsylvania, the second-ranked state in mental patient population.

The relation is replicated for private hospital and emergency admissions, for immigrant patients from each of fifty-one different countries, for the parents of patients originating in fifty-one different countries, for patients of thirty-five different ethnic groups, and for patients admitted to mental hospitals from each of sixty-one different counties. Each of these sets of replications is, in turn, repeated for each sex.

Chapters 7, "Social Stress and the Extent of Economic Loss," and 8, "Economic Change and Role Performance," are attempts to explain the patterns of mental hospitalization of different sociodemographic groups in terms of the probable reactions of each group to fluctuations in the national economy. The central explanatory model is that persons who lose the most in terms of economic and social status during recessions react most consistently to economic downturns with increased mental hospitalization. In this way an effort is made to predict or explain the patterns of mental hospitalization, over time, of groups of persons defined by level of education, ethnic background, subnormal versus normal intellectual ability, age, sex, marital status, and the presence or absence of a history of mental hospitalization.

Chapter 9, "Interpretations of the General Relation," examines the major alternatives to the hypothesis that severe mental disorder actually increases during even slight economic recessions. These alternative hypotheses, involving community intolerance of mental disorders, purely financial considerations, and external phenomena such as wars, are not found, in and of themselves, to explain the basic data of this study.

Chapters 10, "Economic Change and the Structure of Psychiatric Care," and 11, "Conclusions and Implications," deal with the pragmatic and theoretical implications of the findings. It is evident that the pressure of hospital admissions reacting to economic instability is such that the entire organization of psychiatric care experiences continuous waves of change—with important consequences to the mentally ill patient and the community to which he eventually returns. These findings raise questions about the utility of therapies that do not take into account disturbances in the patients' social environment which may have made treatment necessary.

The concluding discussions deal with the implications of the basic findings for the understanding of different types of psychopathology in the areas of crimes of violence, psychosomatic disorders, and specified types of political turbulence. The inverse relation between economic change and an indicator of mental illness is examined as the probable underpinning of the most consistent finding in studies of the distribution of mental disorder in society—namely, its inverse relation to socioeconomic status.

Finally, the question of why the basic findings of this study are difficult to comprehend from a clinical viewpoint is examined. It is argued that a fundamental philosophical flaw has traditionally encumbered the purely individual approach to psychopathology. This erroneous conception has made it all but impossible for many professionals and large segments of the general population to comprehend the influence of sociocultural phenomena on the behavior of individuals.

The logic of arrangement of the book may be most easily followed by a reading of the chapters in distinct groupings: Chapter 1 (theory), Chapters 2–6 (methods, basic findings, replications), Chapters 7 and 8 (explanations of varying behavioral patterns), and Chapters 9–11 (causal interpretations, pragmatic and theoretical implications).

Perhaps the most difficult problem of interpretation in this study revolves around the significance of mental hospitalization trends, as possible indicators of the incidence of mental disorder in the population. There is a long tradition of the use of trends in first admission rates at least to indicate the probable incidence of psychiatric symptoms.[1] While such inferences from trend data have not been criticized in the scholarly literature, concern has developed over the use of hospitalization rates, *at specific points in time,* to indicate the prevalence rate of mental disorder in a population. It has become quite apparent from surveys of non-institutionalized populations that a substantial number of severely disturbed persons are not in any contact with mental health facilities. The question has therefore arisen as to whether hospitalization of the mentally ill is not so much a question of the actual occurrence of illness as of social intolerance.

The data of this study do not support the position that community intolerance of mental illness is the predominant explanation of the *inverse relation* between economic change and mental hospitalization. Those individuals who would theoretically be most subject to intolerance under conditions of great social stress—for example, the aged (especially senile) and persons with a history of hospitalized mental disorder—are in fact the least likely to be hospitalized during an economic recession.

The *exclusive* use of an intolerance argument based on family intolerance also fails on logical grounds. Such an intolerance argument would assume that severe mental disorder is as frequent during economic upswings as during

1. Two of the best known studies in this tradition are Herbert Goldhamer and Andrew W. Marshall, *Psychosis and Civilization* (Glencoe, Ill.: The Free Press, 1949) and Thomas F. Pugh and Brian MacMahon, *Epidemiologic Findings in United States Mental Hospital Data* (Boston: Little, Brown, 1962).

downturns. Further, one would assume that the severely mentally ill are unable to function in ordinary work life and, therefore (accepting both assumptions), the mentally ill, including household heads, would lose their jobs as frequently in prosperous periods as in recessions. But if this were the case, then to the families of the severely mentally ill, *economic* stress (through loss of job or income) should not be specifically related to economic recessions and intolerance of the severely mentally ill should be irrelevant to fluctuations in the national economy. The intolerance argument, by itself, would therefore lead to the incorrect conclusion that hospitalization of the severely mentally ill is unrelated to the behavior of the economy.

From still another point of view, it is difficult to imagine that the same severe stress which would theoretically cause emotional withdrawal or attack directed against the mentally ill would not cause the same stress-reaction in the mentally ill themselves. However, the fact that community intolerance of mental disorder is not the primary factor behind the central finding of this study does not mean that it is altogether inoperative. Intolerance of mental disorder is perhaps present to some degree in all mental hospitalization and may indeed precipitate additional psychiatric symptoms during periods of economic stress.

Problems of interpretation are also encountered in any attempt to analyze trends in hospitalization rates in specific diagnostic categories of mental disorder. This is particularly true of the finer categories of functional psychosis and psychoneurosis for which the difficulty in establishing diagnostic reliability is well-documented. At the same time, the central hypothesis of this study called for a distinction of the functional psychoses from other disorders, since functional psychotic reactions are traditionally thought to respond to proximal stresses in the social environment. In addition, at several points in the study it was necessary to exclude the elderly from the remainder of the population when categories of admission were not subdivided by age, but by major groups of diagnoses that roughly correspond to age levels.

As a result, in addition to observing all available subpopulations admitted to hospitals without reference to diagnosis, whenever possible each subpopulation was examined in terms of the distinction between all disorders and (the sum of) the functional psychoses. Specific diagnostic categories are used infrequently and then to show the overall applicability of the central hypothesis.

Various aspects of the statistical relations themselves are measured by techniques drawn from very different disciplines, including econometrics, geophysics, and epidemiology. Each of the techniques reveals a different aspect of the overall relation. Perhaps more important is that they are all consistent in replicating the basic inverse relation. It should be pointed out, however, that the techniques shown here by no means exhaust even the well-accepted methods of ascertaining relations among time-series. Additional methods by which the central finding of this study has been replicated include use of the business-cycle reference-date program of the National Bureau of Economic Research,[2] moving-average calculations for estimation and removal of trends,[3] and spectral analysis.[4]

In general, two types of inverse relation are observed, and are arbitrarily designated as *relatively stable* and *relatively unstable*. Relatively stable inverse relations, involving approximately 60 percent of mental-hospital admissions, apply to economic fluctuations of all sizes measured in this study, that is, of at least 1–11 years' duration. Relatively unstable inverse relations are fundamentally inverse as judged by reactions to "short" (1–4 year) economic fluctuations, but these short-term inverse relations increase in their impact during longer (7–11 year) economic *upswings*. Thus, the overall relation for the relatively unstable inverse groups often appear to be positive, since the larger economic movements dominate the statistical picture. Some 25 percent of the population of admissions are subject to the unstable inverse relation which is particularly prominent for a large minority of women, ethnic groups of relatively low socioeconomic status, and readmissions. (For these specific groups compare, for example, the multiple correlations presented in Chapters 5, 7, and 8 with those in Appendix II, and with the Fourier analyses).

Unequivocally positive correlations with economic changes are found for approximately 5–7 percent of admissions. These positive correlations apply largely to admissions of elderly, particularly senile, patients and to female admissions with involutional psychosis. A final 6–8 percent of admissions show no significant relation to economic fluctuations.

The most traditional of the graphic analyses, based on estimation and removal of secular trends, was originally used in working with the data extending from 1914 to 1960 (Figs. 16–26). The most highly accurate of the graphic analyses, based on Fourier transformations, was particularly important in examining the effects of the shorter and milder economic fluctuations of the 1950's and 1960's. For this reason, Fourier transformations are used in the graphic descriptions of the 1915–1967 data (Figs. 1–3, 11–15).

The reader will note the use of frequencies of admissions, in addition to admission rates, as the basic data to be explained. Traditionally, the conversion

2. Arthur F. Burns and Wesley C. Mitchell, *Measuring Business Cycles* (New York: National Bureau of Economic Research, 1946).
3. Gerhard Tintner, *Econometrics* (New York: Wiley, 1952), pp. 198–208.
4. Gwilym M. Jenkins and Donald G. Watts, *Spectral Analysis and Its Applications* (San Francisco: Holden Day, 1968).

into rate per unit of population is used in order to transform morbidity, mortality, or treatment data to a form that allows comparisons among different-sized populations. In this study, however, for many categories of data it was not possible to obtain corresponding demographic data on the population base.

In addition, the major purpose in this study, of dividing admissions by the appropriate population base, was to control for the effects of population-base changes of *less than ten years duration* which might affect mental-hospital admissions. This purpose could hardly be realized since no information is available for each of the nine years between census estimates. Our methodology called, in any event, for subtracting the secular trends in both the employment and mental hospitalization data in order to (1) gauge the effects of 1–10 year economic changes on similarly sized fluctuations in admissions, and (2) control for the long-term effects of such factors as changes in the labor force composition, construction of mental hospitals, and public attitudes toward hospitalization of the mentally ill. Thus, even where rate data were available we still needed to detrend in order to remove all secular influences on admissions.

For these reasons, the data transformations, correlations, and graphic analyses of the 1914–1960 data were initially based largely on levels of admission (Chapters 5–8). (The major exceptions are admission rates by county, which were originally in rate form). Subsequent to analysis of the 1914–1960 data, however, a research contract with the National Institute of Mental Health, Division of Epidemiology, provided support for tests of alternative methods of control for long-term trends, several of which included the use of rate-based admissions levels. The reader will therefore find that for the data updated to 1967 (that is, 1914–1967), only admission rates were used (Chapters 3, 4). This subsequent analysis of admission rates was confined to categories of admission for which the population base is readily found in census materials, that is, by sex, age, marital status, and by specific groupings of ethnicity, country of birth, and level of education.

The correlations or graphs representing the relation between economic fluctuations and mental hospitalization are not substantially different whether based on admissions or admission rates, because secular trends have been removed in both instances. (Compare corresponding categories in Figs. 21, 23, 24, and 26 with those in Figs. 7–10, where the data do not contain measurable trends.) While the rate data give an indication of the effects of economic stress on the aggregate of the population, large-scale change in the sheer volume of admissions emphasize these effects on the individuals who, comprising that aggregate, are subject to the consequences of severe mental disorder.

I thank Professors Francis Anscombe, Lester Telser, and Marc Nerlove for their assistance with the statistical and econometric analyses, and Bernard Bergen and Kai Erikson for criticisms of the theoretical interpretations. The manuscript was read by Professors Rashi Fein, Paul Lemkau, Stephen Fleck, Marc Fried, and Gerald Grob. I am very grateful for their valuable suggestions.

Abbott Weinstein and Albert Maiwald of the New York State Department of Mental Hygiene were most helpful in making available statistics on admissions to New York State mental hospitals for the last ten years. The National Academy of Sciences and the Walter Reed Army Institute of Research, and the publisher of *Mental Hygiene,* graciously permitted liberal quotation from articles by (respectively) J. S. Tyhurst, and P. O. Komora and M. A. Clark. Valuable assistance was given by William Leng in computer programming, and by Beatrice Latham and Barbara Bancroft, who were research assistants with the project.

This study was supported in part by National Institute of Mental Health, Division of Epidemiology, Contract PH 43–68–996; U.S. Public Health Service General Research Support Grant PHS RR 05443–11, Yale University Department of Epidemiology and Public Health; and U.S.P.H.S. Grant 5 R01 HS 00090, Operations Research in the Health Services, The Johns Hopkins University.

M. Harvey Brenner

Baltimore, Maryland
April 1973

Contents

Figures

Tables

Mental Illness and the Economy

1 The Problem and Its Setting

Under what historical conditions does society become "unglued," and what society-wide factors (if any) are responsible for basic instabilities in social relations? This general subject has long been a fertile ground for social scientists and historians. Most frequently, the objectives of their research included massive cultural, political, and economic changes; occasionally, disruptions in family life, criminal behavior, and suicide were examined.[1] Such studies have had some success at analyzing disruptions in behavioral patterns in terms of fundamental social change.

Disruptive aspects of society have been traced (within this broad framework) to breakdowns in, or incongruities among, various components of the social structure, including major institutions, values and beliefs, technology, economic structure, and population. The causal factors were frequently regarded as involving the lack of (available) social resources for dealing with such events appropriately. This type of analysis focused on social disruption which had, in the thoughts of the researchers, a "rational" basis. Disruptive political, cultural, or even "pathological" events such as suicide or homicide were thought to be comprehensible to observers of the historical process as a consequence of the societal changes that preceded them.

The subject matter of this book, by contrast, concerns that traditionally most incomprehensible and apparently irrational of human phenomena, the extent to which members of a society are perceived to be, and dealt with as, mentally ill. Are there types of social change which would increase the likelihood that mental illness would be more or less evident in society? Although a good deal of theoretical speculation has been advanced[2] and a number of empirical analyses have been undertaken, very little in the way of systematic evidence has been brought to bear on this question.[3]

The present study focuses on the appearance of mental illness because, as a social label, the concept of mental illness epitomizes social disintegration. A person who is perceived to be mentally ill is not only the subject of disrupted relations, but is also regarded as being unapproachable by appeals to rationality. It might therefore seem difficult, if not illogical, to proceed with an analysis of relatively commonplace changes in society that might lead to the appearance of irrational behavior.

The disruptive element in labeling a person mentally ill reaches its most dramatic and conclusive form in mental hospitalization. This signifies not only a breakdown in the network of communication between the individual and his society, but also a breakdown in social ties and relations and a physical segregation of the individual, so that his role in society consists almost entirely of adjustment to an institution that is cut off from the ordinary functions of society.

Following this perspective, the general question becomes whether social change influences either societal intolerance of mental disorder or the incidence of mental disorder. To increase the incisiveness of the investigation, concentration is on a major component, as well as a major source, of social change, namely, economic change. Indeed, economic change appears to be the classically cited source of social development and disorganization. Economic change is also continuous through time, and it is more dramatic and obvious than many other types of continuous social and cultural change. Social and political historians, however, have traditionally described cultural change in terms of major discrete events. This study is an attempt, by contrast, to understand the continuous impact of one type of social change on mental hospitalization. Under what economic conditions has mental hospitalization been more or less frequent? Put another way, have economic changes had a continuous and significant impact on the extent of mental hospitalization in the population?

There is reason to believe that changes in the economy have the most pervasive impact on the life of a society and its individual members. The varieties of economic change can be described from three perspectives: (1) duration, (2) economic characteristics of the aggregate population involved, and (3) size of the aggregate population involved. The econometrician's view of economic change has traditionally included three components: (1) "long-term" or secular trends, (2) cyclical changes (that is, aggregate fluctuations in parts of the economy that exhibit some regularity and are imposed upon the long-term trends), and (3) seasonal changes.

Finally, independent of continuous economic and social changes are those changes in the society which are so dramatic that they are thought of as unique. Examples of such changes are economic panics (which have occurred in the stock market), riots, wars, the development of social movements, and the destruction of economic and social organizations. Although these events may be pictured as discrete in historical perspective, they may also be understood in terms of the longer-term causes of their relations to continuous changes in the social system.

Of fundamental importance to the perspective of this study is the fact that any societal change, be it cultural (involving norms, values, or beliefs) or social structural (involving social positions and institutions), results in changes in the economic system. The economic system consists of the organization of labor in society, the relation of labor to technology and land, and exchange of goods and services. The economic system in any society is the instrument by which (at least) the fundamentals of life are provided and in which the technology of the society is applied in order to increase the productivity and efficiency of labor.

The economy is, in its early evolutionary phases, the means of survival of the species whereby adaptation to the nonhuman environment is achieved. In later stages of the evolution of human culture, the economy becomes the instrument whereby individuals can be recruited and recompensed in the service of social ideals, advancing knowledge, literature, and the arts. Thus, regardless of the objectives of the society—be they political, literary, scientific, theological, or artistic—the economy is the fundamental means by which these enterprises will be supported. Depending on the types of endeavors a society is interested in, its major institutions will be organized and provided, accordingly, with the resources available to it.

A society's institutions are its largest-scale organizational components within which definite social objectives are accomplished. Our definition of institutions includes such "systems" as the legal system, the health-care system, the religious system, the military system, the educational system, and the communications system. In order to accomplish their various tasks, social institutions make use of the talents of members of the society by recruiting them into organizations of various sizes, such as factories, schools, armies, courts, hospitals, and so on. Each institution, and each functioning social unit within each institution, has, in a sense, a sociological life of its own. It is a small society which, to some degree, approximates the large-scale social system in terms of the types of changes it can undergo. The more complex the organization, the more (in total structure) it resembles the entire society.

An example of an institution that attempts to fill a great variety of human needs with little formal internal organization of units is the family. It is through such social institutions and groupings that the individual functions as a social being—indeed, as a human being. The individual derives from them *whatever* the society is able to provide him, which in most modern societies involves nearly all of the socially valued aspects of life.

This point sets the stage for understanding the relation between the individual and the economic system. What does the individual derive as a result of his participation in the institutional life of the society? He derives, theoretically, a certain measure of social remuneration in terms of economic wealth, prestige, and authority that are attached to his social position.[4] Thus, the rank of a person's social position, as well as his ability to perform in that position, will be largely responsible for the degree to which he enjoys economic goods and services, authority, and prestige.

However, the ability of an individual to obtain a specific position, and to perform effectively in that position, is to a large extent determined by the overall economic performance of the specific industry, occupation, organization, and geographic location in which he is employed. The individual is therefore largely dependent on the behavior of an economic system over which he, as an individual, probably has little (if any) control. Rather, it is through the controlling instrument of the economy that the vast majority of social *and* individual objectives are achieved. Even for the individual living in an economy with a rudimentary division of labor, social recognition, power, or even physical sustenance must be achieved within the confines of the economic system.

Economic Change, Social Mobility, and Individual Role Performance

Social mobility occurs within organizations where individuals increase their social status as a result of rising responsibility, or of large-scale economic change in which a specific variety of economic organization (industry or institution) becomes more important in the society as a whole. (This does not exclude the possibility that noneconomic groups of which the individual may be a member, such as ethnic groups or age groups, may also, as a result of social changes, experience upward or downward mobility.)

Social mobility is, to a very large extent, dependent upon the activity of the economic system as a whole. Thus, during a period in which the job market expands and more highly skilled and better-educated workers are in demand, the opportunity for upward mobility within the economic system becomes available to larger numbers of persons. Such periods of short-term or long-term economic growth provide a major avenue of upward mobility for a large portion of the society. The principal initiating factor is structural change in the economic system as a whole.

Structural change involves organic growth in a particular sector of the economy. Growth in one sector frequently has implications for growth in others. As a consequence of continuous economic growth, the majority of individuals in any society gain rather than lose in terms of social status. This is not to say that during a period of economic growth there are no losers; since the economy grows at an uneven pace, some industries and sectors of it will grow more rapidly than others. It is entirely possible that a large number of persons whose economic position remains stagnant will suffer from both relative and absolute decrease in social valuation. The "normal" situation of the modern economy is that of continuous long-term growth.[5] The minority of the society whose economic positions remain stagnant are therefore a major source of downward mobility in a society whose economy continues to grow.

However, superimposed on the long-term trend of growth are "cyclical" economic changes and major social changes that have a short-term (or middle-range) effect upon change in the economic system. Such short-term economic changes characterize uneven growth. Relatively short-term economic slumps, often referred to as recessions or depressions, are a second major source of downward mobility. Downward mobility is, therefore, to a great extent, a question not of large-scale but of short- or intermediate-term economic downturns on the occupational, industrial, national, or even international level. A large-scale impact on social mobility may originate within the economic system itself, as a result of economic disequilibria, or may follow more pervasive changes in the value system. Changes in the value system create new tastes, motivations, desires, modes of achievement, or ideals.

The literature on causes of short- or intermediate-term changes in the economy is quite extensive in the disciplines of both economics and sociology. There appear to be at least four themes that dominate the explanations offered: (1) structural changes in the economy,[6] (2) disequilibria between the economic system and the social structure,[7] (3) political conflicts between groups within the social structure,[8] and (4) fluctuations in economic activity which represent relative stagnation within the more general trend of economic growth.[9]

Such theories of economic and social structural change are quite different from evolutionary theories of economic and social change. The evolutionary theories are based on such long-term phenomena as urbanization, the development of science and technology, the development of complex organizations, the development or transformation of certain ideological themes, and the structure of population growth or decline.

Apart from the fact that there are many different groups of causes of economic change, there are also many different approaches to measuring the extent of economic change. Theoretically, a large and varied number of measures of economic change should be, and empirically usually are, highly intercorrelated. Examples of such measures of economic activity might include man-hours involved in production, number of persons employed or unemployed, rates of net profit or loss, national product, personal income, interest rates, and levels of utilization of material resources or facilities. As a general rule, economic studies have shown that such measures of economic activity rise and fall together, at least in terms of the moderate-sized economic changes referred to as business cycles.[10]

In this particular study, the major focus is the impact of short-term economic fluctuation on mental hospitalization. It was necessary, therefore, to select an indicator of economic change, or, more precisely, of the level of economic activity, that is fairly consistently representative of the short-term and middle-range expansion and contraction of the total economy. Studies by the National Bureau of Economic Research on indicators of business-cycle fluctuations have shown that rates of employment and unemployment are consistently among the most highly representative indicators of such general economic fluctuations.[11] This is one reason for our interest in employment as a major economic indicator. (A second reason is that *unemployment*, as an economic indicator, has been subject to several changes in definition, and was therefore judged to be less useful than employment in a study that covered more than half a century.)

Another reason for focusing on factors related to employment is that the number of available jobs provides a direct indication of the degree to which family breadwinners will be able to fulfill their roles. An indicator such as personal income, by contrast, is not as secure a (negative) measure of stress because when aggregate income falls that of any one individual or family may fall only a little in relation to the general average. In addition, the extent of employment itself gives prima facie evidence of the well-being of the economy and of the society.

Although productivity and income may fall or prices may rise, if an individual is employed he can at least be remunerated by way of some share of the resources available in his society. The degree to which the human resources of society are not employed perhaps reflects more than any other economic indicator a disequilibrium or breakdown in the relation between members of the society and the economic system.

This work concerns the impact of economic change on social disintegration; we use the term disintegration, or lack of cohesion, as synonymous with the extent of social "deviance." Deviance, in turn, signifies the degree to which individuals are unable or unwilling to conform to the normative (or usual) patterns of behavior that are expected of people playing particular roles in the society. Specifically, it is the deviance that results in mental hospitalization, as well as the concomitant breakdown of the individual's own microsociety, which is particularly representative of social disintegration. In a general sense, then, the initiating research position of this study is that lack of integration of the material and human resources of the economy will have a major adverse impact on the extent of social integration of the small groups and organizations that form a person's immediate link to his society.

Studies involving the relation between economic change and deviant behavior have been of two general types. The most prevalent type includes a group of studies on upward and downward mobility in relation to deviant behavior.[12] These studies focus on the social isolation that social mobility appears to engender for many individuals. The detachment of the individual from previous role arrangements is thought to lead to a situation of partial anomie in which the individual is, to some degree, unfamiliar with the behavior other persons will expect of him. Under these conditions, his actions will frequently not even approximate the expectations others have of him since he is a novice at his new role.[13]

In the situation of downward mobility, the individual not only loses social contacts but also must adjust to a condition in which his social status falls, and the amount of material and emotional sustenance that he can derive from the society will thereby decrease. In the situation of upward mobility, the individual must frequently break ties with his old associates—including, perhaps his family—in order to become accepted in a new social circle. In addition, upward mobility often implies an increase in responsibility, if not in actual work load. The pressure of adjusting to an economic role of higher status may result in both anomie and added life stress.

However, there is an enormous difference between moving into a situation that is clearly of greater desirability and moving into one in which the person and his family are devalued by friends and other role associates. The difference between upward and downward mobility is felt to be so extreme that the present study emphasizes the crisis character of the economic downturn, rather than of economic change in either direction. It argues that as economic activity decreases and the economy contracts (rather than expands), *overall* social stress increases and therefore mental hospitalization should increase.

Economic Changes and Mental Illness

A major theoretical question of this research is how important social factors are relatively in the precipitation of mental illness itself. One way to test the idea that mental illness is probably a response to conditions in the social environment is to examine admissions to treatment facilities in a defined population over a specified period of time and link the treatment data to known conditions existing in the economic structure of society during the same period.

The research hypothesis of this study proposes that *a significant relation exists between economic conditions and admissions to treatment agencies.* Ideally, of course, we should use an indicator of mental status in the population that would include all mentally ill persons, whether or not they are in treatment. Practically, this is impossible since no such data exist. In fact, we must confine our indicator of mental status to admissions to licensed public and private mental hospitals.

In viewing the rate of admissions to mental hospitals as an indicator of the emergence of mental illness in the general population, *over time*, we are dealing with the problem of precipitation; we are considering only the latest, or most immediate, in a series of developmental factors that may be significant in the appearance of mental illness.

In this study, we were able to hold "predisposing" factors constant, and ask simply *when* mental illness appears in the population. A predisposing factor is understood in this discussion as any event in the development of an organism that interferes with the most efficient adaptation to a given environmental stress factor (or precipitating factor) that occurs later in the life of that organism. The precipitating factor is then an event—a stress-producing situation—to which the organism maladapts (or adapts inefficiently) because of the earlier weakness or adaptive handicap engendered by the predisposing factor or set of factors. The appearance of mental illness is seen as *the* maladaptive response to the precipitating stress situation. Thus, regardless of the number and combination of factors that may predispose a person toward mental illness, the question here is why it appears *when* it does.

Our general hypothesis, finally, allows for the following possible sequences in the relation of social stress to the development of mental illness: (1) initial evidence of mental illness in the life history, (2) the flare-up of symptoms of a previously dormant mental illness, (3) the reactivation of symptoms of an illness that appears in cycles, (4) an increase or accentuation of symptoms of a continuous illness, and (5) the superimposition of a psychotic, neurotic, or behavioral reaction upon a previously established mental disorder (thus, for example, if psychosis is present "in" paresis, the psychosis may well be a reaction to additional social stresses).

Now, in addition to the most general problem of the effects of social stresses on the development of mental illness, we are also specifically interested in the operation of *economic* change on the personality. In fact, it is suggested that a substantial fraction of *all* stress factors that precipitate mental illness in American society at present is economic in origin.

Thus, for example, in a general population survey of a sample of 2460 persons, it was found that 29 percent, 27 percent, and 41 percent of the population respectively found "economic and material" reasons among the two most important sources of "happiness," "unhappiness," and "worries." In addition, 14 percent, 11 percent, and 9 percent respectively found their jobs to be among the two most important sources of such feelings.[14]

One method by which downward economic changes bring stress is via unhappiness or worries stemming directly from economic or material loss or job concerns. A second method involves the social implications of a decrease in economic status. Some of these implications can be inferred from the suggestion offered by the authors of the Midtown Manhattan Study in explanation of the inverse relation between socioeconomic status and the prevalence of mental disorder:

In the high SES [socioeconomic status], the widowed mother at least has money in the bank. Children of low intelligence or diligence can be expelled from a school or college, yet parents with financial means can assure their placement in another institution of learning. Physical or mental ailments are less likely to impair the child's general functioning. These conditions are not only more easily recognized by parents who have a better education, but there is a positive attitude toward medical services, more money to pay for the best of such services, and more time available to see that the children get such services when the mother does not work. The high SES person has more freedom to move from jobs which are unsatisfying. Thus, the "hammer blows" that might originally be as damaging to mental health as they seem to be in the low SES could be cushioned by the generally favorable circumstances in which the high SES people find themselves.[15]

The combined influence of stresses stemming from both direct and indirect effects of decreased economic status may be largely responsible for one of the most prominent findings[16] in psychiatric epidemiology, namely, the inverse relation between socioeconomic status and the incidence of treated mental disorder.[17]

Two models of the possible relation between economic change and changes in the rate of appearance of mental illness may be distinguished. The first model treats the economic change as the (or at least one) proximal precipitating factor in the emergence of mental illness. In the second model, the economic change may be far from the proximal factor in the apparent development of mental illness. In this model of economic change as precipitant, it may initiate a fairly lengthy sequence of (say) family, peer-relation, and physical-health problems which may, in turn, snowball and, either singly or as a group, precipitate the visible manifestations of mental illness. Put somewhat differently, in this model the economic change provides a sufficiently stressful climate that any substantial additional stress is critical for the development of mental illness.

Thus, regardless of the temporal proximity of the economic change to the "last" factor in the developmental chain leading to the appearance of mental illness, the theoretical argument here remains that economic change is related to the appearance of mental illness. It is clear, however, that unless the most significant stressful effects of economic change occur within a relatively short period before the appearance of mental illness, it would be quite difficult to observe and chart the extent of changes in mental-hospital admission levels that were related to economic changes.

The question of precipitation, which is the focus of this study, has only recently been treated as something more than trivial in the social sciences and psychiatry. Psychoanalytic developmental theories, as well as biogenetic theories of personality, have tended to treat precipitating stimuli as relatively incidental to personality change. The picture usually presented is that the fundamental structure of the personality either (1) is formed early in life and changes little in response to "adult" problems,[18] (2) is genetically programed so that, regardless of the presence or absence of specific stresses, at some point in the individual's life he will simply "react,"[19] or (3) is genetically such that the individual is particularly vulnerable to specific stress situations. The picture, then, is that of the presence of stressful social events, which are relatively trivial in comparison with inherent weaknesses that force the individual to respond to these events in aberrant ways.

The sociological approach has been only a little more flexible, arguing that, at least in industrialized societies, personality may adapt to the requirements of certain adult roles. Even here, however, the evidence is unclear, and there is some argument as to whether the classic "bureaucratic personality," for example, is not so much formed by the bureaucracy as recruited for its ranks.[20] By contrast, the hypothesis entertained in this investigation is that it is important to identify the specific events that engender stress. The focus is on the chain of social stresses that are specifically brought about by economic change.

Even more fundamentally, however, the position taken in this research is that the specific precipitants are at least as important as predisposing factors. Regardless of how many predisposing factors are present in an individual personality or group structure, without the specific stress that will disorganize individual role performance or group structure the disorganization may not occur at all. Our interest is in understanding whether economic change is a major factor in mental hospitalization, and if so for whom. These two questions are logically interrelated; for example, the fact that there are specific groups for whom the relation does not occur will influence our explanation of the general relation.

To recapitulate, the fundamental hypothesis of the present study is that *mental hospitalization will increase during economic downturns and decrease during upturns.* This hypothesis assumes that social disorganization, reflected in turn in symptoms and intolerance of deviance, will result from the inability of individuals to perform socially designated roles. Inability to fulfill one's social role frequently results from downward shifts in economic activity, during which more people are losing than are gaining income, prestige, and power. The economy provides the fundamental means whereby the individual fulfills the majority of his aspirations, as well as the more immediate social obligations he faces. His inability to maintain his usual or intended life style and social position indicates that he is unable to meet the requirements of other people who form the network of his social relations, responsibilities, and requirements.

2   Methodological Issues and Strategies

The relation between social change and mental hospitalization has been studied largely from an epidemiological viewpoint.[1] Attempts have been made to discover the impact of long- and short-term social change on the incidence and prevalence of mental disorder. The studies involved tended to assume a fairly clear definition of mental illness, and further assumed that factors governing differential utilization of treatment services, rather than influencing mental illness itself, were relatively unimportant for the study.

Whether or not these assumptions reflect the facts remains an open question. It may be, for instance, that the differential tolerance of mental illness among various groups generally influences differential rates of hospital utilization. At the same time, it is possible that social change affects variation in the incidence of mental illness within various population groups only *after* a basic level of hospitalization has been established. Such an "early" level of hospitalization may have been influenced by intolerance of psychiatric symptoms on the part of the public; moreover, the results of these studies are equivocal. In fact, one reviewer writes that "for none of these situations do we have the detailed data that might permit us to formulate conclusive interpretations about the precise factors involved and, indeed, some of the problems of data collection and analysis are so considerable that almost any findings might conceivably be reversed by subsequent evidence or reanalysis."[2]

My attempt in the overall research effort was to explore different statistical and historical approaches to the basic research, for two essential reasons. First, each approach might reveal a somewhat different dimension of the problems, and second, given the controversial nature of this research, I hoped that the results of the various techniques might corroborate or complement one another. The same structural problems that arise from differences in traditions among professional disciplines were evident in my attempt to work out the overall interpretation of the relation and the mechanism by which it takes place. Basic to an understanding of the relation are the viewpoints of researchers in (at least) psychiatry, epidemiology, medical care, and economics. The overall interpretation of the general relation, in addition, involves sociological and historical perspectives.

Apart from the multidisciplinary content of this study, the preeminent analytical problem is to demonstrate the causal sequences involved in the basic relations. In this work, the process of defining the causal sequences occurs in four stages: (1) determination of the direction of the relation, (2) determination of whether external variables are responsible for the relation (that is, the question of "spuriousness"), (3) determination of which variables intervene in the process of the relation, and (4) determination of the general conditions under which the relation takes place.

Studies of the Effect of Recession on Mental-Hospital Admissions

The idea that changes in an indicator of economic activity, especially income and employment, may be related to changes in the occurrence or intolerance of mental illness does not originate with the present writer. There have been several attempts to document possible correlations of economic change and mental-hospital admissions. To date, however, the results have been at worst negative and at best equivocal in support of the idea. These studies sought to determine whether there were unusually high mental-hospital admission rates during the Great Depression years in the United States compared with the years preceding and, in some studies, following.

Perhaps the earliest and most comprehensive study of the effects of the Great Depression on mental hospitalization to date is that of Komora and Clark in 1935.[3] These authors recognize many of the important methodological issues; they do not, however, visualize solutions to the significant procedural difficulties that of necessity occur in the time period of their study. Their equivocal conclusions are stated as follows:

Our inquiry does not show that the depression has produced a notable increase in mental diseases requiring hospital treatment. While most state hospitals reported increases in new admissions and readmissions from 1929 to 1932, many of which were attributed to the economic situation as a *precipitating* factor, such increases were not, on the whole, significant enough to warrant the belief that the depression has exercised a *dominant* influence on hospital admissions.

Nor do the Federal Census returns for the same period show a different picture.

While these figures indicate that the population of state mental hospitals has increased more rapidly since the depression set in, they do not vary sufficiently from the normal trend of increase to prove that the depression has *markedly* affected hospital admissions. The most that can be said is that it has been an important *contributing* factor in causing additional admissions to hospitals and may become an increasingly important one if present economic conditions continue.[4]

Komora and Clark questioned hospital superintendents throughout the country during 1933–34 to determine the effects of the economic crisis on these institutions. In all, 104 hospitals in 35 states and the District of Columbia replied. These represented over one-half of the total number of state hospitals in the United States. Of the 104 institutions replying, 60 reported increases and 31 reported decreases in first admissions between 1929 and 1932 (the period upon which they were questioned). Similarly, a total of 51 institutions reported increases and 35 reported decreases in readmissions during the same period.

To the question, "To what extent do you estimate these changes in population to be attributable to the depression?" the comments were conservative and cautious. Altogether 25 superintendents attributed their increases directly or indirectly to economic conditions, the great majority preferring not to express any opinion on the matter one way or the other.

Komora and Clark report several "typical" comments by the hospital superintendents:

"Very difficult to estimate." "The depression has materially influenced admissions and paroles." "I believe the depression has increased the amount of mental disease." "I feel our increases are due to the general lack of employment." "We are just beginning to see the effect." "No material effect." "Doubt if admissions due to any material extent to depression." "Results of depression beginning to be more in evidence." "Depression has unquestionably increased the demand for admission." "No appreciable extent." "Apparently no effect." "It has no doubt caused some increase in admissions." "Increases due largely in our estimation to depression."[5]

Komora and Clark decline, however, to suggest that their data support the hypothesis of a relation between mental-hospital admissions and the depression. They argue that "various factors of a circumstantial nature which complicate the picture" make it exceedingly difficult to evaluate the recent changes in the mental-hospital population in terms of the depression. They feel that these factors are especially prone to affect changes in mental-hospital admission levels when the individual state hospital is used as the unit of observation:

Changes in population in the individual state hospital are sometimes influenced by factors that have nothing to do with the rate of increase in patients. A spurt in hospital admissions may be due to the fact that new buildings were opened at a given institution, or to transfers from other institutions. Again, some hospitals reported no substantial increases for the simple reason that they were filled to capacity, while in other instances there were longer waiting lists than ever. In one institution admissions were entirely limited to vacancies created by discharges, deaths, and paroles. Others were finding it necessary to refuse new admissions altogether.[6]

The first issue has to do, in general, with the interfering factors of changing hospital administrative and admissions policies, and here the point is well taken.

The second, and more serious, issue is the evaluators' inability to distinguish an increase in admissions due to the depression from a general upward trend in admissions. This problem is not, however, confined to the individual state hospital as the unit of analysis. Nor is the problem limited to data of this type. It is part of the more general problem of distinguishing *any* increase or decrease within data of *any* sort that run over time from the longer-trend movements within the same data. Where does any one trend begin and the other end? And, indeed, how many trends of a different character, or how many factors in a single trend, are there to reckon with?

Deciding, therefore, that no accurate conclusions could be drawn with data from individual hospitals, Komora and Clark go on to suggest that possibly state systems as a whole constitute better units of measurement. The authors review Pollock's study of changes in the level and rate of admissions during the period 1924–1933 for all New York State mental hospitals.[7]

Pollock's study showed the following: (1) The patient population of the New York State mental hospitals increased more rapidly from 1929 to 1934 than it did from 1934 to 1939; the increase was greatest in 1933 (which, incidentally, was the most severe year of the depression in New York State). (2) The trend in the rate of first admissions had been rising since 1924. (3) A slight upward trend was noted in senile first admissions. (4) Extraordinary increases had occurred in the arteriosclerotic group during the preceding 10 years; the most marked change was in 1932. "Part of the increase in this group (senile and arteriosclerotic) is undoubtedly due to the advancing age of the general population.[8] (5) No change in trend is found in the paretic group. (6) A slowly rising trend is noted in the alcoholic group. "The group is more affected by liquor legislation than by economic condition."[9] (7) The trend in the manic-depressive group is slightly upward; a marked increase in the rate of dementia praecox had occurred since 1927; the rate was exceptionally high in 1932 and 1933. "Such rate increases may reflect cumulative effects of the depression."[10]

Pollock's final conclusion is:

The economic crisis does not seem to be the dominant factor in the increase of first admissions *in any one diagnostic group*; it is, however, a precipitating factor in all groups.[11]

In addition to Pollock's conclusion's being somewhat inconsistent, we again find the problem of distinguishing the effects of the depression from those of longer-term movements, such as aging of the general population and the effects of liquor legislation in the case of admissions with alcoholic psychosis. In fact, Komora and Clark quote Pollock's earlier interpretation of the overall increase in the number of patients under care in all New York State mental hospitals since the depression (1929–1934) as follows:

The annual increases of patients have been especially marked in the civil state hospitals since 1927, and are associated with the *vast building program* which has made available additional facilities for the treatment of the mentally diseased. The severe economic depression of the past three years has probably been a contributory factor in causing additional admissions to the hospitals. The excess of admissions over *discharges* and *deaths* is a constant source of increase of population.[12]

Deciding, then, that the state data are as unsatisfactory for their research as the original hospital data, the writers report on the national censuses of patients in state mental hospitals, 1922–1933:

On the surface, the increase shown in the latest enumerations would seem to indicate a correlation with the changed economic conditions in recent years. In the post-war period from 1922–1929, the increases average about 7,000 a year; during the depression period up to 1933 they averaged over 11,000 a year. There is a decided jump from 1930 to 1931, when it may be *assumed* the effects of the depression were beginning to make themselves felt. But this increase can be matched, or nearly so, by the similarly substantial increase of 1926–1929, which were prosperous years. How account for that rise.[13]

Again they find it impossible to distinguish the effects of the depression from a simple extension of the longer trend.

In addition, and as in Pollock's study,[14] questions are raised as to the reaction of mental-hospital admissions to the depression during specific years. The general problem is that no objective and independent indication was obtained of *when* the depression was doing its most significant psychological, or even economic, damage to the population under study (whether local, state, or national).

Nor was even a general idea obtained of the economic effect that the depression had on any of the different ecological areas that were investigated. The effects of any economic change may vary not only by geographical area or industry, but by a large variety of additional demographic and social factors, such as age, sex, occupation, and education. The effects of the depression may also vary by illness. The reason is not only that the differential rates of specific diagnostic categories of mental illness are related to various demographic and social factors, but that the different pathological syndromes may represent qualitatively different reactions—and therefore timing differences—in reaction to economic stress. In fact, it is possible that certain illness categories may respond far more intensively to economic stress than others.

A final point raised in Komora and Clark's study is:

> It would seem, then, that the increases so far observed do not vary *sufficiently* from *the normal* trend to establish the thesis that the depression has markedly affected hospital admissions.[15]

It appears that the authors have some idea of the "sufficiency" or extent to which they feel mental-hospital admissions ought to have increased over and above the increase represented by the normal trend of those admissions. For one thing, we might wonder how the authors planned to estimate the degree to which mental-hospital admissions *ought* to have increased as a result of the depression. For another, of the many trends, both short-term and secular, discussed by the writers, which is the *normal* trend? And finally, we must return again to the question of the mathematical (or other?) method by which one may distinguish the "normal" or any other continuous movement in the data from the variation due to the depression.

To date, hardly any of the several procedural problems raised in the study by Komora and Clark have been sufficiently well worked out that a meaningful study could be made of the relation between economic change and mental-hospital admissions.

Three studies of the effects of the depression on mental-hospital admissions were reported in 1939 and 1940. These studies examined mental-hospital admissions in Chicago, Massachusetts, and New York State in order to ascertain the visible effects of the depression. The important advantage these studies had over the two completed in 1935 was that by 1939–1940 the force of the depression was largely spent. It was, therefore, possible to observe the mental-hospital admissions "before, during, and *after*" the depression—a downturn and an upturn, rather than an upturn only.

Mowrer[16] studied admissions to the Psychopathic Hospital of Cook County (Chicago), Illinois during the period 1929–1935. This hospital would examine all patients from Cook County who entered any of the three state mental hospitals. An additional factor that tended to confound this depression study was that the observations were confined to a *single city*. However, no economic data were used in order to indicate changes in the economy of Chicago during the depression. Now, without at least some basic economic data it is hardly prudent to "estimate" the effects, let alone the exact timing, of a *national* depression on a specific locality.

Mowrer, in fact, found the opposite of what was expected; by his estimate, "the insanity rates decreased toward the middle of the period and declined at the end."[17] Similarly, examining the admission rates by diagnosis, he reports: "It would seem in general, then, that the psychosociogenic types of insanity (dementia praecox, alcoholism, and drug addiction) tend to *decrease* during the *depression*, only to *increase* with the improvement of economic conditions, whereas the bio-physicogenic types (general paralysis or paresis) remain undisturbed.[18]

Dayton[19] studied all admissions to Massachusetts state mental hospitals over the period 1917–1933. Examining first admissions during the years 1929–1932, he argued that "if economic pressures have an effect on the incidence of mental disorders it would seem that these years provide the maximum test."[20] "To our surprise we observe that these very severe conditions, with their many worries and physical deprivations, did not produce a *proportionate* rise in the admission rates for the new cases of mental disorders coming into mental hospitals."[21] But how, indeed, is one to gauge the "proportionateness" of the change in admissions rates? Dayton goes on to suggest that relief programs became a significant factor in aiding the impoverished and unemployed after 1930 and must have mitigated the effects of the depression to the extent that increases in mental-hospital first-admission rates during the period were relatively "slight."[22]

In the third study, Malzberg[23] observed trends of the percentage of first admissions to the New York State mental hospitals in which "loss of employment or financial loss" was considered a causative factor from 1920 to 1937.

Between 1920 and 1928, when allegedly, "economic conditions were stable," there was no significant variation in the annual percentage of patients in whose cases loss of employment or financial loss was considered a causative factor. Between 1928 and 1934, "when the depression appeared," the percentage steadily increased. Between 1934 and 1937 the trend declined, "apparently an answer to the returning prosperity of the epoch." There is consequently a clear suggestion that economic factors influence the rate of first admissions.[24]

In addition, Malzberg found similar trends during those years for manic-depressive psychosis, schizophrenia, and psychoneurosis, but not for the senile psychoses, psychoses with cerebral arteriosclerosis, general paresis, or alcoholic psychosis.

Dunham's report[25] on trends in first-admission rates in mental hospitals for the United States as a whole and separately for New York State,

Massachusetts, Pennsylvania, Michigan, Illinois, California, and Washington directly contradicts Malzberg's earlier findings. Observing the percentage of first admissions without psychosis to all prolonged-care hospitals for the individual states mentioned and the United States, he found that they "took a significant jump between 1923 and 1933"[26] in Massachusetts, Pennsylvania, and Illinois, and for the United States as a whole but not in New York State, Michigan, California, or Washington.

Dunham's report on age-specific first-admission rates *with* psychosis for the United States comparing the years 1923, 1933, 1939, and 1950 finds no comparable increase in these rates.

Dunham did recognize some of the procedural difficulties in employing national data in this investigation:

I am well aware that these rate comparisons for the entire United States are not very meaningful considering the vast geographical area, the marked social changes that forty years have brought about, and the different administrative policies governing mental hospital admissions in the forty-eight states.[27]

Nevertheless, he is prepared to state the "plausible" reason for the differences in rate changes for the first admissions with and without psychosis as follows:

The figures would seem to support the contention that since the beginning of the depression in the 1930's, there has been mounting pressure on mental hospitals to accept persons who are making poor and inadequate adjustments in their communities. The hospitals, while accepting them, have found them upon examination to be "without psychosis" and have so reported them in their statistics. These pressures are possible from organized social services in the various states which have tended to resolve certain problems with clients by committing them to mental hospitals. If this is so, it is a reflection of the increasing multiplication, organization and complexity of social agencies *during this period*.[28]

Pugh and MacMahon appear to have done the most recent and most sophisticated research on mental hospitalization during the Great Depression:

Whether economic depression and its attendant requirement of new adaptations may be a stress which contributes to the manifestation of mental disorder among the population seems a reasonable area of inquiry. There should, perhaps, be no better period in the history of the United States to test this proposition than the prolonged and severe depression of the 1930's.[29]

The authors base their work on age- and sex-adjusted frequencies of first admissions to all United States mental hospitals during the period 1933–1945. From 1933 to 1938, total numbers of first admissions were published without respect to age. Since estimates of the population by age and sex were also available for each year, they computed the number of first admissions expected in each year from 1933 to 1945 if age- and sex-specific admission rates had been the same as in 1922.

It was found that the ratios of observed to expected numbers of admissions increased gradually but consistently from 1933 to 1937; they then déclined until 1941, and increased again between 1941 and 1945. Pugh and MacMahon conclude: "It is evident . . . that the rise and fall of first admissions parallel the depression."[30] They do state a reservation, however:

> We are aware of the possibility that the number of initial admissions during the period of economic depression may well have included a higher than usual complement of illness in existence before the time of stress. The question remains, however, whether this is or is not the full explanation of the findings.[31]

The equivocal, negative, and even positive findings of this group of studies are fraught with serious methodological problems, of which relatively few are even recognized in any individual study. Where the researchers did recognize the methodological pitfalls, unfortunately, they were unable to escape them. The basic objective of these studies, therefore, remains unaccomplished.

The nightmarish issues of method introduced by these studies, moreover, are far from the only ones that confront the student of this problem. We may place the methodological problems in three broad categories: (1) problems of reliability related to the use of proportionate changes in mental-hospital admission rates, (2) problems in the comparison over time of a continuing phenomenon (such as hospital admissions) and an economic indicator, and (3) general problems concerning the correlation of statistical indicators over time.

Hospital Admission Rate as an Indictor of Changes in the Occurrence of Mental Illness

The first major class of problems in this category involves the interference of trends external to those representing the central variables to be correlated. We may distinguish two basic types of trend: (1) "short," nonrecurring movements associated with an unusual event that occurs coincidentally with a particular economic upturn or downturn, and (2) a long-term or secular phenomenon entirely unrelated to any particular upturn or downturn, and running through the entire period, or set of data, under study.

Examples of possible short-term trends would include: changes in mental-hospital admission or discharge policies; increases in discharges that might provide empty beds and thus permit an upswing in admissions of some patients who, because of insufficient hospital space, were unable to gain admission in previous years;[32] decreases in discharges during economic downturns for fear that the former patient could not be financially supported; the sudden expansion or contraction of mental-hospital facilities; the increase or decrease of transfers of mental patients from or to prisons, general hospitals, or convalescent homes; sudden changes in legislative policy concerning, for example, alcoholism, drug addiction, or government-supported medical care for specific age or economic groups; increase or decrease in the activities of social agencies.

Possible secular trends would include any of the above-mentioned short-term factors, but occurring over a long period. Examples are: (1) mental-hospital building programs, which have been increasing at a geometric rate since 1915, (2) the long-term increase or decrease in certain segments of the population at risk, (3) the increase in willingness on the part of the mentally ill and their families to use mental hospitals—possibly related, for example, to increases in the general level of education, (4) the growth of mass communications, (5) the acceptance of psychiatry as a *medical* specialty and of the mentally ill as, indeed, "ill,"[33] (6) the increasing tendency to define various types of deviant behavior as pathological, (7) the possible long-term decrease in certain categories of mental-hospital admissions as a result of increases in the general hospital and clinic care of psychiatric patients.[34]

If neither short-term nor secular trends are distinguished from the specific trends to be correlated, two classes of problems arise. First, if the expected relation does appear, it is possible to argue that the external short-term or secular trend may be the factor causing the trend in the independent or dependent variable or in both variables. Second, if the expected relation is not found, it is possible to argue that the external trend prevented the appearance of the correlation.

Another major group of problems, which involve the accuracy of the measure of changes in mental-hospital admission rates, is peculiar to the problem of investigating a hypothesized relation between economic changes and the incidence of mental illness in the population. This is the problem of estimating the specific time interval necessary for observation of the reaction to the stress engendered by the economic downturn. "Other things being equal," within what period of time after the occurrence of an economic crisis ought we to expect the appearance of the stress reaction on the part of an individual, small group, or large population?

Tyhurst, on the basis of studies of individual responses to community disaster,[35] has arrived at a three-phase conceptual model of reactions to stress situations: (*a*) a period of impact, (*b*) a period of recoil, and (*c*) a post-traumatic period.[36]

The first period (*a*) is characterized by the impact of initial stresses and continues until these stresses are no longer operating on the individual or group. It is the period of maximal and direct effect of initial stresses. The period of recoil (*b*) is characterized by a suspension of initial stresses, and thus begins when the individual has succeeded in avoiding their direct effect for the moment at least, by one maneuver or another, such as escape. Some stresses may continue during this period . . . but from a psychological point of view, and relatively in terms of intensity and type, the stresses are suspended in this period. The stresses of the post-traumatic period (*c*) are derivatives of those of the initial period of impact and are more obviously "social" in nature. This is the period during which first full awareness is possible of what the disaster has "meant" in terms of loss of home, belongings, financial security . . . it begins after the security from initial stresses has been fully established, and when the individual comes to face once again, the matter of daily living but in an environment altered in one of several crucial aspects.[37]

The three periods may be further defined according to duration of the stress reaction peculiar to each:

With regard to duration, (*a*) that of the period of impact may vary within fairly wide margins. However, for acute catastrophe it may last for only 3 to 5 minutes or up to 1 hour . . . (*b*) The time duration of the period of recoil also varies, but to a smaller extent apart from abnormal reaction, being determined more by individual differences than by the nature of the stresses. (*c*) The post-traumatic period lasts, hypothetically at least, *for the remainder of the person's life,* and includes the period of rehabilitation.[38]

In the case of an economic crisis, the stress situation in the "period of impact" may extend for several months to several years as judged by the depression of the 1930's. There may be several periods of "impact" and "recoil," and the "post-traumatic" effect may indeed last a lifetime. As Tyhurst has further indicated:

Further stresses may be of such a type and severity as to impose a prolongation of the first period of impact; or put in another way, as to produce a second impact immediately following the first, and thereby postponing the period of recoil for varying periods of time.[39]

We should, in addition, expect the phases to vary by predispositional factors, social-demographic characteristics, and, as in our particular problem, specific illnesses.

How is one to predict the length of any of these stages of stress reactions to the economic crisis? Furthermore, the present study considers changes in mental-hospital admission rates in relation to the economic downturn. Not only, therefore, must the time interval between the economic crisis and the "stress reaction" be considered, but also the time interval between the stress reaction and its expression in terms of mental hospitalization.

The short-term reactions discussed above are not the only factors that are interposed between the impact of the economic crisis and mental hospitalization. There are, in addition, factors that inhibit or encourage mental hospitalization, such as social stigmatization, the isolation and punishment of the mentally ill, and the structural and economic breakdown of the family. Finally, there are selective factors relating to who, among the mentally ill, are hospitalized at a given time. The family may use such selective criteria as, for example, sex and age,[40] whereas the mental hospital may use prognosis and social status.[41]

Instead of attempting to predict one specific length of time within which the observable stress reaction—namely, mental hospitalization—occurs, it may be more precise to speak about the stress factors and the many possible reactions to them as having a dispersion over a relatively long period. Mental hospitalization, then, would represent the culmination of these various reactions. For a large population, finally, given additional factors of differential reaction time among subgroups, we would expect the dispersion of mental-hospital admissions to be found throughout the entire period of the economic downturn—and perhaps beyond it. The remaining problem concerning reaction time is then to sum up, or concentrate, the dispersed stress reactions (indicated by mental-hospital admission rates)—a certain fraction of which will occur in each of several years—and correlate that sum with the specific economic events that we think may have initiated it.

Some of the more obvious methodological difficulties of the earlier studies of this problem resulted from the absence of any economic indicator by which to measure the extent of covariation with mental-hospital admissions. The earlier studies simply assumed a general period during which the depression ought to have occurred—specifically in the lives of the populations whose rates of mental hospitalization were examined.

The matching of a national economic phenomenon with independent behavior in a subpopulation—whose corresponding economic behavior is essentially an unknown quantity—invites a fundamental methodological difficulty. It is well established that groups in different geographic areas, occupations, industrial groupings, socioeconomic categories, and age and sex categories experience large-scale economic changes at different times, and with varying intensity, relative to the national aggregate.[42] The methodological problem, then, consists in matching an indicator of mental status to the economic behavior of the particular group studied. It is the problem of ascertaining whether a given fraction of the same population that is being damaged economically is also injured in mental status—within a specified period after the initial economic crisis.

Attention having been called to the variety of methodological problems entailed in the analysis of mental-hospitalization statistics as they are related to economic indicators over a defined period of time, it is possible to discuss how the problems are dealt with in the present study.

Indicators Used in the Analysis of the 20th-Century Data

(1) *Mental-Hospital Admissions.* The mental-hospital admission data were abstracted from the *Annual Reports* of the Department of Mental Hygiene (current name) of New York State to the New York legislature.[43] For a 58-year period, 1910–1967, the *Annual Reports* provide detailed information on the sociodemographic, legal, and diagnostic classifications of admissions for each year. This annual census includes the entire population of admissions to all state mental hospitals and all licensed private mental hospitals in New York State for 1910–1967.

(2) *Economic Change.* Theoretically, basic to the concept of changes in aggregate economic activity (and such concepts as economic contraction and expansion) is the extent to which the resources of production are utilized. Furthermore, not only is labor power a central resource of production but it is necessary to the operation of the material resources (capital equipment, raw materials, and semifinished products). If utilization of the material factors of production undergoes a downward shift, so must employment of the human resources. Finally, if the human and nonhuman factors of production become increasingly idle and there is a concomitant decrease in productivity (or real income produced and, ultimately, consumed), then we have an economic downturn or recession.[44]

Although there are several indexes of economic activity for the United States as a whole (Ayres, American Telephone and Telegraph Company, Persons, Axe-Houghton, Snyder, Babson, and others), there are none for New York State in particular. From the standpoint of theory and empirical research, however, *change in the rate of employment in manufacturing industries* is one of the most accurate indicators of change in aggregate economic activity.

Studies conducted by the National Bureau of Economic Research, for example, have shown that changes in manufacturing employment and changes in personal income are two of the most highly representative indicators of the "business cycle."[45] These indicators are highly coincident in chronology and amplitude with the fluctuations of the business cycle. They are therefore also highly correlated over time with each other and with national indexes of total production and productivity.

The lack of an aggregate business index for New York State may be met with regard to *fluctuations over time* by the use of an index of employment for manufacturing industries. Such an index was prepared on a monthly basis by the Department of Labor of New York for the years 1914–1948.[46] In addition, the Department annually prepared monthly employment tables based on an index that originated in 1940.[47]

The two sets of monthly data were combined (by the present writer) to provide a composite manufacturing employment index covering the years 1914–1967. Adjustment of the two employment indexes was accomplished by computing the regression equation, $Y = 97.61 + 12.33\ X$, of the relation between the first index, X, and the second, Y, based on the 9 years of overlap between the two series (1940–1948). The composite index was then represented in terms of the Y series. Finally, since monthly data were available for both employment indexes, the composite employment index was readjusted to conform to the fiscal year used in the accounting scheme of the *Annual Reports* of the New York State Department of Mental Hygiene. This procedure insures accuracy in at least the annual matching of the employment to the mental-hospitalization series.

The procedure of correlating the annually matched economic and mental-hospitalization series over a period of 54 years permits the extension of the specific "depression" problem of the earlier studies to any economic downturn, regardless of magnitude or time of occurrence, within the period 1914–1967. This procedure therefore enables us to argue that economic downturns in general—regardless of size or chronological specificity—will be associated with an upturn in mental-hospital admissions.

By extending the "depression" problem to one of economic downturns in general, and by providing an empirical indicator of various types of economic downturn and correlating it with general fluctuations in mental-hospital admission rates, we are able to eliminate much of the case for a spurious interpretation of the relation.

A major problem of spuriousness encountered by earlier studies was due to the presence of a trend external to the major variables under consideration (for example, an increase in the number, scope, and activity of social agencies during the depression of the 1930's). The existence of the external short trend made it possible to regard an increase in mental-hospital admissions during the depression as "spurious"[48] and as simply reflecting that external trend.

Evidence of a generalized relation between economic change and mental hospitalization eliminates the argument of spuriousness that depends on the possible effect that any of these unusual, external influences may have had during any specific economic downturn.

Statistical and Graphic Analyses

Detrending of Secular (or Long-Term) Trends

In estimating intermediate- or short-term relations in time-series regression analysis, it is frequently necessary to control for the effects of long-term trends. The most common econometric technique for the control of such trends is through algebraic subtraction of a fitted curve that ideally describes the long-term movement. In keeping with traditional econometric discourse, the long-term (or secular) trend is defined as the presence of either a generalized increase or a generalized decrease in a given series of data arrayed over time (time series). Such trends may approximate a linear or a nonlinear mathematical model. A nonlinear long-term trend implies, in this analysis, a generalized increase or decrease of a nonarithmetic character. The restriction in this study on the shape of a nonlinear trend is that it have only one direction, that is, that it not contain an increase as well as a decrease. Five of the most common "families" (or "types") of nonlinear equations would logically be included in our definition of a single linear or nonlinear trend. These five types include a linear equation, three logarithmic equations, $y = a \pm b \log x$, $\log y = a \pm bx$, $\log y = a \pm b \log x$, a reciprocal equation, $y = 1/(a \pm bx)$, and a logistic equation. The three logarithmic equations describe increases or decreases at relatively slow, moderate, or rapid rates of change. The reciprocal equation represents an initially slowly rising or falling trend followed by a much steeper trend in each direction. The salient characteristic of the logistic or "growth" curve is an increase (or decrease) in its rate, beginning at a low (or high) level, reaching a maximum (or minimum) level, and then decreasing (or increasing) so that the growing (or declining) quantity approaches a definite maximum (or minimum) value.

The next procedural questions are: (1) whether a linear or nonlinear equation best fits a given series, and (2) if the nonlinear gives the best fit, which of the five nonlinear types should be used. This problem is resolved by allowing the linear as well as the nonlinear models to compete in fitting the long-term trend, if indeed such a long-term trend is present in the data. Thus, each of the six equations is fitted to any given time series under study, and the Pearsonian correlation coefficient is then used to estimate the relation between the original data and the fitted trend. The best-fitting nonlinear trend competes with the linear equation fitting the data. If the nonlinear fit shows a significantly higher correlation with the original data, it is designated the best-fitting curve to the original series.

The remaining issue of whether this best-fitting curve represents a trend by which the data are not only fitted but also detrended is resolved by a conventional use of the Pearsonian correlation coefficient. If the curve described as best fitting the original data yields a squared correlation coefficient with those original data of less than 0.15, the best-fitting curve is considered not to describe enough of the general shape of the data to be accurate and useful in the eventual detrending process.

Control for trends running through the entire length of each series is then accomplished by an algebraic subtraction of the linear or nonlinear trend line from the original data. The "residual," or detrended series then become the basic data used in all subsequent computations.[49]

Detrending of Intermediate-Sized Trends

Serious questions have been raised whether correlations that might be observed among economic changes and mental-hospital admissions, even after secular detrending, reflect, to some degree, the spurious influence of extraneous large-scale social phenomena. Another related question is whether, in any case, substantial portions of the relations between economic changes and hospitalization are due to a small number of comparatively long (yet not secular) trends. Several techniques have been worked out to deal with these problems. In this study, Fourier analysis is the most frequently used technique. This technique describes a variable number of "cyclical" movements (trends that encompass a period of growth and a period of decline) of variable duration; conventional methods of spectral analysis are used to describe (fit) nonlinear trends of large-scale or short-term duration after the data have been detrended for the secular movement by means of a first-difference transformation.

First differences are also used for preliminary secular detrending of raw time series, which are then examined with the aid of moving-average and polynomial fitting. Fourier analysis of the first-differenced data is used as the initial probe, since the data thus transformed are likely to represent the more usual conception of "cyclical" changes. However, there is really no firm reason to believe that the relation between economic changes and mental hospitalization is best described in an equation involving harmonic terms. Indeed, it is possible that the relations between economic indicators and many social indicators may more accurately be represented in terms of the absolute level of change in one indicator in relation to another. Polynomial and moving-average descriptions of annual changes are used in dealing with this possibility. The difference between these two techniques is that whereas polynomial curvefitting simply describes variations in the magnitude of change, the moving-average procedure is based on the theory that a relation between any two series is best described in annual units of change. For example, if the moving-average procedure were found to be most precise in describing the relation between two series, then 3-year changes in the employment index might be accurately correlated with 3-year changes in the rate of mental-hospital admissions.

Correlation Procedure

Autocorrelation of regression residuals[50] is dealt with by the use of the Durbin-Watson Test[51] and Durbin's subsequent transformation.[52] In addition, a test to derive a "true N"[53] is added as a supplement to the Durbin-Watson regression procedures. Two additional tests and transformations are also added in order to deal with autocorrelation among lagged points in any time series.[54] Through these two traditional procedures, a "true N" may be estimated in view of the degrees of freedom lost by virtue of autocorrelation within any single series. Finally, in addition to regression procedures, a nonparametric test is included to indicate the percentage of years for which the economic indicator moves in the same direction as (or the opposite direction to) the social indicator.

An additional regression procedure follows; it attempts to deal with the general problem of transforming nonlinear time-series relations which can then be subjected to the various linear estimation procedures discussed previously. The method of dissecting a nonlinear or changing relation into several linear relations may be described briefly as follows:

(*a*) The general intention is to define periods of years in which a single, significant, linear relation can be shown. Our method first computes the Pearsonian correlation coefficient from the base year to 5, 6, 7, ... years later.

(*b*) If the base year is part of a series in which a stable linear relation exists, then the correlation sharply decreases as points are added to the series that are not part of the stable group of years.

(*c*) The squares of the correlation coefficients are then scanned by computer to locate the longest periods of time over which a relation of greater than a specific level of significance is measured. Thus, the precise periods of time over which there tend to be substantial relations are estimated.

A Procedure for Dealing with Dispersed Stress Reactions

Two serious obstacles to measurement of the effects of economic stress on behavior have been: (1) the difficulty of estimating the period of time within which the particular stress reaction would occur and (2) the difficulty of isolating those stress reactions in which one is particularly interested from other reactions.

The solution used here makes the assumption that the particular stress reaction we are interested in—admission to the mental hospital—is spread over a considerable period of time, especially when we consider the reactions of a large population. Also, since certain groups experience loss earlier in the economic downturn than others, mental-hospital admissions as a cumulative indicator have the same average or aggregate character as do changes in economic activity. In order to deal with this problem, the research procedure must satisfy two conditions: (1) it must take into consideration the dispersion of mental-hospital admissions over a period of years, in each population that responds to economic change and (2) it must take into consideration differentials in time duration of economic stress among those groups that respond to economic crisis by mental hospitalization.

Time lags and leads of the mental-hospitalization reaction pattern of a particular population group to the pattern of aggregate economic activity can be measured by shifting the economic indicator to the chronological left and right of the hospital-admission series. This backward and forward shift of the economic indicator to mental hospitalization permits optimum matching of the two indicators in annual units. By this matching process we can ascertain the optimum temporal (lag or lead) matching of the indicators.

The comparative measure of goodness of fit of the indicators to one another is the Pearsonian correlation coefficient.[55] It is used to estimate our ability to account for changes in mental hospitalization through changes in an employment index at various leads and lags. Again, since it is difficult to predict whether changes in the aggregate employment index will precede or follow changes in the mental-hospital admission pattern of a particular subgroup, a lead as well as a lag may provide the optimum correlation.

Thus far we have limited the discussion to estimating the optimum lead or lag of mental hospitalization to economic change. In estimating the differences in fit (or relation) at different lags and leads we treat the single economic variable as several different variables, each showing a different relation to mental hospitalization. We have argued, however, that the stress reactions occur over a span of years. Thus, although for a given population subgroup there may be an optimum or average length of time between economic crisis and hospitalization, the predictive optimum is not an aggregate of the stress reactions.

The problem, then, is to match the total stress reaction for a group to the total (or aggregate) pattern of economic change. This may be accomplished by continuing to treat the independent economic variable as several independent variables (the number of variables used depends on the number of lags and leads in question). Thus, several independent variables may be used to predict changes in mental hospitalization. Each of the independent economic variables represents a lag or a lead. The distribution or dispersion of stress reactions to economic changes in terms of mental hospitalization can then be summed by the use of multiple correlation. The multiple-correlation coefficient can be understood to represent the degree to which we are able to account for the *total* stress reaction represented by mental hospitalization, as distributed over as many years lagged or led as we may determine.

In the following chapters we shall compare the different correlation techniques discussed above with regard to how effectively each permits us to predict changes in mental hospitalization from changes in the employment index. Each of these techniques enables us to deal with a different methodological problem. None of these methods is in itself entirely sufficient to deal with all of the methodological problems presented by the original research problem.

Another question has to do with the number of independent populations within which the basic relation can be observed. It is possible that not only the statistically observed but the actual relation may be confined to specific populations and that, therefore, the hypotheses advanced are not universally applicable.

The present study is able to deal with this issue by examining the general relation among 35 ethnic groups for both sexes (and for each ethnic group and sex by 12 diagnostic categories) and among 50 different nationalities for both sexes. In addition, several sociodemographic breakdowns of the total population are found to participate in this relation.

The Ecological Character of the Relations and the Problem of Intercorrelating Data on Different Levels of Analysis

The very detailed breakdowns of the admissions data permit the examination of the effects of economic changes on a large variety of subgroups within the total population admitted to the hospital. The data thus provide the opportunity to examine differential strengths and patterns of relation of each of the subgroups to the large-scale economic change.

Support for the position that the economic changes are acting on the hospitalized population in a specifiable manner can then be demonstrated. Three broad classifications of subgroups of mental-hospital admission can be described: (1) geographical area of residence in New York State (for example, counties, urban versus rural), (2) socioeconomic status (for example, economic classification, educational level, length of residence in the United States of the foreign born), and (3) social role (for example, sex, age, first admission versus readmission to the mental hospital). The strategy of dealing with the methodological problem of interrelating the levels of analysis requires an explanation for each category (geographic areas, socioeconomic groups, and social roles) of which subcategories show greater or less sensitivity to economic change in terms of mental hospitalization.

We might argue, for example, that certain age groups would be unusually sensitive to economic stress (as judged by their pattern of mental hospitalization) because of their differential involvement in economic activity. Should such a differential pattern of sensitivity indeed be found with respect to age, which supports this prediction, then the evidence would also support the general hypothesis relating over-all economic change to mental hospitalization.

A large part of the data is, therefore, devoted to demonstrating the effects of large-scale economic change on specific socioeconomic groups and categories of social roles. By this approach, we not only support the overarching propositions of this study, but also gain additional insight into the mechanisms underlying the relation between economic change and mental hospitalization.

3 Mental Illness and the Economy

An analysis that is based upon appropriately identified population groups, and that controls for the effects of external trends, reveals substantial inverse relations between economic change and mental hospitalization. Thus, for the period 1914–1967 in New York State, for example, state and private mental-hospital admissions are observed to be highly inversely correlated with the index of employment. Furthermore, when groups identified by sex, age, economic status, ethnic group, and diagnosis are specifically examined, the inverse relations appear to be far more predictable.

Strength of the Relation in the 20th Century

When sex, age, and diagnosis are simultaneously controlled, the relation between intermediate-size and short-term trends in mental-hospital admissions and employment usually is at a correlation of less than −0.80, that is, r between −0.80 and −1.00 (controlling for the effects of autocorrelated residuals[1]) during 1914–1960 in New York State.

After the effects of external long-term (secular) trends are controlled for, the correlation (controlling for the effects of autocorrelated residuals) between changes in the level of employment and mental-hospital admissions is less than −0.80 for periods of 35 years or more. This suggests that economic changes may explain the majority of all trend movements in the mental-hospital admissions of various populations for periods of at least 35 years' duration.

A comparison of four methods of detrending—(1) raw data (no detrending), (2) elimination of the linear trend, (3) elimination of the best-fitting linear or curvilinear trend, and (4) elimination of each trend at each observed time span prior to correlation—is shown in Appendix I. Although in many cases these four techniques yield similar results, it is clear in general that the method that requires the least amount of detrending provides the highest estimates of the relation over the longest period of time.

In the aggregate, for nearly any population of admission that is highly sensitive to economic change, and when the effects of autocorrelated residuals are controlled for, (a) r is less than -0.85 for 70 to 85 percent of the years under study; (b) r is less than -0.80 for approximately 80 percent of the years under study; (c) r is less than -0.70 for at least 90 percent of the years under study.

The relation between economic change and mental hospitalization is often predictable on a short-term basis—even on a yearly basis. The extent to which one can predict the short-term relation depends upon how many of the data themselves contain short-term and long-term variation. Thus, for example, one can usually observe the effects of a 1-year change in employment upon admissions within the very same year (Fig. 1). However, a 5-year economic trend may have an impact on mental-hospital admissions lasting considerably longer than 5 years. Nevertheless, the inverse correlations between admissions and economic change are frequently maximized at a lag of 1 year (of admissions behind employment). The highest correlations are generally at zero lag or at a lag of 1 year and the maximum number of years covered by the total relation must usually be estimated by adding the years involved at a lag of zero to those

After breaking up the period 1914–1960 into smaller spans of time, we find involved at a lag of 1 year, disregarding the overlapping years (see Appendix I). that during any given span the correlation between the level of employment and mental hospitalization is on the average at most -0.65 (controlling for the effects of autocorrelated residuals); however, the relation itself may be relatively stable or unstable depending upon the population studied. Thus, regardless of how completely economic change controls the level of mental-hospital admissions, the impact with which economic conditions affect admissions may vary somewhat with the magnitude of the economic change in question and the occurrence of other independent social changes, such as wars, changes in welfare policy, and technological changes.

The interval of time does not seem to matter greatly in the calculation of the over-all relation. The basic relation, therefore, is not grounded on any specific temporal unit of change. For certain populations of admissions that exhibit a lagging response (possibly varying from period to period), calculations based on a very small temporal unit, such as 1- or 2-year changes, may confound our atttemps to observe the relation. For the great majority of populations that were investigated, however, predictability of the relation is quite high even on an annual basis.

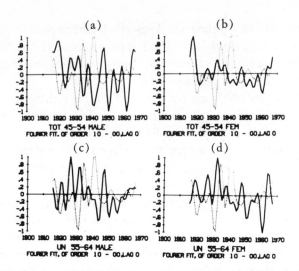

FIG. I. Two- to 4-year fluctuations in employment and in mental-hospital admission rates, 1915–1967: rates of admission with total functional psychosis (schizophrenia, manic-depressive psychosis, and involutional psychosis), ages 45–54, and undifferentiated mental disorder, ages 55–64, by sex. First admission rates to New York civil state hospitals matched with New York State manufacturing employment index; data are smoothed through Fourier transformation of annual changes (first differences) so as to represent 2–4-year changes.

LEGEND:
...... New York State Manufacturing Employment Index
_____ First admission rates:
    (a) male, total functional psychosis, ages 45–54
    (b) female, total functional psychosis, ages 45–54
    (c) male, all mental disorders, ages 55–64
    (d) female, all mental disorders, ages 55–64
SCALE: Fourier curves are scaled for viewing, such that the greatest amplitude from the arithmetic mean of each series (which is set equal to zero) has been normalized to 1.0 if positive, or −1.0 if negative.

This latter finding is most dramatically shown by calculating the fraction of individual annual changes in mental-hospital admissions that move in the opposite direction to changes in the employment index. The only major difference between the predictability of the relation of a small-unit change (1- to 3-year changes) and on a large unit change (10- to 15-year changes) is that the relation based upon large changes tends to show longer lags of changes in the level of admissions with respect to changes in the economy.

Although the relation between economic change and mental hospitalization applies to small temporal units as well as to large intervals, it is best described not in terms of temporal units, such as 1-, 2-, or 3-year changes, but in terms of the magnitude of changes in the economic indicator and in mental-hospital admissions. Thus, we can predict the magnitude of change in hospital admissions as a consequence of the magnitude of change in employment more accurately than we can predict a specific (say a 2-year) change in the level of mental-hospital admissions as a consequence of an opposite change in the level of employment.

Among the various techniques that were applied, Fourier analysis[2] has proved to provide the most precise gauge of the relations. This technique describes a specified number of "cyclical" changes (that is, an increase and a decrease) within a fixed period of time in the variables to be correlated. The research question thus becomes: are a specific number of changes, of variable magnitude and periodicity in the economic indicator, related to the same number of variable changes in the level of mental-hospital admissions.

Lest some readers feel that the statistical techniques discussed here are inordinately complicated, it should be kept in mind that the relations under investigation are themselves complex. Several different computational procedures were required in the present study in order to deal adequately with the major methodological and statistical issues that are peculiar to this type of research.

The impact of economic change on mental hospitalization does appear to vary somewhat, depending on short-term factors as well as on intermediate- and long-term considerations. Along these lines, it is interesting that the specific economic downturn of the Great Depression of 1929–1932 is associated with a much smaller proportionate increase in admissions than any downturn of at least 3 years' duration during the 20th century. Again, interestingly, it does not appear that the influence of factors associated with war affect the overall relation. No unusual increase or decrease was found in the impact of economic change on mental hospitalization during the Civil War, the First World War, the Second World War, or the Korean War.

Economic Change and Mental Hospitalization in the 19th Century

In order to test both the workings of our methods of data transformation on data that were unrelated to our study covering the 20th century and the speculation that external factors (such as wars, hospital admissions policies, changes in cultural and political values, immigration patterns, introduction of welfare) were involved in the relation, an investigation was made to determine whether the inverse relation between economic change and mental hospitalization could be found for the 19th century.

The same techniques of detrending and Fourier analysis were used to investigate the possible relation between changes in the economy and mental hospitalization in New York State for the perod 1841–1915. Since no reliably representative economic index for this period could be found for New York

State, *Ayres' Index of Industrial Production in the United States* was used. The rationale was that evidence available for the 19th and 20th centuries shows[3] that changes in the economy of New York State closely parallel those of the nation as a whole. Since 1841, state commisssioners with the responsibility for psychiatric hospitalization in New York State have published annual reports to the legislature on (statistical) characteristics of hospitals and inmates.[4]

By means of a variety of data transformations, *Ayres' Index* was correlated with admissions to Utica State Hospital, which were cross-classified by several demographic and clinical variables. In general, admissions to Utica State Hospital were found to be highly inversely correlated with the Index of Industrial Production. This general finding demonstrated that the overall inverse relation between economic change and mental hospitalization could be observed for the entire period 1841–1960. Age, sex, and duration of illness prior to admission were the variables that were found to yield the greatest differences in the patterns of mental hospitalization associated with economic change.

In addition to providing effective tests of our data-transformation and correlation procedures, the relations found for the 19th century led to the conclusion that, regardless of any third variable that is independent of both economic change and mental hospitalization, the relation between changes in the economy and mental-hospital admissions in New York State was continuous for 120 years.

The Post-1960 Period

Finally, a third stage of the present study concentrated on the period 1955–1967. The reason that the 1960–1967 data were not part of the initial analysis is that the hospital-admissions data were not as yet available. The findings for 1955–1967 are discussed in detail in Chapter 9. The major finding is that the relations observed for the 19th century and for 1915–1960 continue to be observed through 1967. In fact, for the age groups 15–34, the impact of economic downturns on hospital admissions increased significantly from World War II to 1967, and particularly from 1955 to 1967. The inverse relation between economic changes and mental-hospital admissions can therefore be observed for a period of 127 years.

The implication is that, regardless of variable policies relative to hospital admission, the availability of bed space, the influence of war (including the Civil War, the two World Wars, and the Korean War), the availability of specific treatments (such as drug therapy, psychotherapy, custody) and of hospital staff and facilities, changes in the population composition of New

York State, changes in the population composition of mental hospitals (especially through immigration and migration), definitions by the public and within psychiatry of who is psychiatrically ill, alternative modes of psychiatric treatment relative to hospitalization, attitudes toward the mentally ill and mental hospitalization, the institution of welfare, changes in the capacities of institutions to handle the mentally ill, and so forth, the relation between economic change and mental hospitalization has been reasonably stable for nearly 13 decades.

Economic Changes and Hospitalization for Specific Mental Disorders

A major question, raised by the inverse relation between economic changes and mental hospitalization, is whether or not social stresses originating during economic downturns are instrumental in producing psychiatric symptoms. It might be hypothesized that if the effects of economic downturns were associated with the production of psychiatric symptoms then persons admitted to mental hospitals who were diagnosed as functionally psychotic would be more sensitive to economic changes than those admitted with organic brain syndrome. In order to examine this question in detail we need to distinguish the effects of several sociodemographic factors that are known to affect the inverse relation between economic changes and mental hospitalization. Chief among these external factors are age, sex, and level of educational attainment. If it is true that economic changes affect admissions with different diagnoses in different ways, then we should be able to observe the differential effects of economic changes on the hospitalization of different diagnostic groups within different categories of age, sex, and educational attainment. In the following sections we examine these differential effects.

Our first approach is to examine the relation between economic change and mental hospitalization by categories of illness according to age and sex categories (Table 1 and Figs. 2, 3). Thus, we find that for the schizophrenic group high inverse sensitivity can be observed from the age group 0–15 all the way through 45–54 for males, and through 55–64 for females; after this period, sensitivity drops to a low level, but we still find an inverse relation for both sexes. Admission with a diagnosis of schizophrenia is therefore a typical pattern of response to economic downturns during most of the life span, but gradually ceases as old age approaches. For the manic-depressives we have essentially the same picture as for the schizophrenics, except that for males inverse sensitivity lasts a bit longer than through ages 55–64, whereas for females it lasts only through ages 45–54; thereafter, for both sexes, low inverse

Table 1. Number of years, 1914–1960, during which the correlation between employment and mental-hospital admissions $\leq$ −0.65,[a] by age, sex, and diagnosis.[b]

Illness	0–14		15–24		25–34		35–44		45–54		55–64		65–69		70+	
	M	F	M	F	M	F	M	F	M	F	M	F	M	F	M	F
Schizophrenia	33	29	41	34	35	26	38	37	39	34	15	39	17	14	17	15
Manic-depressive psychosis	31	20	38	39	47	34	47	45	47	47	44	26	12	23	17	24
Involutional psychosis					12	7	22	29	32	0	38	9	33	16	21	19
Total functional psychosis	41	35	41	37	36	29	45	40	47	16	33	20	22	7	32	18
Alcoholic psychosis				10	44	23	42	31	41	24	41	20	28	18	41	23
Senility							14	6	16	16	14	9	14	0	7	8
Psychosis with cerebral arteriosclerosis							43	25	42	27	29	22	37	0	36	31
Paresis	22	14	22	28	45	15	7	36	8	32	37	8	34	26	30	22
Epilepsy	0	0	21	12	21	20	29	28	23	6	24	6	12	13	10	27
Mental deficiency	6	19	16	6	24	26	7	31	22	19	13	17	21	14	10	13
Total admissions	41	33	43	41	42	33	47	39	45	34	34	32	34	19	27	17

[a]r between −0.65 and −1.00. Only correlations not significantly affected by autocorrelation of residuals, as measured by the Durbin-Watson statistic, are included.

[b]First admissions to New York civil state hospitals correlated with New York State manufacturing employment index (secular trend subtracted from both series).

sensitivity to economic change is maintained. It should be pointed out, however, that greater overall inverse sensitivity to economic change is shown by admissions with manic-depressive psychosis than by those in any other diagnostic category.

For involutional psychosis, the males show mild to moderate inverse sensitivity from ages 35–44 through 65–69 and thereafter lose this sensitivity. The females, by contrast, show low to moderate inverse sensitivity beginning at ages 35–44. They then abruptly become highly positively sensitive at 45–54, but during ages 55–64 are somewhat inversely, as well as somewhat positively, sensitive. Thereafter, they lose both inverse and positive sensitivity. Mental-hospital admissions with involutional psychosis represent a typically middle-aged response to economic change. It is interesting that for females in particular the involutional group generally shows high to moderate positive sensitivity, whereas the males show low to moderate inverse sensitivity. However, it appears that for the females high positive sensitivity is confined almost exclusively to the age group 45–54, whereas previous and following decades show only moderate inverse sensitivity.

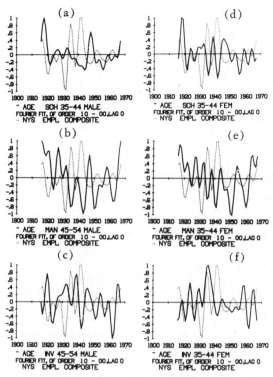

FIG. 2. Two- to 4-year fluctuations in employment and in mental-hospital admission rates, 1915–1967: rates of admission with schizophrenia, manic-depressive psychosis, and involutional psychosis, in critical age groups, by sex. First admission rates to New York civil state hospitals matched with the New York State manufacturing employment index; data are smoothed through Fourier transformation of annual changes (first differences) so as to represent 2–4-year changes.

LEGEND:
...... New York State Manufacturing Employment Index
_____ First admission rates:
    (a) male, schizophrenia, ages 35–44
    (b) male, manic-depressive psychosis, ages 45–64
    (c) male, involutional psychosis, ages 45–54
    (d) female, schizophrenia, ages 35–44
    (e) female, manic-depressive psychosis, ages 35–44
    (f) female, involutional psychosis, ages 35–44
SCALE: Fourier curves are scaled for viewing, such that the greatest amplitude from the arithmetic mean of each series (which is set equal to zero) has been normalized to 1.0 if positive, or −1.0 if negative.

For hospital admissions with alcoholism, moderate to high sensitivity to economic change begins during the period 25–34. Thereafter the males maintain extreme inverse sensitivity, whereas females show only moderate inverse sensitivity. The only exception is that for both sexes during the 35–69

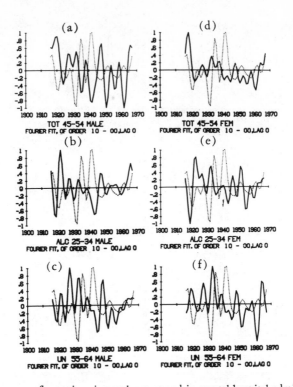

FIG. 3. Two- to 4-year fluctuations in employment and in mental-hospital admission rates,
1915–1967: rates of admission with total functional psychosis (schizophrenia,
manic-depressive psychosis, and involutional psychosis), alcoholic psychosis, and
undifferentiated mental disorder, in critical age groups, by sex. First admission rates to
New York civil state hospitals matched with New York State manufacturing
employment index; data are smoothed through Fourier transformation of
annual changes (first differences) so as to represent 2–4-year changes.

LEGEND:
...... New York State Manufacturing Employment Index
_____ First admission rates:
    (a) male, total functional psychosis, ages 45–54
    (b) male, alcoholic psychosis, ages 25–34
    (c) male, all mental disorders, ages 55–64
    (d) female, total functional psychosis, ages 45–54
    (e) female, alcoholic psychosis, ages 25–34
    (f) female, all mental disorders, ages 55–64
SCALE: Fourier curves are scaled for viewing, such that the greatest
amplitude from the arithmetic mean of each series (which is set equal to zero)
has been normalized to 1.0 if positive, or −1.0 if negative.

period there is a very substantial decrease in inverse sensitivity toward a
low to moderate level.

    The senile diagnostic category does not show sensitivity to economic change
for either sex except for the over-70 age group. During that time, for both
sexes, we find extreme positivity. By contrast, for both sexes we find continuous

and inverse sensitivity for psychosis with cerebral arteriosclerosis from age 35 upward. In the case of males, inverse sensitivity is high to extreme (especially between 35 and 54), whereas for females it is continuously moderate.

For both sexes, admissions with paresis show continuously moderate inverse sensitivity from ages 0–14 upward, and the inverse sensitivity seems to be greatest after age 25. Epilepsy shows low to moderate inverse sensitivity, especially between ages 15 and 64 for males and 15 and 44 for females, and once again over 70. For the mentally defective males, we find low to moderate sensitivity between the ages of 15 and 54, whereas for the females low to moderate sensitivity occurs between ages 25 and 44.

Our second approach is to identify the relation between economic changes and mental hospitalization by illness within categories of educational attainment and sex (Table 2). For admissions with schizophrenia, the grammar-school, high-school, and college-educated groups tend to be equally

Table 2. Number of years, 1914–1960, during which the correlation between employment and mental-hospital admissions ≤ −0.65,[a] by level of education, sex, and diagnosis.[b]

| Illness | Education | | | | | |
| | Grammar school | | High school | | College | |
	Male	Female	Male	Female	Male	Female
Schizophrenia	41	36	29	26	21	36
Manic-depressive psychosis	41	40	41	38	41	30
Involutional psychosis	24	6	30	7	14	8
Total functional psychosis	41	40	34	28	36	33
Alcoholic psychosis	39	32	23	27	28	27
Senility	12	6	19	7	0	12
Psychosis with cerebral arterio- sclerosis	39	7	15	14	7	6
Paresis	35	40	36	28	11	19
Epilepsy	36	19	12	0	12	25
Mental deficiency	35	38	18	10	10	25
Total admissions	38	35	38	31	36	35

[a]r between −0.65 and −1.00. Only correlations not significantly affected by autocorrelation of residuals, as measured by the Durbin-Watson statistic, are included.
[b]First admissions to New York civil state hospitals correlated with New York State manufacturing employment index (secular trend subtracted from both series).

sensitive at a high order of inverse sensitivity; the females, as usual, tend
to be less sensitive than the males. For the manic depressives, interestingly, the
male groups show identical sensitivity of extremely high inverse matching
with the employment index. In the case of the females, the high-school group is
somewhat less sensitive than either the grammar-school or the college groups.
For males, the involutional psychotics appear to be moderately inversely
sensitive, the three educational groups being quite sensitive in response. Among
the females, however, we note either complete lack of inverse matching or
moderate positivity in relation to economic change.

Thus, among hospital admissions for functional psychosis, neither
schizophrenia, manic-depressive psychosis, nor involutional psychosis represents
a typical diagnostic response pattern to the economic change of any particular
educational group. In addition, manic-depressive psychosis seems to provide the
sharpest and most uniform inverse response pattern to economic change
among educational groups. Admissions with schizophrenia also show a very
strong pattern of response to economic downturns, whereas those with
involutional psychosis are the least likely to increase during economic downturns,
especially among females. In fact, for females over age 45 admitted with a
diagnosis of involutional psychosis, admissions increase sharply during economic
upturns and decrease during downturns.

For both sexes, admissions in the category of (total) functional psychosis
show strong inverse sensitivity to economic change. The pattern of response of
the functional psychotics as a group ("psychotic disorder of psychogenic origin
or without clearly defined physical cause or structural change in the brain") [5]
to economic change has been extensively reviewed throughout the present
work. In summary, however, among the educational groups, it was found
that patients with a grammar-school or college education show a considerably
stronger inverse relation between economic change and mental hospitalization
than do those with a high-school education or less than a grammar-school
education.

Admissions for alcoholic psychosis, for both sexes, show a pattern in which
the grammar-school educated display somewhat greater sensitivity to economic
change than either the high-school or the college educated. On the basis
of differential strengths of relation among different educational groups, psychosis
with alcoholism appears to be most typically a lower socioeconomic status
response to the economic downturn. However, it is resorted to occasionally by
the high-school and college educated.

For admissions (of both sexes) with a diagnosis of senility, there is a
moderately strong positive relation to economic changes, with little difference
among educational groups. In addition to the majority of admissions who were

diagnosed as involutional psychotics, the other major group of admissions that appears to increase during economic upturns is the senile group.

For admissions of patients diagnosed as suffering from cerebral arteriosclerosis, among males the grammar-school educated show strong inverse sensitivity to economic change relative to mild inverse sensitivity among the high-school and college educated. Among females, we see moderately positive sensitivity to economic change among the grammar-school educated relative to mild positivity and negativity among high-school and college educated women. Psychosis with cerebral arteriosclerosis is, therefore, typically a relatively lower socioeconomic status response among males, but a high socioeconomic status response for females. In general, admissions for cerebral arteriosclerosis are less sensitive to economic change than are admissions for functional psychoses or alcoholism, but more sensitive than any other organic brain syndrome.

For paresis, admissions of males in each of the three major educational groups react with high inverse sensitivity to economic change. However, among females the grammar-school educated react to economic change with strong inverse sensitivity, the high-school educated, with moderate inverse sensitivity, and the college educated with only mild inverse sensitivity. Admissions for paresis are, in general, quite sensitive to economic change, though not quite so sensitive as are admissions for functional psychosis, alcoholism, or psychosis with cerebral arteriosclerosis. Though paresis is not a typical response of any specific socioeconomic status group, there is a tendency for admissions of paretics of lower socioeconomic status to react with greater sensitivity to economic change.

Male admissions with a diagnosis of epilepsy show moderate inverse sensitivity to economic change for the grammar-school educated group, which gradually declines as the level of education increases. Females show moderate inverse sensitivity for the grammar-school educated, mild to moderate inverse sensitivity for the college educated, and moderate positivity for the high-school educated. Admissions with epilepsy are among the groups that are relatively mildly sensitive to economic change. For males, admission due to epilepsy tends to be a lower socioeconomic status response, whereas for females socioeconomic status does not seem to exert a significant influence on the admission patterns.

For the mental defectives, among male admissions there is strong inverse sensitivity for the grammar-school educated, mild sensitivity for the high-school educated, and very little inverse sensitivity for the college educated. For females, by contrast, we find moderate inverse sensitivity for each of the educational groupings. The response pattern of admissions for mental

deficiency is very similar to that for epilepsy. We find a relatively low overall
sensitivity to economic change, but with the greatest sensitivity among
lower socioeconomic status groups for males, whereas for females the response
pattern is not associated with socioeconomic status.

Economic Stress and Specific Mental Disorders

It was suggested initially that, if social stresses which originated during
economic downturns were instrumental in producing psychiatric symptoms,
then admissions to the mental hospital that were diagnosed as functional
psychotic might be more sensitive to economic change than admissions with
organic brain syndrome. This hypothesis is, to a great extent, supported by the
data. The major diagnostic categories of functional psychosis taken as a
group (including schizophrenia, manic-depressive psychosis, and involutional
psychosis) react more sharply to economic downturns than any other
diagnostic group.

It is also significant that the second most sensitive diagnostic groups to
economic changes, in terms of hospital admissions, are those with alcoholic
psychosis. Much as increases in functional psychiatric illness might be thought to
be related to economic stress, we might expect that stress resulting from an
adverse economic situation would provoke a significantly increased rate
of alcohol intoxication. Additional support for this possibility is found in a study
of the relation between downward movement in socioeconomic status and
alcohol intake in New Haven.

It is also true, on the other hand, that admissions for any psychiatric diagnosis
are, to some degree, sensitive to economic change. However, we do not really
know the total configuration of the psychiatric syndrome with which
patients diagnosed as suffering from organic brain syndrome are admitted. It is
entirely possible that, in addition to the organic brain syndrome as the underlying
condition, the patients in question may have been admitted with superimposed
"psychotic, neurotic, or behavioral reactions."[6] Thus, although social stresses
may not have been instrumental in introducing new evidence, or exacerbated
symptoms, of organic brain syndrome, such stress may have led to increased
hospital admissions which may have been provoked by an increased rate
of psychotic, neurotic, or behavioral reactions. This possible explanation may be
especially useful in accounting for increased admissions during economic
downturns of patients diagnosed as cerebral arteriosclerotic, senile, epileptic, or
mentally defective.

Admissions of two major diagnostic groups appear to show the opposite pattern of reaction to economic change to those of all other diagnostic groups. Patients of both sexes diagnosed as senile, and female patients (particularly over the age of 45) diagnosed as involutional psychotics, show definite and consistent trends of increased admissions during economic upturns and decreased admissions during downturns.

The case of the seniles lends itself to speculation concerning the possibly severe impact of economic upturns upon the elderly. It is possible, first of all, that the rate of inflation would show particularly sharp increases during economic upturns. Such increases in inflation would be particularly damaging to the fixed incomes of the elderly, thus producing considerable economic stress for them during economic upturns. It is also possible that many young families, in response to increased economic opportunities geographically removed from their present homes, would move to a new location, and necessarily, though not intentionally, abandon their elderly parents living with them. This situation of abandonment might be particularly critical for the senile, as distinguished from the patient with cerebral arteriosclerosis, since the senile patient is likely to have been almost childishly dependent on the family during the economic upturn. (It should be pointed out, however, that there is also a tendency for admissions of females with relatively low socioeconomic status to be positively related to economic changes.)

The case of admissions of females who are diagnosed as having involutional psychosis and who show increased rates during economic upturns also requires some explanation. An interesting related finding is that admissions of involutional psychotic males are not nearly as strongly inversely related to economic change as are admissions of males for other classes of functional psychosis. At least two explanations may be suggested. First, we may note that the increases in admissions for involutional psychosis during the economic upturn occur largely among female patients over 45 years of age. We have also observed that the age range of approximately 45–60 is the period in the life span most sensitive to economic change in terms of mental-hospital admissions. In addition, among the three major classifications of functional psychosis (schizophrenic, manic-depressive psychotic, and involutional psychotic), involutional psychosis is probably the mildest illness in that it has the best prognosis and the least severe symptoms.[7]

Now it is possible that there is a certain segment of the population that reacts with a variety of psychotic symptoms to environmental stress. In the early stages of this psychotic stress reaction, it may not be possible to distinguish the specific type of the psychotic syndrome so that a precise diagnosis could be made. In fact, it is likely that only if this stress reaction persists could a definite diagnosis be established.[8] Perhaps under the relatively mild stress of an economic upturn we are seeing some increase in admissions with psychosis within the 45–60-year range—but only in its mildest form, namely, involutional psychosis. If this were true, then we would find the more severe functional psychoses, such as schizophrenia and manic-depressive psychosis, increasing during economic downturns for this age group. It should be emphasized, however, that a basic assumption underlying this suggestion is that there indeed exists a population which, depending upon the severity of environmental stress, will react with a wide range of psychotic symptoms which may resemble relatively mild, moderate, or severe forms of functional psychosis. The further underlying assumption is that a definite personality-based distinction among population groups who would be predisposed toward one form of functional psychosis rather than another has only partial validity.

A second possible explanation is based on the reverse assumption, namely, that there are three fundamental character types which, under certain conditions, exhibit distinctly different psychotic reactions. The group predisposed toward involutional psychosis would be of particularly compulsive personality structure,[9] and would be especially sensitive to changes that involve movement from the home by the individuals themselves or by their children.[10] The extraordinary stress on this group of "leaving the nest" would be especially severe during economic upturns. It is during such upturns that the tendency toward geographic mobility among the population would sharply increase owing to the increased availability of economic opportunities in areas outside the immediate area of residence. This latter explanation would support the psychiatric basis for distinguishing the diagnostic groups among the functional psychoses and thereby provide a psychiatric rationale for explaining one feature of the general relation between economic change and mental hospitalization. In any case, the two suggestions that have been offered in explanation of increased admissions of female involutional psychotics during economic upturns are highly speculative, and we will require additional research in order to be able to confirm or reject them.

4   Long-Term Trends and the Basic Relation, 1850–1967

The 19th Century

Our analysis of the 19th-century relation between economic changes and mental hospitalization utilizes transformations of admissions and economic data that are based on percentage changes. The Fourier transformation of percentage changes was found to be particularly useful for the 19th-century material, since our fundamental indicator of economic changes is based on *Ayres' Index of Industrial Production* for the United States as a whole. Although fluctuations in this index of production are known to correlate well with changes in the national business cycles, there was some concern that these correlations might be specific only to particular intervals of economic changes for New York State.

The Fourier transformations provide a cyclical representation of both the economic and mental-hospital admissions data at specific levels of change, and thereby allow us to examine the issue of whether the 19th-century relations are confined to specific time intervals. In comparing the 19th and 20th centuries, therefore, consideration is given to both large and intermediate-sized cycles, which indicate changes of relatively great magnitude, and very small cycles, which indicate relatively strong short-term predictability as well as a rapid response of admissions to economic changes.

However, some relations appear to be so strong during the 19th century, even when a national index of industrial production is used, that they can be measured in terms of absolute levels in addition to percentage changes and Fourier transformations. (Specific age groups and categories of duration of illness prior to hospitalization are examples.) In our comparison of the 19th and 20th centuries, specific populations are examined in relation to their sensitivity to economic change in terms of mental hospitalization. The question is whether different age, educational, and other classifications of admissions

were more or less sensitive to economic changes during the 19th century than
they are during the 20th century. For example, does the middle-aged
group, which tends to show the greatest sensitivity to economic change as
compared with other age groups (during the 20th century), show the same
prominence among age groups during the 19th century?

Age and Marital Status

An examination of the different reaction patterns of hospital admissions
to economic change shows a somewhat similar set of patterns among the various
age groups during the 19th century (Table 3). Apart from the fact that,
in general, female admissions are somewhat less sensitive to economic change
than male admissions, only occasionally (and episodically) do we find inverse
relations between admissions and economic change that are neither reasonably
predictable nor consistent. There does not appear to be any distinctive
pattern among age groups in terms of sensitivity to economic change. This
contrasts sharply with the picture for the 20th century, in which a distinctive
pattern emerges of the middle-aged groups showing considerably more consistent
and reliable relations to economic change than the younger or older age groups.

It may of course be true that the mechanism underlying the relation
between economic change and mental hospitalization among different age
groups is different for the 19th and 20th centuries. On the other hand, it may be
that during the 19th century, in general, age was not as important a factor
in distinguishing social position as it is in the 20th century. Rather, during the
19th century, factors that stem from family background were perhaps
intrinsically more significant in determining socioeconomic status (and other
aspects of social position) than was age. If this is the case, then the major source
of sensitivity of admissions to economic changes may have depended upon
such factors as occupation and education. Although we find that the age
categories show patterns of reaction to economic changes during the 19th and
20th centuries, marital-status categories show similar patterns of reaction during
the two centuries. In both centuries, it is the married groups that show the
most reliable inverse relations of mental-hospital admissions to economic change,
whereas the single groups show only a moderately reliable relation. On the
other hand, the widowed and divorced, overall, show only fair inverse matching
of mental-hospital admissions with patterns of economic change.

Occupation

For the 19th century, occupational categories are particularly reliable for
examining the predictability of the relations between economic changes and

Table 3. Number of years, 1852–1908, during which the correlation between industrial production and mental-hospital admissions $\leq$ −0.65,[a] by age, marital status, and sex.[b]

Category	Male	Female
Age (years)		
0–14	51	52
10–19	50	46
20–29	53	48
30–39	52	45
40–49	56	46
50–59	46	43
60–69	48	43
70–79	43	45
80+	51	25
Marital Status		
Single	51	49
Married	53	48
Widowed	41	43
Divorced	46	43

[a]r between −0.65 and −1.00. Only correlations not significantly affected by autocorrelation of residuals, as measured by the Durbin-Watson statistic, are included.
[b]First admissions to Utica State Hospital correlated with Ayres' Index of Industrial Production for the United States. Data are smoothed through Fourier transformation of annual changes (first differences) so as to represent 2–4-year changes.

mental hospitalization. Theoretically, occupation ought to be important in distinguishing relative sensitivity to economic change among the total population of admissions. Occupation is, first of all, a reasonably good indicator of socioeconomic level, a variable that we know to discriminate sharply between groups in the population that actually gain or lose income during economic downturns. Second, different industrial groups tend to show varying degrees of lag in patterns of economic change in comparison with national economic cycles.[1]

During the 19th century, the major classifications of occupation for males recorded by the Utica State Mental Hospital are laborers, merchants, salesmen, lawyers, doctors, and farmers. For females, the categories listed are housewives, domestics, seamstresses, and housekeepers.

Among the male groups we find relatively clear and even some extraordinarily precise relations within occupational categories (Table 4; Fig. 4). Generally speaking, farmers, laborers, and salesmen show the most highly reliable inverse relations of hospital admissions to economic changes. The

Table 4. Number of years, 1852–1908, during which the correlation between industrial production and mental-hospital admissions $\leqq$ −0.65,[a] by occupation, level of education, and sex.[b]

Occupation	Male	Occupation	Female
	(1853–1907)		(1853–1886)
Laborer	52	Housewife	31
Merchant	44	Domestic	28
Salesman	48	Seamstress	26
Lawyer	23	Housekeeper	29
Doctor	44		
Farmer	55		
Education (1852–1907)		Male	Female
College		56	52
High school		44	42
Grammar school		51	50
Reads and writes		56	51
Reads only		49	47
Illiterate		50	50

[a] r between −0.65 and −1.00. Only correlations not significantly affected by autocorrelation of residuals, as measured by the Durbin-Watson statistic, are included.

[b] First admissions to Utica State Hospital correlated with Ayres' Index of Industrial Production for the United States. Data are smoothed through Fourier transformation of annual changes (first differences) so as to represent 2–4-year changes.

relation for farmers is most reliable, the merchants and doctors show somewhat less substantial relations, and for the lawyers the relation is altogether too difficult to discern clearly. There is a suggestion in these data that the relatively high-status and high-earning occupations (merchants, doctors, and lawyers) do not show nearly as strong inverse relations as do the occupations of lower socioeconomic status (laborers, salesmen, and farmers).

Admissions of females show a fairly concrete pattern of differences among occupational categories in terms of sensitivity to economic change. Among the four groupings, housewives show a moderately good relation only for intermediate-sized fluctuations in admissions; the other occupational groups show relatively reliable inverse relations for small as well as large changes. This would indicate that many of the larger changes in the level of mental-hospital admissions have been influenced by economic changes that affect each of the four occupational groups. Nevertheless, the inverse relation between economic change and mental-hospital admissions is far more predictable over the short

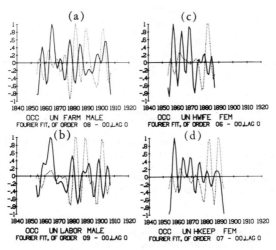

FIG. 4. Fluctuations in industrial production and in mental-hospital admissions, 1853–1907: male and female admissions in selected occupations. First admissions to Utica State Hospital matched with Ayres' Index of United States Industrial Production; data are smoothed through Fourier transformation of annual changes (first differences) so as to represent 2–4-year changes.

LEGEND:
...... Ayres' Index of Industrial Production, United States
_____ First admissions, by occupation:
  (a) male, farmers
  (b) male, laborers
  (c) female, housewives
  (d) female, housekeepers
SCALE: Fourier curves are scaled for viewing, such that the greatest amplitude from the arithmetic mean of each series (which is set equal to zero) has been normalized to 1.0 if positive, or −1.0 if negative.

range for the three groups of women who are economically dependent on personal earnings, namely, domestics, seamstresses, and housekeepers.

Level of Educational Attainment

   Three major classifications of educational attainment may be distinguished in terms of their relations between economic changes and mental hospitalization: the college educated, the high-school educated and those of grammar-school education or less (including the grammar-school educated, those who are able to read and write, those who are only able to read, and the illiterate). Among these three major groups of admissions, those of grammar-school education or less show far more impressive inverse relations than do the high-school or college educated groups; between the college and high-school educated, regardless of sex, the college educated show far more sustained inverse relations (Fig 5).

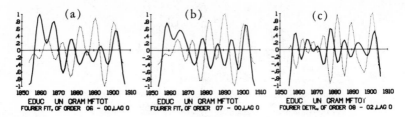

FIG. 5. Fluctuations in industrial production and in mental-hospital admissions, 1852–1907: admissions with grammar-school education. First admissions to Utica State Hospital matched with Ayres' Index of United States Industrial Production; data are smoothed through Fourier transformation of annual changes (first differences) so as to represent 1–3-, 2–3-, and 2–4-year changes.

LEGEND:
...... Ayres' Index of Industrial Production, United States
_____ First admissions of grammar school educated:
    (a) 2–4 year changes
    (b) 2–3 year changes
    (c) 1–3 year changes
SCALE: Fourier curves are scaled for viewing, such that the greatest amplitude from the arithmetic mean of each series (which is set equal to zero) has been normalized to 1.0 if positive, or –1.0 if negative.

This pattern in one way is identical to, and in another contrasts sharply with, the sequence observed for the 20th century. As in the case of the 20th century, mental-hospital admissions patterns of the college, high-school, and grammar-school groups show the high-school group to be less sensitive than either the college or grammar-school groups; also, the grammar-school group is more sensitive than the college group. The group that enters the hospital with less than a grammar-school education shows inverse relations with economic changes that are frequently more reliable than are those for even the grammar-school group. This contrasts sharply with the situation in the 20th century, where hospital admissions with less than a grammar-school education generally show the poorest relations—occasionally even increases of admissions during economic upturns.

It may be productive to speculate on the similarities and differences in these patterns of relations as they occur in the 19th and 20th centuries. Let us first distinguish those with less than a grammar-school education, who probably account for the bulk of the 19th-century relation, from the high-school and college educated, who show considerably less inverse sensitivity to economic changes. We shall assume, to begin with, that educational level is positively related to socioeconomic status not only because increased education leads to increased income, but also because (particularly in the 19th century) education itself had to be privately financed. It is possible that patients of grammar-school education or less experience the greatest economic devastation during the economic downturn and probably possess least in the way of economic resources to fall back on in comparison with the high-school and college educated.

Henry and Short's hypothesis,[2] that groups of relatively high socioeconomic status lose more status and income during economic downturns because they have more to lose, may be operative to some extent in this instance. This explanation, on the other hand, clearly does not extend to the extremely low-income groups, who live on the borderline of economic survival and for whom even a minor downward move in economic status might be life-threatening. In fact, generally speaking, we find that patients admitted with a grammar-school education or less are far more sensitive than those admitted with more than a grammar-school education; this finding is the reverse or what would be expected if Henry and Short's position were entirely correct.

The interpretations offered above would not follow the same argument as those given for the 20th-century data on differential sensitivity among educational groups. In fact, the data for the 19th and 20th centuries show significant contrasts. The principal difference is that in the 20th century admissions for the very lowest educational group (those with less than a grammar-school education) are not highly sensitive to economic downturns, and actually show some positivity in their relation to economic changes. Even if we disregarded the literal meaning of the specific educational levels, which obviously may vary considerably from generation to generation, we still find that admissions for the lowest socioeconomic group in the 19th century tend to be extremely sensitive to the economic downturn, whereas there is a questionable relation for this group in the 20th century.

Now, it is possible that the absolute economic level of, and the resources available to, persons of very low socioeconomic status were considerably poorer in the 19th century than in the 20th century. During much of the 20th century, for instance, there has been a much more extensive provision of unemployment and welfare services.[3] Then, too, in the 20th century we are dealing with a far more highly urbanized population, one that would find it relatively easier to obtain alternative work among a greater variety of industries during periods of high unemployment.[4] This point is important in its relevance to the 20th-century situation of the lowest socioeconomic groups actually showing income gains during major economic downturns, especially during the Great Depression. Our explanation was that these low socioeconomic status groups, especially younger workers and relatively unskilled laborers, would experience an increase in employment and income at the very bottom of the economic downturn or, in other words, as the economy just began to repair itself. Employment of these groups at such a time would not be an imprudent investment since they would demand comparatively low wages.

These same groups, however, might be replaced, as the economy advanced,

Table 5. Number of years, 1870–1907, during which the correlation between industrial production and mental-hospital admissions $\le$ −0.65,[a] by duration of illness prior to admission and sex.[b]

Duration	Male	Female
1 month	32	30
3 months	36	38
6 months	31	32
1 year	37	36
0–1 year	36	35
1–2 years	37	34
2 years	30	29
2 years and over	32	15
2 years and chronic	34	18
Chronic	35	32

[a] r between −0.65 and −1.00. Only correlations not significantly affected by autocorrelation of residuals, as measured by the Durbin-Watson statistic, are included.

[b] First admissions to Utica State Hospital correlated with Ayres' Index of Industrial Production for the United States. Data are smoothed through Fourier transformation of annual changes (first differences) so as to represent 2–4-year changes.

in favor of more highly skilled and better-paid workers and managerial staff. This general explanation of the 20th-century data is clearly more pertinent to a highly urbanized economy, one that would allow for a fairly rapid turnover of employees in and out of the labor force. Such high levels of turnover would especially require fairly rapid communication as to the availability of jobs in certain industrial sectors and occupations, and particularly among the underemployed and lower-income workers.

To try to use the explanation that was suggested for interpreting the 20th-century data for the 19th-century findings would needlessly stretch comparability between the two centuries. For example, it was suggested that in the 20th century the high-school educated group would be most nearly representative of skilled workers and lower-level management, where higher levels of management and professionals would be statistically represented through their college backgrounds. During the 19th century, however, the college-educated person was relatively rare, and the small number in question would probably have trained for academia, the ministry, law, medicine, or perhaps life as a cultured gentleman or gentlewoman. The far more numerous high-school educated might have been among the elite of the business world, a world that was hardly analogous to the large-scale bureaucratic setting

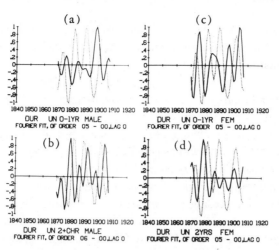

FIG. 6. Fluctuations in industrial production and in mental-hospital admissions, 1870–1907: males and females by critical duration of illness preceding admission. First admissions to Utica State Hospital matched with Ayres' Index of United States Industrial Production; data are smoothed through Fourier transformation of annual changes (first differences) so as to represent 2–4-year changes.

LEGEND:

...... Ayres' Index of Industrial Production, United States
_____ First admissions, by duration of illness preceding admission:

   (a) males, under 1 year
   (b) males, at least 2 years or chronic
   (c) females, under 1 year
   (d) females, at least 2 years

SCALE: Fourier curves are scaled for viewing, such that the greatest amplitude from the arithmetic mean of each series (which is set equal to zero) has been normalized to 1.0 if positive, or −1.0 if negative.

of the 20th century. The structure of education and industry are therefore so different in the 19th and 20th centuries that it would probably be grossly inaccurate to use the total 20th-century model of replacement of upper-middle personnel for high-level personnel in order to explain the 19th-century data.

Duration of Illness Prior to Admission

For mental-hospital admissions during the 19th century, duration of illness prior to admission appears to be a major factor in discriminating between individuals who will respond more or less sharply to economic change. Our data on duration of illness prior to admission are subdivided into nine categories, ranging from 1 month through 2 years (or chronic). The original data were recategorized as follows: under 1 year, 1 to 2 years, 2 years, over 2 years but not chronic, and over 2 years and chronic. When the admissions data are thus recategorized, a clear picture emerges of the differential extent of inverse relations to economic changes (Table 5; Fig. 6). We find that admissions with duration of illness up to and including 2 years show highly predictable and consistent inverse relations, whereas those whose illnesses lasted more than 2 years prior to admission (but were not chronic) show only a moderately strong inverse relation to economic changes. Finally, those whose illnesses are listed as having lasted over 2 years (and as chronic) again shows highly predictable and consistent inverse relations with economic changes.

At least two major interpretations may be offered in an attempt to explain these patterns. First, it is possible that we are observing truly different personality-based representations of stress reactions by persons who have mental disorders of different severity and duration. We may be finding, therefore, that sensitivity to any significant environmental stress may be greatest for patients whose illnesses are either of relatively recent origin or of very long duration (that is, chronic). If this explanation is correct, then it is possible that the group of mentally ill whose illnesses have passed through the first stages of stress reactions but have not as yet become chronic may have been able to accommodate their life styles to such environmental stresses without the need for hospitalization and without their illnesses neccessarily become chronic accompaniments of their behavior.

A second type of interpretation involves a two-level model of response to economic changes based on duration of illness. In this model, the explanation of the highly sensitive pattern of admissions of those with relatively short-lived illnesses is based on actual reactions of illnesses to precipitating economic and other social stresses. Patients with chronic illnesses, on the other hand, would respond sharply to economic downturns because, in their case, the hospital might be used either as an almshouse or as a haven from the intolerance of their families and other members of the society. This explanation assumes that the chronically mentally ill person probably is economically dependent on his family or on a welfare institution or may perhaps be a marginally employed worker. The financial burden imposed by such individuals on their families, friends, employers, or charitable institutions might be such that their mentally disturbed condition would not be easily tolerated during periods of economic stress.

On the other hand, the groups whose illnesses lasted over 2 years but were not chronic might represent individuals who were neither reacting to economic stress of short or intermediate range nor were mentally ill for a sufficiently long period to have been placed in a dependent economic position; in that case, their pattern of hospital admissions might be unclear in relation to economic changes. Our 19th-century information on duration of illness prior to hospital admission may be, to some degree, analogous to the 20th-century data in which first admissions and readmissions were distinguished. To the extent that these data are analogous, we may be observing a real difference between reaction patterns of admissions of the chronically ill in the 19th century as compared to the 20th century. Whereas the chronically ill patient of the 19th century is sharply responsive to economic changes, for most of the 20th century admissions of the chronically ill are only moderately sensitive to economic change. The result of this comparison suggests that intolerance of the chronically mentally ill during economic downturns might have been considerably more severe during the 19th century than it has been during the 20th century.

Long-Term Changes in the Relation Between Economic Fluctuations and Mental-Hospital Admissions, 1915–1967

In our discussion of the impact of economic change on mental-hospital admissions, estimates were provided of the degree to which fluctuations exist in admissions when the effects of long-term trends were controlled. Having obtained the estimates of intermediate and short-term variation in mental-hospital admissions, and knowing the correlation between such variation in admissions and economic fluctuations, we were then able to estimate the extent of change in admissions that could be attributed to economic fluctuations.

We were also able to find several cases of mental-hospital admissions (particularly among ethnic groups) for which no measurable long-term trend could be found. For these cases, it was argued that, theoretically, nearly the entire variation in admissions might be attributable to economic changes if the correlation were sufficiently high. For example, if the correlation between a series of mental-hospital admissions (which did not require removal of the long-term trend) and economic fluctuations were at the level of -0.90, then as much as 81 percent of the variation in admissions might be attributable to economic fluctuations.

Apart from the technique of removing long-term trends through algebraic subtraction, another method that is frequently useful is based upon admissions rates, rather than admissions levels. In this study rates have frequently been used in the detrending process where the existence of a long-term trend in admissions is largely a result of secular growth or decline in the base population. Rate data were obtainable for mental-hospital admissions in the following sociodemographic categories: age, sex, marital status, and ethnic background (based largely on the classifications of country of nativity of the foreign born).

Age–Specific Trends

Among the various age groups, sharply rising secular trends in admission rates are seen in the population below age 15 and above age 65. Very gradual, and very mild, upward trends are seen in admissions for 15–24- and 25–34-year-olds of both sexes. In fact, the trend is barely noticeable to the naked eye for the 25–34-year-olds. For the 35–44- and 45–54-year-olds of both sexes, no trends are noticeable among admissions rates. Similarly, no trend occurs in admissions rates for 55–64-year-old males, and only a barely measurable trend occurs for 55–64-year-old females. Thus, even without regard to diagnosis, the entire middle-age range of 35–64 years for both sexes contains almost no secular trends (Figs. 7, 8).

An analysis of the relation between admission rates among age groups that do not show a trend and fluctuations in the economy does, in fact, support the suggestion that for these groups short- and intermediate-range economic fluctuations tend to control variations in the admissions rate. It is possible, then, that, apart from the effects of long-term changes in population size, the great majority of fluctuations in the level of mental-hospital admissions is also attributable to economic change for these groups (see Chapter 5, Table 6).

Trends by Marital Status

An examination of rates of mental hospitalization by marital status complements the picture for long-term trends that is found among age groups (Fig. 9). These data provide additional evidence that long-term upward trends in admission rates are to be found only in the case of the relatively young and old. Thus, single males and females show moderate and continuous upward trends in hospitalization rates from 1910 to 1960; even sharper upward trends are observed for widowed males and females. On the other hand, no trend is observed in the case of married males for the same period, and married females show an extremely mild, barely noticeable upward trend. At the same time, no trend in admission rates is observable for divorced and separated males, whereas a very sharp decreasing trend is found for separated and divorced females.

If we now examine the relation between economic change and admission rates for these marital-status categories for which no trend, or a barely noticeable trend, is present, we again find that for major groups of the patient population, most of the variation in mental-hospitalization rates is related to changes in the economy (see Appendix I).

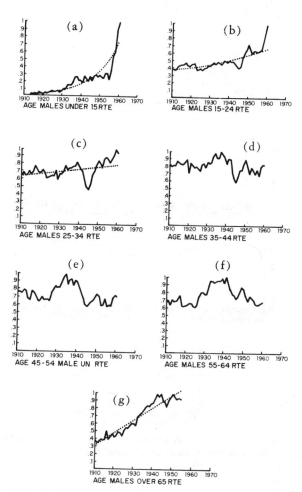

FIG. 7. Secular trends in mental-hospital first admission rates, 1910–1960, by age group for males. Best estimate of linear or nonlinear trend is fitted to admission rates where data contain measurable trend.

LEGEND:
———— Male first admission rates, by age
· · · · · · Plot of best-fitting estimate of trend
Equation models of trend:
(a) log Y=a+bx (b,c) Y=1/(a+bx) (d,f) no measurable trend (g) Y=a+bx
SCALE: Rates per 100,000 are expressed as fractions of the highest rate, which is set equal to 1.0, for each population group. Scalar range describes relative magnitude of variation in each series.
Range of actual rates per 100,000:
(a) 0.37–31.11 (b) 51.09–140.56 (c) 57.25–124.56 (d) 71.94–121.45
(e) 80.94–137.42 (f) 107.54–176.11 (g) 150.61–435.43

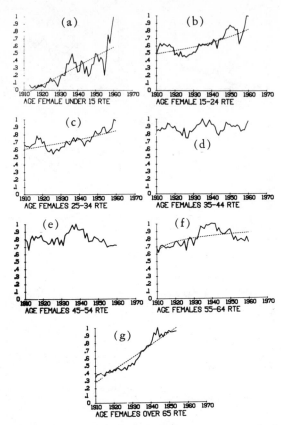

FIG. 8. Secular trends in mental-hospital first admission rates, 1910–1960, by age group for females. Best estimate of linear or nonlinear trend is fitted to admission rates where data contain measurable trend.

LEGEND:
_____ Female first admission rates, by age
...... Plot of best fitting estimate of trend
Equation model of trend:
(a) Y=a+bx (b,c) Y=1/(a+bx) (d,e) no measurable trend
(f) log Y = a + b log x (g) Y=a+bx
SCALE: Rates per 100,000 are expressed as fractions of the highest rate, which is set equal to 1.0, for each population group. Scalar range describes relative magnitude of variation in each series.
Range of actual rates per 100,000:
(a) 0.34–11.16 (b) 37.95–85.08 (c) 61.17–112.85 (d) 76.08–101.72
(e) 81.21–122.56 (f) 86.72–138.57 (g) 149.23–426.68

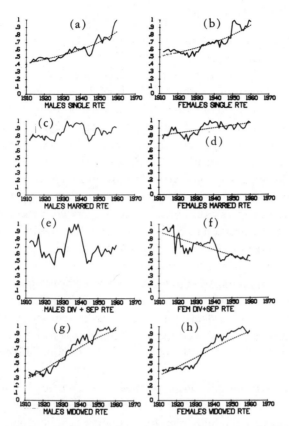

FIG. 9. Secular trends in mental-hospital first admission rates, 1912–1960, by marital status and sex. Best estimate of linear or nonlinear trend is fitted to admission rates where data contain measurable trend.

LEGEND:
———— First admission rates, by marital status
······ Plot of best fitting estimate of trend
Equation model of trend:
(a,b) $Y=/_1(a+bx)$ (c,e) no measurable trend (d) $Y=a+bx$ (f) $Y=a-bx$
(g,h) $Y_t=a/(1+bx^{-ct})$
SCALE: Rates per 100,000 are expressed as fractions of the highest rate, which is set equal to 1.0, for each population group. Scalar range describes relative magnitude of variation in each series.
Range of actual rates per 100,000:
(a) 101.46–248.11 (b) 75.05–152.16 (c) 59.90–82.55
(d) 54.50–75.17 (e) 91.71–202.92 (f) 658.31–1298.70
(g) 169.83–520.99 (h) 132.62–336.37

Trends for Selected Ethnic Groups

At several points in the present study, it has been observed that the most "pure," or homogeneous, groupings of the patient population with respect to the relation between hospitalization and economic change were based on a highly specific classification of ethnic background. In an attempt to investigate more closely the effect of long-term trends on mental hospitalization, first-admission rates by country of nativity of the population of patients were compiled. For each of the 35 countries involved, and for both sexes in each case, at least moderate and occasionally strong upward trends were observed. These data, however, did not provide sufficiently great differences among populations, in secular trends, to permit a long-term comparative analysis.

Since the factor of age, as we have seen, exerts a very great influence on long-term trends in admission rates, the next logical step was to decompose the ethnic-nationality data by some classification that would allow us to distinguish age groups. Such a classification does not exist in the case of the nationality groupings, but an approximation to it can be obtained by using data based on ethnic background, where these data are cross-classified by diagnostic groupings. This second set of data, based on ethnicity, includes categorizations of the patient population according to ethnic stocks, broad nationality groupings, and the parents of each patient, as well as a separate classification of Negroes and Jews.

Although it was technically uncomplicated to obtain base population data in order to compute admission rates for Negroes and Jews,[5] a somewhat unusual procedure was used in obtaining rates for other major ethnic groups. The assumption was made that the secular trend in population growth or decline of ethnic groups categorized by nationality would parallel the population trends of the foreign born of the respective nationality groupings. On this assumption, admission rates for ethnic groups whose classification was based upon nationality categories were computed by dividing first admissions of each nationality-based ethnic group by the foreign-born population present in New York State of each respective nationality classification. Rates for the following major ethnic categories were included in the final analysis: English, French, German, Irish, Italian, Jewish, and Negro.

In order to avoid a concentration on either the very young or the aged population of patients, rates were computed on patients diagnosed as having some form of functional psychosis (including schizophrenia, manic-depressive psychosis, and involutional psychosis). Among the seven ethnic groups studied, only two show strong upward trends in first-admission rates, namely, Negroes and Italians (of both sexes). For the other five ethnic groups, admission rates for functional psychosis show no measurable trend whatever.

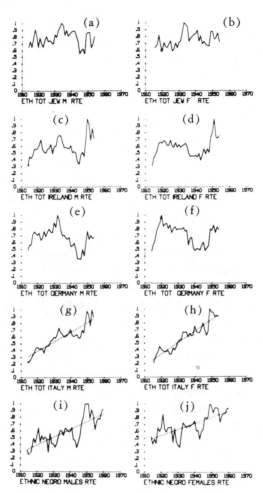

FIG. 10. Secular trends in mental-hospital first admission rates, 1913–1955: Jewish, Irish, German, Italian, and Negro ethnic groups with functional psychosis (schizophrenia, manic-depressive psychosis, and involutional psychosis), by sex. Best estimate of linear or nonlinear trend is fitted to admission rates where data contain measurable trend.

LEGEND:

_____ First admission rates with functional psychosis, by ethnic group

...... Plot of best fitting estimate of trend

Equation of model of trend:

(a–f) no measurable trend (g–j) $Y = a + bx$

SCALE: Rates per 100,000 are expressed as fractions of the highest rate, which is set equal to 1.0, for each population group. Scalar range describes relative magnitude of variation in each series.

Range of actual rates per 100,000:

(a) 180.99–323.42 (b) 233.95–400.92 (c) 82.9–268.1
(d) 74.98–260.83 (e) 41.13–116.41 (f) 68.77–150.59
(g) 24.16–110.31 (h) 25.39–140.79 (i) 24.13–101.65
(j) 43.87–107.08

This analysis clearly indicates that among the major ethnic groups for which it is possible to estimate rates of admission with functional psychosis, several show variation that is nearly entirely related to changes in the economy (Fig. 10; Chapter 5, Tables 10–12).

In general, we have seen that for the cases in which no long-term trends were present, a large part of the variation in mental-hospital admission rates is associated with economic changes. But what of those cases whose admission rates do show secular trends? An explanation of such trends will doubtless involve long-term changes in noneconomic phenomena. However, there is a possibility that the existence of some of the secular trends in admission rates may be due to long-term increases in the sensitivity of the population to economic change as expressed through mental hospitalization.

Our technique of assessing whether or not there has been an increase or a decrease in sensitivity of mental hospitalization to economic changes utilizes Fourier analysis. Fluctuations in hospital admission levels based upon annual percentage changes are transformed into their cyclical representations and matched with similarly sized cyclical representations of the Employement Index. The size of these cycles is determined on the basis of estimates, obtained through independent methods of analysis, of the smallest time interval for which the relation between economic change and mental hospitalization is clearly observable. In general, approximately 8.5 cycles in mental-hospital admissions can be readily observed (and measured through correlation procedures) to match inversely with the same number of cycles during the period 1915–1967. These cyclical representations describe either increases or decreases of approximately 2–3 years' duration.

Long Term Sensitivity of the Relations

These transformations of the data allow us to compare many different groups with respect to a possible increasing or decreasing trend in amplitude of the cycles of mental-hospital admissions that are found to be inversely related to cycles of employment. In this way we examined mental-hospital admissions of the various age and marital-status groupings for the presence of trends in amplitude, for the same number of cycles, in each sociodemographic group during the period 1915–1967.

Among the various age groups, we find that since the Second World War there has been a marked increase in the magnitude of reaction to economic change for 15–24- and 25–34-year-olds of both sexes, whereas there has been only a mildly increasing trend for 35–44-year-olds of both sexes. The age groups 0–15, 45–54, and over 65 years do not show rising trends of increase in the sensitivity of mental hospitalization to economic change. Since 1955, there has been a marked increase in sensitivity to economic change for the age groups 15–24, 25–34, and 35–44 years of both sexes, and only a modest increase among 45–54-year-olds of both sexes. No increasing trend in sensitivity to economic change since 1955 is shown for age groups under 15 or over 55 years of either sex.

These findings force us to reject the hypothesis that the increasing trend in rates of mental hospitalization, particularly among the young and the old, are due to increasing sensitivity among those age groups to economic change. On the other hand, we have seen that the age groups 15–34 years in particular do show an increasing trend of sensitivity to economic change after World War II, whereas the 15–54-year-olds show such increased sensitivity since 1955. So great, in fact, are the proportionate increases in mental-hospital admissions for 15–34-year-olds during the two relatively small economic downturns in the period 1955–1967 that they dwarf the magnitude of increased admissions during the Great Depression. Furthermore, the increases in sensitivity since World War II and 1955, among specific age groups, can be measured through Fourier analysis regardless of whether levels or rates of mental hospitalization are used. Since World War II we have clearly embarked upon a period in which even minor economic downturns occurring during periods of large-scale prosperity are producing enormous increases in mental-hospital admissions.

A summary of the situation among age groups since 1955 would indicate that, first, although for males we continue to find a somewhat stronger inverse relation for the late-middle-age group, in general the relation between economic change and mental-hospital admissions shows substantially less tendency for the different age groups to reveal different relations. Second, in general, admissions for females in each age group seem to yield relations with economic changes that are closer to those shown for the males in their respective age groups than has been true during earlier periods of the 19th or 20th centuries (see Table 3 and Figs. 11, 12).

Among the marital-status groups, only single males and females show increasing trends of sensitivity to economic changes since World War II. Both single and married males and females, however, show increased sensitivity to economic change since 1955, whereas the widowed, separated, and divorced do not (Fig. 13). The fact that there is an increasing trend in sensitivity since World War II only among single males and females may reflect the fact that it is the younger age groups, except for the 0–15-year group, whose hospitalization has become increasingly sensitive to economic downturns since World War II.

At least two possible explanations may be offered for the increases in

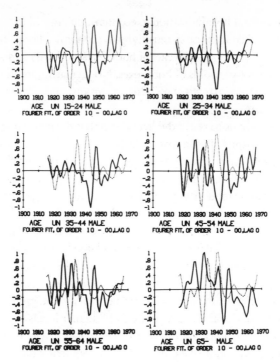

FIG. 11. Two- to 4-year fluctuations in employment and in mental-hospital admission rates, 1915–1967, by age group for males. First admission rates to New York civil state hospitals matched with New York State manufacturing employment index; data are smoothed through Fourier transformation of annual changes (first differences) so as to represent 2–4-year changes.

LEGEND:
...... New York State Manufacturing Employment Index
_____ Male first admission rates, by age group
SCALE: Fourier curves are scaled for viewing, such that the greatest amplitude from the arithmetic mean of each series (which is set equal to zero) has been normalized to 1.0 if positive, or −1.0 if negative.

sensitivity to economic change since World War II among the 15–24 and 25–34-year-olds. There are indications that supportive mechanisms in family life that have traditionally protected family members from stresses of the social environment have declined in influence as the family itself declines in size and influence relative to other social institutions.[6] In addition, the decline in the utilization of socially integrative mechanisms inherent in religion may also have increased the sensitivity of the population to the socially disruptive impact of economic downturns.[7]

Second, it is possible that with the decline of such integrative mechanisms as are inherent in the family and in religion the population has increasingly

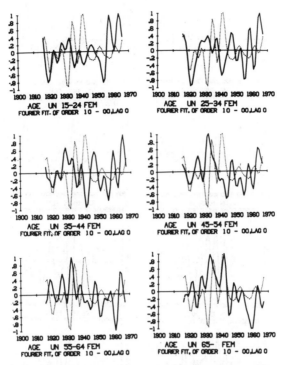

FIG. 12. Two- to 4-year fluctuations in employment and in mental-hospital admission rates, 1915–1967, by age group for females. First admission rates to New York civil state hospitals matched with New York State manufacturing employment index; data are smoothed through Fourier transformation of annual changes (first differences) so as to represent 2–4-year changes.

LEGEND:
...... New York State Manufacturing Employment Index
———— Female first admission rates, by age group
SCALE: Fourier curves are scaled for viewing, such that the greatest amplitude from the arithmetic mean of each series (which is set equal to zero) has been normalized to 1.0 if positive, or −1.0 if negative.

turned to medicine, and particularly psychiatry, to deal with problems of personal and social disorganization. Thus, as a result of economic stresses we may find an increasing tendency to utilize psychiatric institutions as sanctuaries. Trends of increasing breakdown in traditional institutions of social cohesion or the increased utilization of professional therapists would apply particularly to the population under age 40, since these younger age groups are more likely to have been raised under the more recent methods of accommodation to stress. Since 1955, however, we see that the increased sensitivity to economic change has expanded to include the age groups 35–44 and 45–54, among married persons of both sexes.

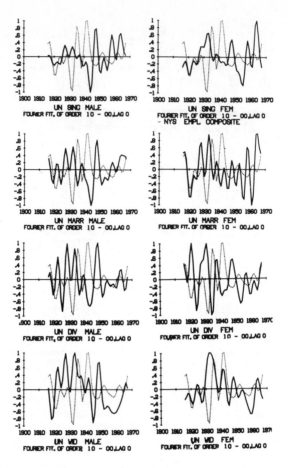

FIG. 13. Two- to 4-year fluctuations in employment and in mental-hospital admission rates, 1915–1967, by marital status and sex. First admission rates to New York civil state hospitals matched with New York State manufacturing employment index; data are smoothed through Fourier transformation of annual changes (first differences) so as to represent 2–4-year changes.

LEGEND:
...... New York State Manufacturing Employment Index
———— First admission rates by marital status: single, married, divorced, widowed
SCALE: Fourier curves are scaled for viewing, such that the greatest amplitude from the arithmetic mean of each series (which is set equal to zero) has been normalized to 1.0 if positive, or −1.0 if negative.

Though there are no trends in increased sensitivity to economic change of admissions below age 15 and above age 65, we do find very sharp increases in rates for both groups during the period 1910–1960. One is tempted to try to explain away these increasing trends by reference to the expansion of facilities and administrative policies of increased admissions for the young and the aged during the 1950's. Although these factors may indeed have been partly responsible for increased admissions during the 1950's and beyond, they certainly will not explain the secular trend that shows steady linear increases since 1910.

It is possible that the secular trends in admission rates for these particular age groups especially result from declines in the integrative functions of the family. Such declines might be reflected most sharply in a decreased dependence of the young and the elderly upon what has come to be called the nuclear family. Though the integrative functions of the family might have declined over the secular trend in the 20th century, it appears that such a decline has not adversely affected the situation of the separated and divorced woman. Rather, trends of increasing separation and divorce clearly reflect a long-term decrease in the importance of the family as the most basic economic and social unit. We find, in fact, that among all marital status categories, age groups, and even ethnic groups the single group whose admission rates show a strongly declining trend during the 20th century is separated and divorced females.

The general secular decline in admission rates of divorced and separated females may be the result of several social trends that have occurred over the past century. There is little doubt, first of all, that we have witnessed an increasingly greater acceptance of the status of the divorced or separated woman. Such women are no longer severely stigmatized for their marital status, are not necessarily isolated from their friends and associates at the time of the marital schism, and are probably able to return without disgrace to the families of their parents.

Second, the economic situation for the divorced or separated woman has substantially improved over the long term. Alimony and child-support monies are available to divorced women, as are support funds for the families of legally separated women. In addition, since the late 1930's we have witnessed a very substantial increase in the rate of entrance of women into the labor force.[8] It has become increasingly less difficult for women to earn an independent income at significantly higher levels and at jobs of increasingly greater social prestige.[9]

Unfortunately, since the data on ethnic background are available only through 1954, it is not possible to ascertain with accuracy whether there have been increases in sensitivity to economic change among these groups since World War II. We have noted, however, that among several major ethnic groups Italians and Negroes show very sharply rising secular trends in hospitalization for functional psychosis.

Part of the reason for the sharply increasing secular trends for Italians and Negroes may lie in the possibility that there would ordinarily be increased secular trends for admission rates among all ethnic groups, except that second- and third-generation ethnic groups tend to assimilate quickly into the population at large and admissions of the different ethnic groups include more than only the foreign born and their children, whereas the population denominators by which rates are described are based on only the foreign-born population.

Thus, assimilation of the major ethnic groups might tend to be so rapid that their absolute numbers do not increase over time in comparison with the increase in size of the foreign-born population of their ethnic group. In fact, for most of the major ethnic groups, admission rates for functional psychosis do not show increases over the secular trend. However, the Italian ethnic group, with a strong family structure, has relatively low rates of interethnic marriage, and Negroes similarly show relatively low rates of intermarriage because of racial and socioeconomic barriers. Relatively low rates of interethnic assimilation for the Italians and Negroes might be responsible for an increasing population of these ethnics (including second, third, and additional generations) in comparison with population trends based on waves of migration to the United States for Italians, and from South to North among Negroes.[10]

This answer is at best a partial one, however, since Jews, who do not show increased rates over the secular trend, are also known to have relatively low rates of intermarriage. In addition to the previous explanation, therefore, we may look to the types of factors that distinguish Jewish, Italian, and Negro groups. In a later section on the relation between economic change and mental hospitalization among ethnic groups (see Chapter 7), it is pointed out that Jews tend to be of relatively high socioeconomic status, whereas Italians are of relatively lower-middle class status and Negroes are among the ethnic groups of lowest socioeconomic status. This suggests that ethnic groups whose socioeconomic status has traditionally been even moderately low, relative to the population at large, have been experiencing increasing difficulties as higher education has tended to become a prerequisite to both high professional status and economically stable occupational positions.

Another possible explanation might be based on different subcultural orientations toward psychiatry among Jews, Italians, and Negroes. There is some evidence that Jews have for a long time shown favorable attitudes toward psychiatry as a means of dealing with emotional problems.[11] Italians, on the other hand, are known to have made extensive use of the institutions of the church and family to deal with such problems,[12] whereas Negroes until very recently have been somewhat isolated from medical care in general and from psychiatry in particular.[13] The dramatically increased trends in rates of psychiatric hospitalization of Italians and Negroes as compared with Jews may therefore reflect acculturation to distinctively American styles of coping with emotional disorder on the part of groups who have traditionally used alternative methods.

Educational Attainment

Ideally, we would have liked to examine secular trends in mental-hospital admission rates for different socioeconomic status groups, as defined by level of educational attainment. For New York State, unfortunately, data on educational attainment for the base population are unavailable for the period covered by the long-term trend in admissions. As to the question of possible long-term changes in sensitivity to economic change, however, several generalizations can be made. First, among the three major categories of educational attainment, namely, grammar school, high school, and college, no major changes in sensitivity to economic change appear to distinguish the pre- and post-World War II eras. Since 1955 we find a marked increase in sensitivity to economic downturns for mental-hospital admissions with a high-school educaton (Table 4; Fig. 14). Thus, as distinguished from most of the 20th century, in which the high-school educated are considerably less sensitive to economic change than either the grammar-school or college educated, since 1955 it is difficult to distinguish the level of sensitivity of the high-school group relative to the other two educational groups.

This may be due in part to the fact that the significance of educational background, as an indication of socioeconomic position, has undergone considerable change. Within the last 20 years, it has become relatively common for the children of even poor families to obtain a college education, and the high-school dropout has nearly acquired the status of a deviant.[14] Moreover, as one might imagine, the group of patients who have had less than a grammar-school education is now so small that a separate classification of their mental-hospital experience is of questionable value.[15] The significance of grammar-school, high-school, and college education must obviously be reinterpreted in the light of changes in the levels of technical skill and income potential that they have come to represent. Occupations held earlier by precondition of only a grammar-school education now require high-school education; those that formerly required a high-school education now demand collegiate training.

Secular trends in technological development result in an increasingly finer specialization of labor as well as in the accumulation of countless areas of technical knowledge associated with increasing numbers of occupations. At the same time we have witnessed the increased routinization of many unskilled,

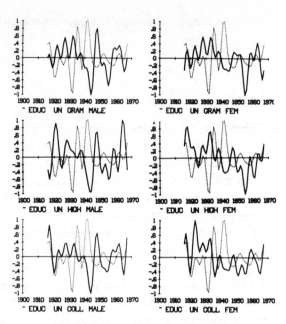

FIG. 14. Two- to 4-year fluctuations in employment and in mental-hospital admission rates, 1915–1967, by level of education and sex. First admission rates to New York civil state hospitals matched with New York State manufacturing employment index; data are smoothed through Fourier transformation of annual changes (first differences) so as to represent 2–4-year changes.

LEGEND:
...... New York State Manufacturing Employment Index
———— First admission rates, by level of education: grammar school, high school, college
SCALE: Fourier curves are scaled for viewing, such that the greatest amplitude from the arithmetic mean of each series (which is set equal to zero) has been normalized to 1.0 if positive, or −1.0 if negative.

as well as relatively skilled, jobs which can now be performed more efficiently and effectively by machine.

The high-school educated person of today may therefore occupy a similar position within the present economy to that of the grammar-school educated of predepression, or even pre-World War I, days. It is therefore likely that the high-school educated would increasingly resemble the grammar-school educated of an earlier day in terms of unusually great sensitivity to economic change. Thus, the high-school educated person may have become more expendable to business firms during economic downturns—firms that have increasingly adopted automated procedures and may find it economical to replace even the high-school educated foreman by a low-level administrator with a college degree.

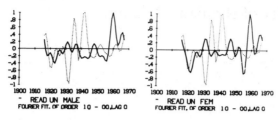

FIG. 15. Two- to 4-year fluctuations in employment and in readmission rates to mental hospitals, 1915–1967, by sex. Readmission rates to New York civil state hospitals matched with New York State manufacturing employment index; data are smoothed through Fourier transformation of annual changes (first differences) so as to represent 2–4-year changes.

LEGEND:
...... New York State Manufacturing Employment Index
———— Readmission rates
SCALE: Fourier curves are scaled for viewing, such that the greatest amplitude from the arithmetic mean of each series (which is set equal to zero) has been normalized to 1.0 if positive, or −1.0 if negative.

Readmissions

We observed earlier that several major categories of first admissions among age, marital status, and ethnic groups do not show increased secular trends of admission rates. On the other hand, there are strong increases in trends of readmission rates since 1910, and particularly since World War II. An analysis of changes in the size of the inversely matched cycles of readmissions with those of employment also indicates a marked increase in sensitivity since World War II, with an acceleration of this increase since 1955. The overall trend of increases in admission rates may therefore be partially accounted for by increased sensitivity of readmissions to changes in the economy (Fig. 15).

The possibility must be raised that increased readmission rates may also partially result from the increased use, since the 1950's, of tranquilizing drugs.[16] Extensive use of such drugs has provided greater control over patients' symptoms without the necessity of long-term hospitalization. The discharge of increasingly large numbers of patients to the general community, however, also brings with it the danger of exposing these former patients to the same kinds of social and economic stresses that may have brought them to a hospital in the first place. It is further possible, if not probable, that patients who have had relatively brief hospital stays will not readjust as well to community life as those who stay somewhat longer. The underlying reason may have to do with the sanctuary effects of even minimal custodial care or to the stabilizing effects of a structured and routinized social environment. In any case, the possibility is clear that early discharge of patients into a hostile economic environment might rapidly result in extraordinarily high rates of readmission.

5 Stability of the Basic Relation

In this chapter we shall examine in detail the types of patients whose mental-hospital admissions have shown a highly stable and predictable inverse relation to economic changes for the period 1914–1960. The statistical procedures on which the analysis of stability is based contrast somewhat with the procedure for determining the number of years over which relations exist at varying levels of correlation. The latter procedure was used in the previous chapter, where we were interested in establishing whether or not relations actually existed over specific periods of time for a large number of categories of the population of admissions.

We found that, in general, for nearly any population of admissions that is highly sensitive to economic changes, the correlation coefficient tends to be less than −0.85 (r between −0.85 and −1.00) for approximately 70 to 85 percent of the years under study, and less than −0.70 for 90 percent of the years under study. These findings are based on a procedure that identifies the precise spans of time for which the relations approach a predetermined level of correlation (which has been corrected for possible autocorrelation of residuals). The procedure takes into account the fact that for certain populations of admissions the relation may be quite stable at a specified level of correlation, whereas for other populations it may vary widely during the period 1914–1960; for certain spans it may be exceedingly high; for others it may involve a change in direction (from inverse to positive) that may be at variance with the rest of the relation.

In the present chapter we attempt to identify those populations of admissions for which the basic inverse relation can be easily identified, and therefore easily replicated. Thus, we are interested in describing those categories of admissions that give evidence of stable relations over a relatively long period.

The component of stability in the relation between economic change and mental hospitalization is important in its pertinence to our original hypothesis, which maintained that economic change per se, rather than any other major external social variable, would inversely influence mental-hospital admissions. However, although many of the populations were referred to in the previous chapter as having identifiable relations with economic change for specific periods of time, many of these relations may have been highly unstable. A relation that extends over even a fairly lengthy period, but is unstable, indicates that there are external variables which definitely influence the magnitude of impact of economic change upon mental-hospital admissions and, frequently, the degree to which a correlation exists between economic change and admissions. In fact, it is quite possible that for a highly unstable relation the very existence of that relation may depend on factors extrinsic to the variables under study.

For this reason, our conception of easy replication is very rigidly confined to relations of demonstrable stability. The determination of stability in a relation uses the simplest and most traditional methods of correlation. It makes use, first of all, of the multiple-correlation coefficient, which takes into account the possibility of a relation involving distributed lags, but does not make allowance for an unstable relation, that is, one in which the correlation or impact varies through time. Second, it uses the simple (zero-order) correlation coefficient as an estimate of the stability of the relation for 47 years, 1914–1960.

We would like, ideally, to be able to make some general statement about the reaction pattern of the total population under study (in terms of mental hospitalization) to changes in the economy. However, any attempt to describe a general reaction pattern is likely to be fruitless—if, indeed, such a pattern exists. The difficulty is that any or all of the individual subgroups which constitute total mental-hospital admissions may have a unique relation to economic change. Wilson expresses it thus:

> To assess the meaning of disaster, it is of course not enough to think in terms of global stress. Rather, one must question the time-and-space coordinates of stress, asking what particular events occurred when. Differentiation of disaster events, in turn, demands differentiation of the target population by area, time, age, and sex, ethnicity, and as many elements as possible of the total life history. Connections between stress and illness can never be established "in general."[1]

More specifically, in this particular problem of stress-reactions, we must be particularly sensitive to possible occurrences of unique subgroup reactions according to: (1) the interval of time involved in the reaction, (2) the dispersion of the effects of the stress over time, (3) the differential reaction to

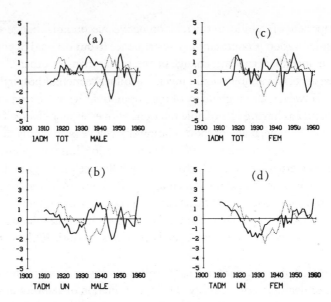

FIG. 16. Fluctuations in employment and in mental-hospital admissions during 1914–1960: total admissions and first admissions with functional psychosis (schizophrenia, manic-depressive psychosis, and involutional psychosis), by sex. Admissions to New York civil state hospitals matched with New York State manufacturing employment index (secular trend subtracted from both series).

LEGEND:

...... New York State Manufacturing Employment Index
_____ First admissions and total admissions:
    (a) male first admissions, functional psychoses
    (b) total male admissions
    (c) female first admissions, functional psychoses
    (d) total female admissions

SCALE: Deviations from secular trend in admissions and in the employment index are expressed in standardized normal scores. Scalar range describes relative magnitude of variation in each series.

economic changes of varying magnitude, and (4) the differential distribution of the effects of economic change among the various subcategories of the population, such as age, sex, socioeconomic status, or illness (see, for example, Fig. 16). Thus, any statement of the general reaction pattern of the total population to economic change can be stated only in terms of a summary or arithmetic summation of the various subpopulation reactions.

In estimating the subpopulation reactions to economic change, we shall be concerned with: (1) the importance of economic change relative to other influences on mental-hospital admissions over time, (2) the relative importance of large and small economic changes in the fluctuation of mental-hospital admissions over time, and (3) a measure of the impact of economic changes on mental-hospital admissions.

The Relative Importance of Economic Change in Mental Hospitalization

The importance of economic change relative to other influences on mental-hospital admissions over time may be gauged by the Pearsonian correlation coefficient, which provides a measure of the stability of the relation (or the average fraction of variation in mental-hospital admissions accounted for by inverse variation in the employment index).

The very best estimate of stability is theoretically given by the multiple correlation, which allows for dispersion of the effects of economic stress through time. Another appropriate measure of the relation is the optimum correlation from which an estimate of the average timing of the reaction can be obtained. Although this measure is not as sophisticated as the multiple correlation, it has a long tradition of reasonably successful use, and can be more readily compared with correlations obtained in other studies. In addition, the optimum correlation involves the fewest mathematical manipulations of the data and is closest to the concept of a raw correlation. Finally, we employ the optimum correlation, using serially independent data, to obtain an estimate of the statistical significance of the relations.

These three estimates of predictability are computed for the two finest, and possibly most diverse, classifications of first admissions to civil state hospitals, namely, age and level of educational attainment. Our argument is that the more highly differentiated the subpopulations are, the greater is the possibility that different patterns of reaction to economic change will appear.

The Multiple Correlation

Multiple correlations between changes in the employment index and changes in mental hospitalization were computed for thirteen age and six educational-attainment categories over the periods 1914–1955 and 1914–1960 respectively (see Tables 6, 7).

Taking a multiple correlation of ±0.50 as evidence of stable sensitivity of mental hospitalization to economic change, we find that 65.6 percent (based on the mean number of admissions per year) of male first admissions show a stable inverse correlation and 19.2 percent show a positive correlation over the full period 1914–1960; 6.7 percent show neither a predictably positive nor a predictably inverse correlation. Thus, 84.8 percent of the population of male first admissions, when categorized by age groups, show stable sensitivity to economic changes.

On the average, the data show that in the great majority of conditions a unit (percentage) decrease in the employment index is accompanied by at

Table 6. Correlations between employment and mental-hospital admissions during 1914–1960, by age and sex.[a]

Age (1914–1960)	Optimum correlations[b]					Multiple correlations[c]		Mean number per year	Per cent
	r_1	r_2	r_3	r_4	n	R	B		
Male									
0–14	+0.10	+0.09	−0.16	−0.25	40	−0.35	−0.04	116.4	2.4
15–19	− .35	− .67	− .32	− .31	39	− .45	− .38	235.8	4.3
20–24	− .48	− .57	− .59	− .62	41	− .61	− .39	418.1	7.6
25–29	− .38	− .45	− .58	− .61	35	− .48	− .28	466.3	8.5
30–34	− .68	− .82	− .71	− .67	40	− .75	− .67	455.1	8.3
35–39	− .80	− .91	− .77	− .60	44	− .83	− .91	483.8	8.8
40–44	− .86	− .96	− .78	− .60	45	− .90	−1.06	453.9	8.2
45–49	− .88	− .95	− .80	− .71	45	− .92	−1.11	411.4	7.5
50–54	− .79	− .93	− .71	− .63	44	− .85	− .80	383.0	6.9
55–59	− .71	− .88	− .58	− .55	37	− .78	− .62	350.5	6.4
60–64	− .63	− .82	− .62	− .61	34	− .76	− .44	347.1	6.3
65–69	− .52	− .64	− .58	− .55	34	− .76	− .03	335.2	6.1
70+	+ .47	+ .71	+ .30	+ .43	27	+ .50	+ .34	1059.6	19.2
Total								5516.2	100.0
Female									
0–14	−0.18	−0.33	−0.36	−0.41	33	−0.42	−0.20	54.5	1.0
15–19	+ .42	+ .48	− .38	− .48	41	+ .50	+ .13	198.6	3.8
20–24	+ .28	+ .33	− .25	− .39	20	+ .29	+ .02	345.7	6.7
25–29	+ .43	+ .51	− .29	− .54	26	+ .43	+ .35	422.7	8.1
30–34	+ .15	− .34	− .26	− .34	33	− .47	− .04	435.6	8.8
35–39	− .55	− .65	− .70	− .78	41	− .72	− .36	447.3	8.6
40–44	− .68	− .86	− .58	− .54	39	− .76	− .86	407.0	7.8
45–49	− .75	− .87	− .68	− .65	34	− .82	− .52	391.2	7.5
50–54	− .61	− .82	− .50	− .37	35	− .67	− .35	358.3	6.9
55–59	− .43	− .63	− .30	− .40	33	− .66	− .12	295.2	5.7
60–64	+ .46	− .54	− .48	− .49	31	+ .75	+ .13	284.6	5.5
65–69	+ .66	+ .74	+ .65	− .54	19	+ .86	+ .31	301.0	5.8
70+	+ .54	+ .66	+ .40	+ .37	17	+ .64	+ .51	1255.0	24.1
Total								5196.7	100.0

[a]First admissions to New York civil state hospitals correlated with New York State manufacturing employment index (secular trend subtracted from both series).

[b]r_1, detrended data; r_2, 5-year moving averages of detrended data; r_3, 5-year moving changes (differences); r_4, detrended by subtracting 5-year moving averages; n, number of years that correlations $\leq$−0.65. Correlations based on data transformed to control for autocorrelated residuals.

[c]R, multiple correlations; B, sums of beta weights based upon multiple regressions; both include 0–3-years lagged admissions. Detrended data.

Table 7. Correlations between employment and mental-hospital admissions during 1914–1960, by educational attainment and sex.[a]

Educational attainment (1914–1960)	Optimum correlations[b]				n	Multiple correlation[c]		Mean number per year	Percent
	r_1	r_2	r_3	r_4		R	B		
Male									
Illiterate	−0.57	−0.77	−0.37	−0.30	18	−0.62	−0.43	289.1	5.7
Reads	− .47	− .74	− .24	+ .40	16	− .61	− .62	31.3	0.6
Reads and writes	+ .62	+ .74	+ .46	+ .33	19	+ .65	+ .46	431.0	8.5
Grammar School	− .89	− .96	− .84	− .72	38	− .93	− .92	3148.8	62.3
High School	+ .38	+ .35	− .56	− .68	38	− .50	+ .13	926.4	18.3
College	− .64	− .74	− .69	− .68	36	− .73	− .36	226.7	4.5
Total								5053.3	100.0
Female									
Illiterate	+0.42	+0.62	−0.32	−0.47	16	+0.65	+0.13	350.2	7.3
Reads	− .34	− .43	− .22	− .23	13	− .37	− .29	38.5	0.8
Reads and writes	+ .74	+ .86	+ .64	+ .53	6	+ .79	+ .68	406.8	8.5
Grammar School	− .85	− .95	− .76	− .57	35	− .90	− .74	2732.6	57.2
High School	+ .67	+ .71	+ .43	− .49	31	+ .68	+ .62	1043.7	21.9
College	+ .53	+ .60	− .42	− .68	35	+ .56	+ .24	201.9	4.2
Total								4773.7	100.0

[a]First admissions to New York civil state hospitals correlated with New York State manufacturing employment index (secular trend subtracted from both series).

[b]r_1, detrended data; r_2, 5-year moving averages of detrended data; r_3, 5-year moving changes (differences); r_4, detrended by subtracting 5-year moving averages: n, number of years that correlations ≦−0.65. Correlations based on data transformed to control for autocorrelated residuals.

[c]R, multiple correlations; B, sums of beta weights based upon multiple regressions; both include 0–3 years lagged admissions. Detrended data.

least a 1/3-unit (percentage) increase in mental hospitalization. In a large fraction of the age and educational-attainment subcategories (40–60 percent), however, the ratio is about 1.00, and the unit (percentage) change is of approximately the same magnitude. These proportionate increases in the ratio of changes in admissions to changes in the employment index are expressed in summations of the beta weights.[2] However, proportionate increases and decreases in hospitalization that are inversely related to economic change are not directly interpretable in terms of either the absolute number or the fraction of persons employed or unemployed. Our employment statistics for New York State are based on samples of persons employed in selected manufacturing industries, beginning in 1914. Data on total unemployment are not available for New York State until 1929.

Lack of stable correlation in some cases indicates simple lack of sensitivity to the stresses of economic upturns or downturns. It may also indicate that the stresses of the upturn and the downturn are equal, so that no dominant positive or inverse relation appears.

Correlation Based on Optimum Lag

Of the various methods used, the data on which the optimum correlation is performed have undergone the least amount of transformation; except for elimination of the secular trend, the data are in their raw form. The correlations appear to be only slightly lower than those found for the multiple correlation (Tables 6 and 7). Also, a somewhat smaller fraction of first admissions (approximately 10 percent in each case; see Tables 8 and 9) is sensitive either to the downturn or to the upturn than with the multiple correlation. We conclude, then, that, even with the more traditional correlation technique, the correlations are quite high by conventional standards, but somewhat less than when the dispersed effects of economic stress are estimated.

The F test of statistical significance[3] was used to determine whether the magnitudes of the optimum correlations were significant at the 0.01 probability level. To perform this test the detrended data were transformed by Durbin's method[4] to control for the effects of autocorrelation as estimated by the Durbin-Watson statistic.[5] This same data transformation was employed in determining the absolute number of years over which correlations could be found at specific levels (see Chapter 4). After data transformation, all of the age and educational-attainment series were found to fall within the limits indicated for absence of autocorrelated residuals.

Since the time series used in this test have been reconstructed so as to be serially independent, the independent and dependent series (or variables) are

Table 8. Percentage of mental-hospital admissions that are sensitive to economic changes, by age and sex during 1914–1960.[a]

Correlation[b]	r_1	r_2	r_3	r_4	n	R
			Male			
$r \leq -0.50$ or $\geq +0.50$						
Negative	58.0	69.9	74.1	74.1	100.0	65.5
Positive	0.0	19.2	0.0	0.0	0.0	19.2
Total	58.0	89.1	74.1	74.1	100.0	84.7
$r > -0.50$ or $< +0.50$	42.0	10.9	25.9	25.9	0.0	15.2
			Female			
$r \leq -0.50$ or $\geq +0.50$						
Negative	30.8	41.7	30.5	37.8	84.6	40.0
Positive	29.9	38.0	5.8	0.0	0.0	35.4
Total	60.7	79.7	36.3	37.8	84.6	75.4
$r > -0.50$ or $< +0.50$	39.3	20.3	63.7	62.2	19.2	24.6

[a]First admissions to New York civil state hospitals correlated with New York State manufacturing employment index (secular trend subtracted from both series).

[b]r_1, detrended data; r_2, 5-year moving averages of detrended data; r_3, 5-year moving changes (differences); r_4, detrended by substracting 5-year moving averages; n, number of years that correlations ≤ -0.65, based on data transformed to control for autocorrelated residuals; R, multiple correlations include 0–3-year lagged admissions; detrended data.

being matched point for point (or year for year). Thus, the optimum correlation represents the best fit, independently, of every single year's employment index number to an opposite year's number of first admissions.

As expected, the optimum correlations with serially independent data are moderately lower (approximately 10 to 15 correlation points) than those found for the linearly detrended data. Over the full period 1914–1960, however, 100.0 percent of male first admissions classified by age show inverse sensitivity to economic changes, at $r \leq -0.65$ (between -0.65 and -1.00) for at least 25 years. Similarly, 84.6 percent of female first admissions classified by age show sensitivity to economic change, and all to the downturn (see Table 8). We may conclude that even where the economic series is matched against the various mental hospitalization series independently, year for year during the entire period 1914–1960, the majority of the male and one-third of the female first admissions, as classified by age, show stable tendencies to increase during economic downturns.

Table 9. Percentage of mental-hospital admissions that are sensitive to economic changes, by level of education and sex during 1914–1960.[a]

Correlation[b]	r_1	r_2	r_3	r_4	n	R
Male						
$r \leq -0.50$ or $\geq +0.50$						
Negative	72.5	73.2	85.2	85.2	85.1	91.5
Positive	8.5	8.5	0.0	0.0	0.0	8.5
Total	81.0	81.7	85.2	85.2	85.1	100.0
$r > -0.50$ or $< +0.50$	19.0	18.3	14.8	14.8	14.9	0.0
Female						
$r \leq -0.50$ or $\geq +0.50$						
Negative	57.2	57.2	57.2	61.4	83.3	57.2
Positive	34.6	42.0	8.5	8.5	0.0	42.0
Total	91.8	99.2	65.7	69.9	83.3	99.2
$r > -0.50$ or $< +0.50$	8.2	0.8	34.3	30.1	16.7	0.8

[a]First admissions to New York civil state hospitals correlated with New York State manufacturing employment index (secular trend subtracted from both series).
[b]r_1, detrended data; r_2, 5-year moving averages of detrended data; r_3, 5-year moving changes (differences); r_4, detrended by subtracting 5-year moving averages; n, number of years the correlation ≤ -0.65, based on data transformed to control for autocorrelated residuals; R, multiple correlations include 0–3-year lagged admissions; detrended data.

Correlations for the education categories yield similar results. In this case, 85.1 percent of male and 83.3 percent of female first admissions show statistically significant inverse relations for at least 25 years. None of the male or female first admissions show statistically significant positive correlations (see Table 9). In general, it appears that, although much of the population responds very sharply to even a single year's economic downturn, increases in admissions during the upturn—when they occur—seem to be a response to relatively long-term (8–10-year) upward economic movements.

The Relative Importance of Large and Small Economic Changes to Mental Hospitalization

We have seen that for many groups the relation between economic changes and mental hospitalization is highly stable. We now ask whether this relation is primarily related to relatively large economic cycles of approximately 8–10 years in duration (but not periodic), or equally sensitive to shorter movement of 1–5 years in duration.

We may distinguish the effect of the large economic cycle from those of smaller economic movements by correlating the 5-year moving averages of the linearly detrended series. The optimum correlations are as high for the 5-year moving averages as for the multiple correlations (Tables 6–9). The implication, then, is that at least a significant part of the reaction of mental hospitalization to economic change represents reaction to the economic cycle.

Having seen that a substantial number of groups show highly stable relations between the level of mental-hospital admissions and the level of employment, we may inquire whether there is as stable a relation with changes in employment of moderate size, that is, over 5-year intervals. Transformation of the economic and admissions data into 5-year changes (that is, five-point moving averages of first differences) provides the possibility for such an investigation.

The optimum correlations (see Tables 6–9) for the age and educational-attainment categories show that first admissions are, in general, just as sensitive to 5-year changes as they are to variations in the absolute level of the economic indicator. The patterns of sensitivity to the 5-year changes are somewhat different (though less for the educational-attainment categories) from those to the absolute levels of the economic indicator. (Explanations of this particular response to the economic cycle are offered in Chapters 6 and 7.) It appears, then, that the relation between mental-hospital admissions and intermediate-sized economic changes need not be based on the method of eliminating the secular trend that has been used to produce most of the estimates of relation that are used in this study.   •

We may also eliminate the largely cyclical component of economic change, as well as all economic trends of at least 5 years' duration, by subtracting the linearly detrended 5-year moving average from the raw series. This leaves us with only economic changes of less than 5 years' duration. We may now inquire whether mental-hospital admissions respond *only* to the broad contours of cyclical economic changes and other large-scale economic changes of at least 5 years' duration.

The data (Tables 6–9) show that both the optimum correlations and the percentages of the population of admissions whose sensitivity to economic change is stable are almost identical when we compare the relations, based on decycled and 5-year change data. The clear implication is that a substantial number of categories of mental-hospital admissions show stable relations that are as sensitive to small as to large economic changes.

Replication of Procedure Among Different Total Populations

By subclassifying the total population of mental-hospital admissions according to age and educational attainment, we have been able to observe some of the differences in the way specific groups may react to economic change with mental hospitalization. By adding the fractions of the total population of admissions (indicated by specific groups) that show stable sensitivity to economic change, for the full 41 or 47 years, we arrive at estimates of the fraction of the total population that show predictable sensitivity.

Repeating the statistical procedures for 13 male and 13 female age groups and on 6 male and 6 female educational-attainment categories enables us to demonstrate that a stable relation exists between economic change and mental hospitalization among nearly all of these groups (provided one examines each of these sociodemographic categories separately). However, to first combine the categories and then note the fraction responding is to "add" what are often quite unique (and therefore dissimilar) relations. Therefore, when one examines the "reaction of a total population," he works in a way that is equivalent to summing the reactions of variously categorized subgroups within that population. Unless these subgroup reactions are very similar to one another, the "total" reaction (sum of reactions) will consist of a series of unrelated phenomena that, when added together, would not be meaningful.

Nevertheless, for the sake of demonstrating that a general relation does exist among a sizable number of "total populations," it is necessary to examine the various reaction patterns of entire populations; the reason is that, although admissions to the mental hospital are classified by ethnic background and country of patients' (and their parents') nativity, they are not cross-classified by either age or socioeconomic status. Our examination of the reactions of independent total populations must, then, proceed under the caveat that the substantial limitations of the available data may lead us to grossly underestimate the number of populations whose mental hospitalization exhibits stable sensitivity to economic change. With this warning before us, we turn to an examination of specific categories.

Ethnic Groups

First admissions to all New York State mental hospitals are described according to the "racial" or ethnic background classifications of the U. S. Bureau of Immigration.[6] Thirty-four classifications tabulated by sex are available for analysis.

The optimum correlation over the 5-year moving average and the multiple correlation based on raw data (except for detrending) show, respectively, that 28 and 24 male ethnic groups exhibit highly stable sensitivity (where R is at least ± 0.50). The 28 male populations are equal to 82 percent of the entire set of 34 populations. Of these stably sensitive populations, 2 and 4 respectively show a positive correlation. For the females, the 5-year moving average and the multiple correlation show that 21 and 15 populations respectively exhibit stable sensitivity. The highest female number, 21 populations, is equal to 62 percent of the 34 populations in question. Of the stable relations for female populations, 12 and 7 respectively show positivity (Table 10).

With the series that have been transformed so as to eliminate major sources of autocorrelation, 29 of the male and 25 of the female populations show inverse sensitivity to economic changes at $r \leq -0.65$ (between -0.65 and -1.00) for at least 25 years. None of the male and 5 of the female relations show positivity (Tables 11 and 12).

It is interesting that the 5-year moving average yields much higher correlations than the multiple correlation (Table 10). One interpretation of these findings is that the greatest uniformity among stress-reactions would be found, among a variety of subpopulations, in response to the large 5-year average changes in the economy. Less uniformity among subpopulation reactions might be found in response to economic change regardless of magnitude, even though dispersion of stress was accounted for to some extent. Even less uniformity might occur where the subpopulations were reacting to small changes, with no allowance for the effect of dispersion of economic changes; not more than 14 male and 8 female populations, however, show stable reactions to each yearly change in the economic indicator for the 41-year period.

Replication Among 47 Countries of Nativity of Admissions

The optimum correlation over the 5-year moving average and multiple correlation based on raw data (except for detrending) show that 40 and 29 of the 47 male populations of different countries of nativity respectively exhibit highly stable sensitivity (Table 13). The highest male number (40 populations) includes 80 percent of the 47 populations. Of these sensitive populations, 3 and 1 respectively show positive correlations. For the females, these correlations show that 28 and 25 populations respectively exhibit stable sensitivity. The highest female number (28 populations) is 60 percent of the 47 populations. Of the stable relations for females, 9 and 7 respectively show positivity.

Table 10. Correlations between employment and mental-hospital admissions during 1914–1960, by ethnic group and sex.[a]

| | Multiple correlations[b] | | Optimum correlations | | | |
| | | | 5-year moving average | | Data not averaged | |
Ethnic group	Male	Female	Male	Female	Male	Female
Negro	−0.37	+0.49	+0.17	+0.53	+0.25	+0.48
American Indian	+ .63	+ .38	+ .37	+ .37	+ .23	+ .26
Armenian	− .63	− .64	− .91	− .86	− .60	− .59
Bulgarian	− .33	− .45	− .38	− .62	− .20	− .28
Chinese	+ .54	+ .52	+ .61	+ .64	+ .40	+ .34
Cuban	− .42	− .27	− .51	− .41	− .18	− .13
Dutch and Flemish	− .49	− .42	− .64	− .74	− .41	− .38
East Indian	+ .39	− .27	+ .30	− .19	+ .18	− .11
English	+ .51	+ .61	+ .45	+ .69	+ .38	+ .55
Finnish	− .54	− .52	− .59	+ .36	− .39	+ .30
French	− .45	+ .41	− .56	+ .53	− .33	+ .25
German	− .77	+ .54	− .89	+ .71	− .69	+ .51
Greek	− .58	+ .42	− .84	+ .60	− .49	+ .32
Jewish	− .79	− .75	− .81	− .71	− .67	− .61
Irish	− .90	+ .50	− .95	+ .79	− .82	+ .54
Italian	− .76	− .69	− .90	− .69	− .73	− .54
Japanese	− .40	+ .55	− .77	+ .84	− .30	+ .43
Korean	− .52	+ .21	− .79	+ .15	− .43	+ .12
Lithuanian	− .69	+ .64	− .94	+ .75	− .57	+ .43
Magyar	− .59	+ .29	− .79	+ .41	− .50	+ .35
Mexican	− .51	− .34	− .65	+ .16	− .37	− .08
Pacific Islander	− .71	− .39	− .94	− .45	− .64	− .17
Portuguese	− .36	+ .45	− .59	+ .51	− .31	+ .22
Rumanian	− .60	− .51	− .68	− .62	− .39	− .30
Scandinavian	− .73	+ .38	− .89	+ .39	− .70	+ .25
Scotch	− .57	− .53	− .72	− .49	− .37	− .28
Slavic	− .74	+ .33	− .83	+ .78	− .73	+ .40
Spanish	− .46	− .55	− .66	− .81	− .43	− .50
Spanish American	+ .59	+ .53	+ .74	+ .69	+ .58	+ .52
Syrian	− .67	− .46	− .81	+ .19	− .60	− .16
Turkish	− .52	− .53	− .72	− .55	− .35	− .34
Welsh	− .29	+ .23	− .48	+ .41	− .25	+ .08
West Indian	− .52	− .53	− .65	− .69	− .51	− .52
Mixed	− .62	− .47	− .71	− .31	− .57	− .30

[a]First admissions to New York civil state hospitals correlated with New York State manufacturing employment index (secular trend subtracted from both series).
[b]The sign of R depends on the signs of the beta weights.

Table 11. Number of years, 1914–1955, during which the correlation between employment and mental-hospital admissions $\leq$ −0.65:[a] male admissions, by ethnic group.[b]

Ethnic group	Number of years				
	36–41	30–35	25–29	20–24	Under 20
Pacific Islander	41				
Italian	41				
West Indian	41				
Mixed	41				
American Indian	40				
Armenian	40				
German	40				
Irish	40				
Mexican	40				
Scandinavian	40				
Slavic	39				
Spanish	39				
Spanish American	39				
French	39				
Negro	39				
Scotch	37				
Jewish	36				
Magyar	36				
Bulgarian		35			
English		35			
Lithuanian		35			
Cuban		34			
Greek		34			
Turkish		33			
Japanese		30			
Finnish			28		
Portuguese			28		
Syrian			27		
Dutch and Flemish			26		
Korean				24	
Rumanian				23	
Chinese				21	
East Indian				21	
Welsh					18
Number of groups	18	7	4	4	1
Cumulative number		25	29	33	34
Fractions of total number of groups	0.529	0.206	0.118	0.118	0.029
Cumulative fractions		.735	.853	.971	1.000

[a]r between −0.65 and −1.00. Only correlations not significantly affected by autocorrelation of residuals, as measured by the Durbin-Watson statistic, are included.

[b]First admissions to New York civil state hospitals correlated with New York State manufacturing employment index (secular trend subtracted from both series).

Table 12. Number of years, 1914–1955, which the correlation between employment and mental-hospital admissions $\leq$ −0.65:[a] female admissions, by ethnic group.[b]

Ethnic group	Number of years				
	36–41	30–35	25–29	20–24	Under 20
West Indian	41				
Mixed	41				
Armenian	40				
Spanish American	40				
Negro	39				
English	37				
Scotch	36				
Bulgarian		35			
Jewish		35			
Turkish		35			
Italian		34			
Finnish		33			
Irish		33			
Magyar		33			
Rumanian		32			
French		30			
German		30			
Greek			29		
Mexican			28		
Scandinavian			28		
Spanish			28		
Portuguese			27		
Cuban			26		
Dutch and Flemish			25		
Lithuanian			25		
Welsh				24	
Syrian				22	
East Indian				20	
Slavic					19
Pacific Islander					17
Japanese					16
American Indian					13
Chinese					0
Korean					0
Number of groups	7	10	8	3	6
Cumulative number		17	25	28	34
Fractions of total number of groups	0.206	0.294	0.235	0.088	0.176
Cumulative fractions		.500	.735	.823	.999

[a] r between −0.65 and −1.00. Only correlations not significantly affected by autocorrelation of residuals, as measured by the Durbin-Watson statistic, are included.

[b] First admissions to New York civil state hospitals correlated with New York State manufacturing employment index (secular trend subtracted from both series).

Table 13. Correlations between employment and mental-hospital admissions during 1914–1955, by country of birth.[a]

Country of birth	Optimum correlation, 5-year moving averages		Multiple correlation,[b] data not averaged	
	Male	Female	Male	Female
United States	−0.72	+0.73	−0.71	+0.64
Africa	− .69	− .87	− .54	− .69
Armenia	− .80	− .87	− .64	− .63
Asia	− .53	− .22	− .45	− .43
Atlantic Islands	− .81	− .76	− .69	− .69
Australia	− .94	+ .43	− .70	+ .40
Austria	− .50	+ .58	− .38	+ .57
Belgium	− .40	− .49	− .42	− .30
Bulgaria	− .54	− .57	− .37	− .45
Canada	− .83	+ .47	− .61	+ .42
Central America	− .58	− .20	− .28	− .45
China	+ .59	+ .40	+ .49	+ .45
Cuba	− .53	− .68	− .48	− .43
Czechoslovakia	− .83	− .47	− .49	− .40
Denmark	+ .20	− .45	+ .33	− .46
England	− .71	+ .27	− .49	+ .40
Finland	− .65	+ .59	− .48	+ .44
France	− .58	+ .45	− .53	+ .27
Germany	− .90	+ .77	− .76	+ .66
Greece	− .66	− .40	− .51	− .50
Hawaii	− .30	+ .65	− .41	+ .44
Holland	− .16	− .30	− .27	− .53
Hungary	− .61	− .65	− .46	− .53
India	− .85	− .69	− .58	− .55
Ireland	− .95	+ .68	− .86	+ .64
Italy	− .79	− .73	− .69	− .54
Japan	− .89	+ .80	− .54	+ .46
Yugoslavia	− .54	− .86	− .43	− .58
Lithuania	− .90	− .78	− .79	− .56
Mexico	− .84	− .74	− .71	− .67
Norway	− .31	+ .42	− .46	+ .40
Philippines	− .83	− .50	− .63	− .34
Poland	− .83	− .81	− .79	− .67
Puerto Rico	+ .52	+ .54	+ .38	+ .40
Portugal	− .84	+ .08	− .60	+ .32
Rumania	− .53	− .61	− .28	− .62
Russia	+ .61	+ .56	+ .63	+ .68
Scotland	− .82	+ .50	− .64	+ .52
South America	− .57	− .79	− .32	− .70
Spain	− .47	− .47	− .29	− .45
Sweden	− .78	+ .37	− .67	+ .52
Switzerland	− .39	− .25	− .55	− .28
Syria	− .83	− .80	− .70	− .69
Turkey	− .60	− .71	− .50	− .65
Virgin Islands	− .68	− .34	− .59	− .33
Wales	− .23	+ .35	− .20	+ .45
West Indies	− .75	− .77	− .60	− .58

[a]First admissions to New York civil state hospitals correlated with New York State manufacturing employment index (secular trend subtracted from both series).
[b]The sign of R depends on the sign of the sums of the beta weights; R includes 0–3-year lagged admissions.

Table 14. Number of years, 1914–1955, during which the correlation between employment and mental-hospital admissions $\leqq$ −0.65:[a] male admissions, by country of birth.[b]

Country of birth	Number of years				
	36–41	30–35	25–29	20–24	Under 20
Africa	40				
Bulgaria	40				
Ireland	40				
Italy	40				
Poland	40				
Puerto Rico	40				
West Indies	40				
Armenia	39				
Australia	39				
Philippines	39				
United States	38				
Yugoslavia	38				
Canada	37				
Czechoslovakia	37				
France	37				
Germany	37				
Denmark	36				
Mexico	36				
England		35			
Japan		35			
Sweden		35			
India		34			
Turkey		34			
Hawaii		33			
Spain		33			
Russia		32			
Atlantic Islands		31			
Austria		31			
Hungary		31			
Lithuania		31			
Virgin Islands		31			
Greece			29		
Portugal			29		

Table 14. *(continued)*

Country of birth	Number of years				
	36–41	30–35	25–29	20–24	Under 20
Wales			29		
China			28		
Holland			28		
Syria			28		
Asia			27		
Scotland			27		
Finland			26		
South America				24	
Belgium				22	
Cuba				22	
Rumania				20	
Norway					19
Central America					16
Switzerland					13
Number of countries	18	13	9	4	3
Cumulative number		31	40	44	47
Fractions of total number of countries	0.383	0.277	0.191	0.085	0.064
Cumulative fractions		.660	.851	.936	1.000

[a] r between −0.65 and −1.00. Only correlations not significantly affected by autocorrelation of residuals, as measured by the Durbin-Watson statistic, are included.

[b] First admissions to New York civil state hospitals correlated with New York State manufacturing employment index (secular trend subtracted from both series).

Among the series that have been transformed so as to eliminate major sources of autocorrelation, 40 of the male and 34 of the female populations show inverse relations at $r \leqq -0.65$ for at least 25 years. None of the male and one of the female relations shows positivity (Tables 14 and 15).

The same systematic differences among results are shown by the two statistical techniques. In comparing the results of the ethnic and nativity groups, however, we do find a significantly larger number (rather than fraction) of sensitive populations among the nativity groups. This comparison is most important for our task of replication since we are primarily interested in the absolute number of populations for which a stable relation is found.

Table 15. Number of years, 1914–1955, during which the correlation between employment and mental-hospital admissions ≤ −0.65:[a] female admissions, by country of birth.[b]

Country of birth	Number of years				
	36–41	30–35	25–29	20–24	Under 20
Central America	40				
India	40				
Lithuania	40				
Puerto Rico	40				
West Indies	40				
Africa	39				
Atlantic Islands	39				
Poland	39				
South America	39				
Austria	38				
Finland	37				
United States		35			
Yugoslavia		35			
Mexico		35			
Scotland		35			
Sweden		35			
Italy		33			
Belgium		32			
Holland		32			
Virgin Islands		32			
Bulgaria		31			
Czechoslovakia		31			
Hungary		31			
Rumania		31			
Wales		31			
Syria		30			
Canada			28		
Germany			28		
Australia			27		
Ireland			27		
Portugal			27		
Switzerland			27		
Asia			26		
China				22	

92   Mental Illness and the Economy

Table 15.   *(continued)*

Country of birth	Number of years				
	36–41	30–35	25–29	20–24	Under 20
Cuba				22	
Philippines				22	
Denmark				21	
England				20	
Turkey				20	
Armenia					19
Hawaii					19
Japan					16
Greece					15
France					13
Norway					11
Spain					6
Number of countries	11	15	8	6	7
Cumulative number		26	34	42	47
Fractions of total number of countries	0.234	0.319	0.170	0.128	0.149
Cumulative fractions		.553	.723	.851	1.000

[a]r between −0.65 and −1.00. Only correlations not significantly affected by autocorrelation of residuals, as measured by the Durbin-Watson statistic, are included.

[b]First admissions to New York civil state hospitals correlated with New York State manufacturing employment index (secular trend subtracted from both series).

Replication Among 47 Countries of Nativity of Parents of Admissions

In the last section, we examined the relation among U. S. born and immigrants from 46 different countries; in this section, we observe the relation among populations of different origin (or country) of the second generation. These are the countries of nativity of both parents of each patient.

The optimum correlation over the 5-year moving average and the multiple correlations based on raw data (except for detrending) show that 41 and 29 respectively of these 47 male populations exhibit highly stable sensitivity (Table 16). The highest male number (41 populations) is equal to 87 percent of the 47 groups. Of these sensitive populations, 1 and 0 respectively show

Table 16. Correlations between employment and mental-hospital admissions during 1914–1955, by country of parents' birth.[a]

Country of parents' birth	Optimum correlation, 5-year moving averages		Multiple correlation,[b] data not averaged	
	Male	Female	Male	Female
United States	−0.57	−0.59	−0.58	−0.51
Africa	− .54	− .75	− .45	− .39
Armenia	− .80	− .86	− .64	− .65
Asia	− .64	− .35	− .48	− .49
Atlantic Islands	− .72	− .59	− .61	− .68
Australia	− .66	− .50	− .52	− .52
Austria	− .75	− .84	− .50	− .67
Belgium	− .29	− .48	− .48	− .36
Bulgaria	− .50	− .34	− .41	− .46
Canada	− .71	− .33	− .50	− .47
Central America	− .11	+ .29	− .37	+ .36
China	− .42	+ .67	− .40	+ .52
Cuba	− .55	+ .65	− .43	+ .38
Czechoslovakia	− .67	− .30	− .48	− .34
Denmark	− .36	− .12	− .37	− .51
England	− .82	+ .39	− .63	+ .47
Finland	− .82	− .26	− .69	− .48
France	− .82	+ .42	− .60	+ .25
Germany	− .92	+ .58	− .77	+ .63
Greece	− .72	+ .62	− .48	+ .48
Hawaii	− .17	+ .29	− .47	+ .30
Holland	− .29	− .72	− .32	− .49
Hungary	− .80	− .73	− .60	− .60
India	− .92	− .38	− .69	− .24
Ireland	− .93	− .32	− .88	− .44
Italy	− .86	− .78	− .74	− .71
Japan	− .89	− .80	− .50	+ .64
Yugoslavia	− .60	− .80	− .43	− .44
Lithuania	− .96	− .63	− .84	− .57
Mexico	− .81	− .76	− .68	− .63
Norway	− .44	+ .23	− .45	+ .31
Philippines	− .86	+ .29	− .63	+ .30
Poland	− .90	− .77	− .83	− .65

Table 16. *(continued)*

Country of parents' birth	Optimum correlation, 5-year moving averages		Multiple correlation,[b] data not averaged	
	Male	Female	Male	Female
Puerto Rico	− .54	+ .55	− .40	+ .40
Portugal	− .76	+ .27	− .50	+ .29
Rumania	− .74	− .81	− .51	− .63
Russia	− .87	− .76	− .69	− .68
Scotland	− .74	− .43	− .62	− .53
South America	− .56	− .69	− .53	− .60
Spain	− .56	− .57	− .46	− .41
Sweden	− .91	+ .33	− .74	+ .57
Switzerland	− .67	+ .42	− .60	+ .34
Syria	− .82	− .61	− .72	− .63
Turkey	− .53	− .81	− .44	− .67
Virgin Islands	− .64	− .44	− .57	− .43
Wales	− .58	− 39	− .36	− .32
West Indies	− .75	− .77	− .61	− .64

[a]First admissions to New York civil state hospitals correlated with New York State manufacturing employment index (secular trend subtracted from both series).
[b]The sign of R depends on the signs of the beta weights; R includes 0–3-year lagged admissions.

positive correlations. For the females, these techniques show that 28 and 22 respectively of the female populations exhibit predictable sensitivity. The highest female number (28 populations) is equal to 60 percent of the 47 populations. Of the stable relations for females, 5 and 4 respectively show positive correlations.

With the series that have been transformed so as to eliminate major sources of autocorrelation, 38 of the male and 25 of the female populations were found to have correlations of $r \leqq -0.65$ for at least 25 years. All of these stable relations were inverse (Tables 17 and 18).

Once again, in this third set of categories, we see the systematic differences produced by the different statistical techniques. In this last breakdown, as many as 39 male populations show stable sensitivity to the 5-year average economic changes. This represents 85 and 55 percent respectively of the number of male and female populations. The lowest estimate of stable sensitivity places the number of stable male and female relations at 38 and 22 respectively.

Table 17. Number of years, 1914–1955, during which the correlation between employment and mental-hospital admissions $\leq$ −0.65,[a] male admissions, by country of parents' birth.[b]

Country of parents' birth	Number of years				
	36–41	30–35	25–29	20–24	Under 20
Africa	40				
Bulgaria	40				
England	40				
France	40				
Ireland	40				
Italy	40				
Mexico	40				
Poland	40				
Puerto Rico	40				
Spain	39				
Sweden	39				
United States	38				
Germany	38				
Holland	38				
India	37				
Philippines	37				
Russia	37				
Syria	37				
Lithuania	36				
Denmark	36				
Canada		35			
Japan		34			
Hungary		34			
Scotland		34			
Atlantic Islands		33			
Austria		33			
Central America		33			
Hawaii		33			
Turkey		33			
Yugoslavia		31			
West Indies		31			
Armenia		30			

Table 17. *(continued)*

Country of parents' birth	Number of years				
	36–41	30–35	25–29	20–24	Under 20
Asia		30			
Greece			29		
China			28		
Finland			28		
Virgin Islands			28		
Wales			27		
Cuba				24	
Rumania				24	
South America				24	
Portugal				23	
Switzerland				20	
Belgium					18
Czechoslovakia					16
Norway					15
Australia					6
Number of countries	20	13	5	5	4
Cumulative number		33	38	43	47
Fractions of total number of countries	0.426	0.227	0.106	0.106	0.085
Cumulative fractions		.703	.809	.915	1.000

[a] r between −0.65 and −1.00. Only correlations not significantly affected by autocorrelation of residuals, as measured by the Durbin-Watson statistic, are included.

[b] First admissions to New York civil state hospitals correlated with New York State manufacturing employment index (secular trend subtracted from both series).

Additional Tests of Stability

An additional set of tests has been devised as a gauge of the replicability of the finding of stability in the relation between economic change and mental hospitalization. A first set of tests examined classifications of admissions by county of residence and economic status. In a second set of tests, we ask whether the general relations extend to several specific populations of first

Table 18. Number of years, 1914–1955, during which the correlation between employment and mental-hospital admissions $\leq$ −0.65:[a] female admissions, by country of parents' birth.[b]

Country of parents' birth	Number of years				
	36–41	30–35	25–29	20–24	Under 20
Mexico	40				
Puerto Rico	40				
Atlantic Islands	39				
West Indies	39				
Austria	38				
Germany	37				
Belgium	36				
Holland	36				
Bulgaria		35			
Australia		34			
Canada		34			
Italy		34			
Rumania		34			
Czechoslovakia		33			
Denmark		33			
Yugoslavia		33			
Turkey		33			
United States		32			
Russia		32			
Sweden		32			
Virgin Islands		32			
Wales		31			
Africa		30			
Central America		30			
Finland		30			
Asia			29		
Poland			29		
Hungary			28		
Lithuania			28		
Syria			27		
South America			27		
Portugal			26		
Scotland			26		

Table 18.   *(continued)*

Country of parents' birth	Number of years				
	36–41	30–35	25–29	20–24	Under 20
Switzerland			26		
Norway				23	
Spain				23	
Greece				22	
India				22	
Cuba				21	
England					19
France					18
Japan					14
Armenia					13
China					6
Hawaii					0
Philippines					0
Number of countries	8	17	9	5	7
Cumulative number		25	35	40	47
Fractions of total number of countries	0.170	0.362	0.213	0.106	0.149
Cumulative fractions		.532	.745	.851	1.000

[a]r between –0.65 and –1.00. Only correlations not significantly affected by autocorrelation of residuals, as measured by the Durbin-Watson statistic, are included.

[b]First admissions to New York civil state hospitals correlated with New York State manufacturing employment index (secular trend subtracted from both sides).

admissions (admissions to private licensed hospitals, emergency admissions, and different diagnostic categories of mental illness).

Distribution of the General Relation Among the Counties of New York State

Another method of replication would make use of the fact that mental-hospital admissions in New York State were classified according to county of residence. Here again, despite our inability to establish a control for the serious disturbances (introduced by age and socioeconomic status

Table 19. Multiple correlations between employment and mental-hospital admissions during 1914–1960, by county of residence and sex.[a]

Industrial area	County	Multiple correlation[b]		1940 Population (thousands)	Percent
		Male	Female		
I. Albany-Schenectady-Troy	Montgomery Warren	−0.69	−0.30	59	0.4
II. Binghamton	Broome	− .72	+ .44	166	1.2
III. Buffalo	Niagara	− .64	+ .28	160	1.2
IV. New York	Bronx	− .78	− .72	1395	10.3
	Kings	− .79	− .69	2698	20.0
	New York	− .81	+ .69	1890	14.0
	Queens	− .81	+ .69	1298	9.6
	Richmond	− .88	− .73	174	1.3
V. Rochester					
VI. Utica-Rome	Madison	− .83	+ .28	40	0.3
	Oneida	− .77	− .74	204	1.5
	Otsego	− .62	− .34	46	0.3
					60.4
	Albany	− .57	− .40	221	1.6
	Chautauqua	− .53	+ .45	124	0.9
	Chenango	− .59	+ .37	36	0.3
	Jefferson	− .57	− .37	84	0.6
	Nassau	− .59	+ .33	407	3.0
	Putnam	− .55	+ .33	17	0.1
	Saratoga	− .50	+ .37	66	0.5
	Schuyler	− .54	+ .37	13	0.1
	Steuben	− .56	− .21	85	0.6
	Ulster	− .52	− .50	87	0.6
Total				13,479	68.7

[a]First admissions to New York civil state hospitals correlated, at 0–3-year lags, with New York State manufacturing employment index (secular trend subtracted from both series).
[b]The sign of R depends on the signs of the beta weights.

differentials) in the overall relation between economic change and mental hospitalization, we may examine the set of "total population" reactions according to area of residence.

An additional problem introduced by this ecological classification is that each county's mental-hospitalization level is to be correlated with the *aggregate* employment index for New York State as a whole. The aggregate character of the employment index is best represented in counties that have large populations and industries so diversified as to be representative of the aggregate industrial activity of the entire state. Given this population size and industrial diversity we may, in addition to simply estimating the number or fraction of populations showing stable sensitivity, predict the differential stability of sensitivities shown by the specific populations: the counties having the largest populations and most diversified economic activity (matching as closely as possible the character of diversification for the entire state) should show the most stable correlations of their mental-hospital admissions to the aggregate employment index.

The multiple correlations for males of all counties with a population of over 1 million in 1940 are $\leqq -0.78$ (Table 19). This finding supports our emphasis on the importance of large populations in terms of matching the mental hospitalization with the (aggregate) New York State employment index.

The importance of large-scale (and diverse) economic activity is likewise supported by the data. *All* counties showing multiple correlations for males of at most -0.78 either have large populations or contain large-scale industry. An additional ten counties show multiple correlations for males of between -0.50 and -0.59. This means that a total of only 22 counties show stable multiple correlations for males; these counties, however, have such large populations that together they account for nearly 70 percent of the total population of the State (see Table 18). More striking still is the fact that the 12 counties showing multiple correlations for males of at most -0.64 account for 60.4 percent of the state population.

With the series that have been transformed so as to eliminate major sources of autocorrelation, 38 of the male and 33 of the female populations were found to show inverse sensitivity to economic changes, at $r \leqq -0.65$, for at least 25 years (Tables 20 and 21). One of the stable correlations for males and four of those for females were positive. However, exactly according to the prediction, of the 61 counties examined, the only ones showing high stability with both the multiple correlation and the optimal correlation based on serially independent data are those with populations of at least 250,000. (The fact that the ecological findings of highest sensitivity occur in counties having very large populations is not due simply to the possibility that rural populations are

Table 20. Number of years, 1914–1960, during which the correlation between employment and mental-hospital admission rates $\leqq$ −0.65:[a] male admission rates, by county of residence.[b]

County	Number of years					
	40–46	35–39	30–34	25–29	20–24	Under 20
Oneida	46					
Putnam	46					
Richmond	45					
Madison	44					
Queens	44					
Broome	43					
Rockland	43					
Nassau	42					
St. Lawrence	41					
Warren	41					
Chatauqua	40					
Chenango	40					
Clinton	40					
Westchester	40					
Kings		39				
Montgomery		39				
Chemung		38				
Dutchess		38				
Lewis		38				
Monroe		38				
Sullivan			31			
Cortland			30			
Niagara			30			
Rensselaer			30			
Schenectady			30			
Columbia				29		
Cattaraugus				28		
Delaware				28		
Onondaga				28		
Tioga				28		
Jefferson				27		
Livingston				26		
Schuyler				26		
Fulton					24	
Ontario					24	
Saratoga					24	
Franklin					23	
Greene					23	
Allegany					22	
Essex					20	

County		County	
New York	38	Seneca	20
Schoharie	38	Washington	20
Ulster	38	Wyoming	18
Orange	37	Cayuga	16
Oswego	36	Herkimer	16
Suffolk	36	Yates	15
Otsego	35	Genesee	12
Albany	34	Orleans	7
Erie	34		
Steuben	34		
Tompkins	33		
Wayne	32		
Bronx	31		

Number of counties	14	13	11	8	9	6
Cumulative number		27	38	46	55	61
Fractions of total number of counties	0.230	0.213	0.180	0.131	0.148	0.098
Cumulative fractions		.443	.623	.754	.902	1.000

[a] r between −0.65 and −1.00. Only correlations not significantly affected by autocorrelation of residuals, as measured by the Durbin-Watson statistic, are included.

[b] First admissions to New York civil state hospitals correlated with New York State manufacturing employment index (secular trend subtracted from both series).

Table 21. Number of years, 1914–1960, during which the correlation between employment and mental-hospital admissions $\leq$ −0.65:[a] female admissions, by county of residence.[b]

County	40–46	35–39	30–34	25–29	County	20–24	Under 20
	\multicolumn{4}{Number of years}		\multicolumn{2}{Number of years}
Rockland	44				Bronx	24	
Tioga	40				Broome	24	
Ulster	40				Delaware	24	
Wayne		39			Fulton	23	
Suffolk		38			Jefferson	23	
Genesee		37			Monroe	23	
Nassau		37			Erie	22	
Schenectady		37			Saratoga	22	
Warren		37			Kings	21	
Cattaraugus		36			Niagara	21	
Oneida			34		Tompkins	21	
Lewis			33		Greene	20	
Washington			33		Schuyler		19
Columbia			32		Chatauqua		18
Franklin			22		Putnam		18
New York			31		Clinton		17
Westchester			31		Schoharie		15
Albany			30		Allegheny		14
Livingston			30		Seneca		14
Richmond			30		Chemung		13

County			County	
Orange	29		Chenango	13
Otsego	29		Orleans	12
Rensselaer	29		Yates	12
Cortland	27		Essex	8
Onondaga	27		Montgomery	8
Steuben	27		Ontario	6
Dutchess	26		St. Lawrence	6
Madison	26		Wyoming	0
Oswego	26			
Queens	25			
Cayuga	25			
Herkimer	25			
Sullivan	25			

Number of counties	3	7	10	13	12	16
Cumulative number		10	20	33	45	61
Fractions of total number of counties	0.049	0.115	0.164	0.213	0.197	0.262
Cumulative fractions		.164	.328	.541	.738	1.000

[a] r between −0.65 and −1.00. Only correlations not significantly affected by autocorrelation of residuals, as measured by the Durbin-Watson statistic, are included.

[b] First admissions to New York civil state hospitals correlated with New York State manufacturing employment index (secular trend subtracted from both series).

more sensitive than urban populations regardless of diagnostic category of illness on admission; see Chapter 6.)

*Distribution of the General Relation by Economic Classification
Determined Upon Admission to the Mental Hospital*

It is pertinent to determine whether the strong relation between mental-hospital admissions and economic conditions is similar to what is observed from within the mental hospital. If, as has been argued, there is a strong relation between aggregate economic change and mental hospitalization, then economic changes occurring in the general population should be observable from within the hospital.

The state mental-hospital admissions officer categorizes patients by economic status, on admission to the hospital, as "comfortable," "marginal," or "dependent." These categories reflect the degree to which the patient is economically self-sufficient or self-supporting upon admission. "Comfortable" is defined as "having accumulated resources sufficient to maintain self and family for at least four months";[7] "marginal" signifies "living on earnings but accumulating little or nothing, being on the margin between self-support and dependence"; "dependent" is defined as "lacking in the necessities of life or receiving aid from public funds or persons outside the immediate family."

If income changes in the general population are reflected in the economic status of mental-hospital admissions, then the number of persons categorized as "comfortable" by the admissions officer should generally decrease in the economic downturn and increase in the upturn. The reverse should be true for patients classified as marginal and dependent.

The multiple correlations reveal that, as suggested, the number of admissions in the "comfortable" category decreases during the economic downturn, whereas those in the "marginal" and "dependent" categories increase during these periods. The relations are highly stable, even with controls for diagnosis and the use of tests based on the serially independent data (see Fig. 17).

First Admissions to Private Licensed Mental Hospitals

A sharp response of private-hospital admissions to the economic downturn might represent the most dramatic evidence of the general relation hypothesized in this study. To be sure, in admission of a breadwinner to the state hospital

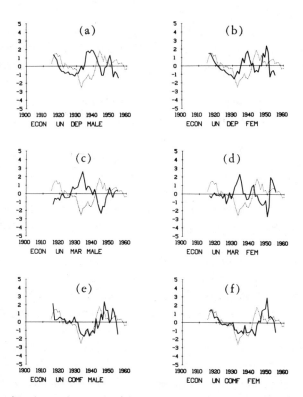

FIG. 17. Fluctuations in employment and in mental-hospital admissions during 1914–1960: first admissions by preadmission economic situation and sex. First admissions to New York civil state hospitals matched with New York State manufacturing employment index (secular trend subtracted from both series).

LEGEND:
...... New York State Manufacturing Employment Index
_____ First admissions, by pre-admission economic situation:
      (a,b) dependent (c,d) marginal (e,f) comfortable
SCALE: Deviations from secular trend in admissions and in the employment index are expressed in standardized normal scores. Scalar range describes relative magnitude of variation on each series.

during economically depressed periods, the family suffers the loss of much potential income when it can least afford this loss. Moreover, in the case of the private hospitals not only is there loss of the patient's income but also the additional great cost of long-term, private psychiatric treatment in a mental hospital. Thus, if a stable inverse correlation were found between economic fluctuations and private psychiatric hospitalization, it would signify that precisely at the moment when economic resources are at their *lowest,* the *most* money is spent on psychiatric hospitalization.

The multiple correlations for first admissions to private licensed mental hospitals (1941–1960) are −0.89 and −0.91 for males and females respectively. (Prior to 1940, only court-committed private admissions, less than 10 percent of total private admissions, were recorded in the Annual Reports of the Commissioner of Mental Hygiene.) Similarly, the correlations based on serially independent data yield highly stable correlations: −0.75 and −0.91 respectively for males and females.

Emergency Admissions

Among the various classifications of admissions to mental hospitals, the one that perhaps best indicates the acute emergence or "outburst" of disturbed behavior is the emergency admission. This classification, above all others, should indicate that something new and unusual has occurred in the patient's behavior just prior to admission.

An examination of the relation between economic change and emergency first admissions to a mental hospital for the years 1919–1940 (the entire period for which these data are available) shows multiple correlations of −0.82 for males and −0.56 for females. These correlations are "stable" according to our earlier definition. However, the correlations based on the serially independent data show only the male relation to be stable. Thus, the frequent pattern of a less pronounced relation for females again emerges. (The male-female differential sensitivity to economic change is discussed in detail in Chapter 7.)

Summary

The basic relation between economic change and mental hospitalization does not greatly depend on the interval of change measured. Detrended, but otherwise untransformed, data show similar relations to those data based on large (5-year) cyclical changes or on year-to-year changes. For a large fraction of admissions, the correlations are so high ($r \leq$ −0.71) that, statistically speaking, economic changes are the predominant factor.

Our general findings have been internally replicated for 34 ethnic groups, immigrant groups of 47 nationalities, and the foreign stock of 47 countries of origin. Among the 61 New York counties examined, those whose economic structure most closely resembled the diverse industrial economy of New York State showed the highest inverse correlations. Other internal checks of validity showed that emergency and private-hospital admissions respond sharply and in stable patterns to the economic downturn, and that admissions classified by the state hospital as economically comfortable increased during an upturn. However, those classified as marginal or dependent increased during downturns; this finding implies that, in general, there is little lag between changes in the economic characteristics of the general population and those of the mental-hospital population.

Controls for the effects of differential socioeconomic status and age grades were found to be critical for an accurate description of the general relation. Indeed, without such controls, it is often impossible to find the basic relation. Clearly, the patterns of reaction to the economic downturn vary strongly according to these two factors (at least).

Private hospitalization, one of our most sensitive indicators of validity, similarly showed the strong inverse relation. The implication here is that, even among the socioeconomic strata that are left during a downturn with sufficiently large incomes to be able to afford private hospitalization, some economic loss leads to admission. Even emergency admissions, which perhaps best indicate the acute emergency or outburst of symptoms, showed the same strong inverse relation to the economic indicator.

6 Impact of Economic Change on Mental-Hospital Admissions

Until now, we have been mainly concerned with one specific measure of the relation between economic change and mental hospitalization—the correlation coefficient. This measure represents only one dimension of the overall relation, albeit a major one—the relative directness of the relation. In other words, the more nearly direct the relation between economic change and mental hospitalization is, the smaller will be the number of intervening noneconomic factors in this relation.

The intervening factors in question are those that are initially brought to life through the stimulus of economic change and have, in turn, a secondary (or tertiary) effect on mental-hospital admissions. An economic downturn may, in the first instance, result in loss of employment and income; but these initial losses may not generate sufficient immediate stress to bring about mental hospitalization. However, for certain individuals, loss of employment or income may, for example, lead to severe disruption in family relations. The disruption may then have the effect of profoundly isolating these individuals and may, in this second stage, result in their mental hospitalization.

There is substantial evidence from the present study that at least three major factors are involved in producing a strongly direct relation between economic change and mental hospitalization, as represented by the multiple-correlation coefficient. These factors are: (1) whether or not economic loss occurred, (2) the relative amount of economic loss sustained, and (3) the degree of exclusive concern of an individual's social role with economic achievement. The fact that a strong direct relation does not exist between economic change and mental hospitalization does not imply a total lack of relation between these two phenomena. We have seen, in fact, that the linear-correlation coefficient (which may vary in magnitude over time) is the more appropriate measure of the extent of the relation, and that this measure is frequently unrelated to the measure of directness of the relation.

We shall now examine in greater depth the general impact of economic change on mental-hospital admissions in terms of the actual proportionate increase in admissions that occurs during an economic downturn, and the proportionate decrease in admissions during an economic upturn. The data on impact were approached with the understanding that they might indeed show apparent conflict with the earlier findings on directness of the relation. For example, it was initially felt that the 35–54-year age groups might experience the most direct effects of economic loss, because other age groups (particularly the very young and the aged) were less directly concerned with maintenance and furtherance of their family's socioeconomic status. Although the most direct relations between economic change and mental hospitalization among age groups were indeed found for males and females in the 35–54-year range, we did not necessarily expect that during a given economic downturn these particular age groups would experience a greater proportionate increase in their mental-hospital admissions than other age groups. It was, rather, thought that possibly the indirect effects of an economic downturn might also be severe for individuals whose social roles were not very directly involved with issues of socioeconomic status.

Consideration was given to the possibility that a senile man or woman, who might become a substantial financial and emotional burden to the family during a period of economic crisis, might not be tolerated as well as would a mentally disturbed head of the household who was a family's only hope for economic survival. Although there were few strong preconceptions as to what the data on impact of economic change would show in terms of mental hospitalization, there was nevertheless the general feeling that the impact would tend to be strongest where the relation between economic change and mental hospitalization was most direct.

Such a general tendency never actually appeared in the data; in fact, the tendency was rather in the opposite direction. The indications are generally that a very direct relation to economic change—one that contains few if any intervening factors—tends to produce a considerably smaller overall impact on mental hospitalization than does a relation that involves a number of important intervening factors. In other words, those social groups that experience a number of important side effects, or secondary effects, of economic change (rather than only the immediate stresses of the economic loss itself) show the greatest likelihood of experiencing a major increase in mental-hospital admissions during an economic downturn.

The indirect effects of economic loss on mental hospitalization are so considerable that it is probably true that the greatest part of change in mental hospitalization (which is related to economic changes) occurs as a result of these indirect effects rather than of the more immediate and obvious implications of economic loss. Indeed, in very few cases do we find that the specific groups among the mentally hospitalized population who experienced the most *direct* impact of economic change also experienced the *greatest* impact. Explanations of the findings based on impact may frequently appear to be at variance with those based on directness of the relation. Tentative explanations of both components of the relation have been based on empirical evidence and theoretical considerations found in the social-science literature. There is little doubt that alternative explanations which may be offered at a later time will be found to be particularly pertinent to these data. Nevertheless, it was felt that at least tentative explanations that would place the data within an interpretable framework were justified, especially where such a framework could be supported by previous research.

Age

Data on variation in hospital-admission patterns by age of males indicates that the younger and older age groups, specifically those below 30 and over 65 years, show substantially greater proportions of increases during periods of 3 and 5 years. This phenomenon of relatively higher levels of change in the younger and older age groups is not nearly so visible for proportional decreases in admissions for 3- and 5-year periods. We may note, in general, that proportional short-term decreases in admissions are not nearly as large as proportional increases. In addition, when we consider relatively strong relations between economic change and mental hospitalization for all age groups, we may conclude that economic change is probably having a greater impact during economic downturns (by increasing admissions) than during economic upturns (by protecting the population against the need for admissions).

Much as in the case of the males, data on the extent of short-term variation (changes of 3 and 5 years' duration) for females indicate that the younger and older age groups show far greater variability in their admissions pattern than the middle-range age groups (especially for 5-year changes). One can observe a pattern of gradually increasing variation in admissions with increasing age beyond the 20–34-year groups. This pattern of intense variation for the younger groups is far more pronounced for increases in admissions than for decreases. In the case of females, we again find that, in general, the magnitude of short-term decreases in admissions is smaller than that of short-term increases, which indicates that economic change has a sharper impact on the precipitation of admissions than it has on the prevention of hospitalization. In other words, the economic downturn may have more damaging impact on the population than the economic upturn.

An examination of the differential impact of economic change on the mental hospitalization of different age groups shows a very different picture from that seen in terms of the directness of the relation between economic change and mental hospitalization. We noted earlier that for both sexes the basic relation appeared to be most direct as one approached late middle age, and gradually decreased as one approached the youngest and oldest age groups. The explanation offered was that the age groups whose social roles were most concerned with maintaining and advancing the family's socioeconomic status would show the most direct relations between economic change and mental hospitalization. In other words, direct involvement in issues of socioeconomic status would lead to a preponderance of stress (resulting from an economic downturn), which would be most closely concerned with economic loss. Thus, the very young and the elderly, whose social roles are less directly involved in economic affairs, would be affected by an economic downturn most particularly in terms of subsidiary issues indirectly related to economic loss, which would intervene between the occurrence of the economic change and their consequent hospitalization.

The findings on the impact of economic change show a pattern opposite to that indicated in the findings on directness of the basic relation. In terms of impact, it is precisely the young—ages 0–15 for males and 0–19 for females— and persons over age 70 who show the greatest proportionate change in mental hospitalization in relation to economic change (Table 22). It is clear that in the case of the young and the elderly, on whom the impact of economic change is very strong, this impact occurs through one or more factors that intervene between the economic stress and subsequent hospitalization. Not only are the social roles of the very old and the very young far less concerned with issues of employment and earnings than is the case for other age groups, but these two age groups contribute the least and have the lowest social status among age groups within their respective families and the society at large.

Speaking more generally, and somewhat brutally, the very young and the elderly are the most expendable members of the society at a time when emotional and financial resources are in critically short supply. One might therefore imagine that the stresses of an economic downturn, apart from those directly involved with maintaining or advancing the economic status of the family, might fall heavily upon the young and the aged in the society. This might be the case particularly if, as some of the literature in this field

Table 22. Percentage changes in the level of New York civil state mental-hospital admissions during periods of maximal change in the New York state employment index, 1914–1960, by age.

Age (years)	Male				Female			
	3-year change		5-year change		3-year change		5-year change	
	Maximal increase	Maximal decrease	Maximal increase	Maximal decrease	Maximal increase	Maximal decrease	Maximal increase	Maximal decrease
0–15	189.75	57.63	294.57	78.79	222.12	56.03	273.32	60.21
15–19	37.62	23.84	36.82	25.64	125.04	33.90	182.52	20.22
20–24	69.79	35.43	97.46	41.59	18.96	18.13	16.09	13.38
25–29	70.23	47.09	126.72	48.74	22.47	22.91	19.99	16.94
30–34	29.26	30.96	48.86	37.26	15.16	12.73	16.21	15.66
35–39	41.59	32.07	61.38	35.89	26.13	19.86	27.56	21.30
40–44	43.17	18.42	54.47	31.47	15.19	20.21	28.60	23.78
45–49	37.65	33.80	37.13	29.52	30.83	25.39	39.18	29.26
50–54	43.67	37.19	73.14	44.57	30.26	23.13	32.58	23.31
55–59	40.87	21.80	56.16	29.00	46.50	35.18	38.15	26.43
60–64	30.85	40.26	60.60	28.69	43.11	32.66	44.27	22.16
65–69	76.20	48.34	62.02	42.76	24.88	17.97	50.69	44.90
70+	598.89	63.71	507.80	64.35	675.65	49.44	492.37	48.93

emphasizes, a major factor possibly relating social stress to mental hospitalization is intolerance of psychiatric symptoms on the part of family and friends. It would therefore not be difficult to imagine that the psychiatric symptoms of the young and the aged would be less well tolerated than those of the higher-status age groups, and therefore that mental disturbance among these two age groups would become a particularly heavy burden on the emotional and financial resources of the family during an economic downturn. Many families, for instance, might find it easier to make excuses for the paranoia of a member who was desperately needed in order to maintain at least a marginal financial position.

A similar explanation of the impact of economic change on the mental hospitalization of different age groups may be useful in a more detailed examination of these data for females in general. When we observe the female age groups between 20 and 69 we find a gradually rising trend of impact as age increases. For example, the maximal increases for the age groups 20–24, 25–29, and 30–34 lie between 16.09 and 19.99 percent in a 5-year period; the maximal 5-year percentage increases for the age groups 35–39, 40–44, 45–49, and 50–54 lie between 27.56 and 39.18; and the 5-year percentage increases for the age groups 60–64 and 65–69 are 44.27 and 50.69 respectively.

We appear to be finding that (apart from the very young and the elderly) as the age of the females increases beyond approximately 20, the impact of economic change sharply increases. It is possible that the impact of economic change on the mental hospitalization of females is related not only to their husbands' and families' socioeconomic status but perhaps even more strongly to the age-defined social position of the females themselves. There has been a good deal of research suggesting that, apart from a woman's social position as determined by the occupations of her husband and her father (and occasionally her children), the female role itself carries its own internal status based upon a specific set of considerations.

The role of the female, as distinguished from that of the male, has traditionally revolved around motherhood and nurturance of the newborn. In many societies the utility of the female is to a large extent related to her ability to bear young and to provide a certain measure of sexual satisfaction to her male partner. It is interesting that in Western societies the male sexual partner is not imagined as a symbol of sexuality to nearly the same extent as is the female. Furthermore, in Western societies it is generally the male head of the family who is directly responsible for the socioeconomic status of the family, while the female spouse and her children play economically dependent roles. Whereas the adult male must therefore confront the economic world in order to provide sustenance for himself and his family, the adult female must confront the male in order to provide for her personal requirements. Now if, within the family, the status of the female depends to a large extent on her sexual attractiveness, ability to bear children, and function in the role of mother, then as her age advances beyond the child-bearing years this status will gradually decrease.

This phenomenon of decreasing status for the adult female as she grows older may have the effect of placing her in a social position that ever more closely resembles that of the very young and the aged. As in the case of the young and the elderly, psychiatrically disturbed women who are gradually losing status through the processes of aging may be increasingly less well tolerated over time. During a period of economic crisis the family may therefore offer more emotional support to the younger rather than to the older adult woman, and still less to the elderly woman or the very young girl. Nevertheless, we find that, in general, the impact of economic change is substantially more severe on males than it is on females in terms of percentage changes in mental hospitalization that is related to economic changes. Except for the age groups 0–15, 45–49, and over 70, for which the impact of economic change is similar for both sexes, the nine other 5-year age groups all show the males as absorbing a substantially larger impact of economic stress in terms of mental hospitalization.

In other words, even though we may argue that the status of women is generally lower than that of men, the impact of economic change is greater on men despite the fact that psychiatric symptoms may be less well tolerated for women. The major factor behind the greater sensitivity of the male to economic change may lie in the measure of the relation of economic change to mental hospitalization expressed in multiple-correlation coefficients. In terms of the multiple-correlation coefficient, which expresses directness of the relation, the males show far stronger relations than the females. This more direct relation for males may be immediately reflected in the data on impact. In general, then, it may be that the factors directly implicated in an economic downturn, such as a decrease in income or job status, ultimately have a greater impact upon males than upon females.

A very different picture of the impact of economic change on mental hospitalization is found for males (as distinguished from females) between the ages of 20 and 69. Whereas the female pattern showed that the impact of economic change increases with increasing age, no similar trend of increasing or decreasing impact with age occurs for males. Instead, for males there are two major points between the ages of 20 and 69 at which there is an extraordinarily great impact of economic change on hospitalization, whereas the other age groups between 20 and 69 show relatively moderate and similar impact. The age groups 20–29, and especially 25–29, show the largest impact of economic change on mental hospitalization apart from that which is observed for the young (0–15) and the elderly (70+). The second age group that shows an extraordinarily large measure of impact is the 50–54 group.

In the case of the differential impact on male age groups, the explanation proposed may be somewhat more speculative than that advanced in the case of females, but perhaps not less reasonable. If we consider the career of a working man in terms of several basic stages, then it may be possible to identify certain critical points that serve to allow progression from one stage to another. We might then further imagine that social stresses which have a major impact on economic performance may be particularly severe during these critical junctures in the career span. Three fundamental stages in the working life may be suggested: "apprentice," "qualified worker," and "senior workman or official."

The two critical bridges between stages are those involving movement to the status of a qualified worker and to a senior position. Movement across the first critical bridge is perhaps the more important of the two, since it involves the issue of whether or not the apprentice will ever assume the status of a qualified worker in a specific profession or industry. If he is unable to assume a qualified-worker status, then presumably he will leave, or not be allowed to remain in, the profession or industry. Movement across the second bridge toward a status of seniority may not be as basic an issue as that of whether the younger worker will become qualified and ultimately capable of earning a reasonable living. However, whether a qualified worker can progress toward the higher status that a long-term career would ordinarily warrant is a major issue for many persons whose jobs occupy many of the predominant concerns of their daily lives. An examination of the data on the impact of economic change on mental hospitalization would appear to indicate that the impact of an economic downturn is most severe during these two periods of transfer in the work life of the male. It may then be that for males the sharpest impact of an economic downturn results in deprivation of the opportunity to progress beyond the relatively junior stages of a career, encompassed in the age groups 20–29, and the qualified-worker stages, which occur, on the average, during the early 50's.

The tentative explanation offered for the extraordinary impact of economic change on males in the age groups 20–29 and 50–54 is very different from the explanation offered earlier for the finding that the relation between economic change and mental hospitalization reached a peak of directness for the age groups 45–54, and decreased as one approached the higher and lower ends of the age spectrum. It was suggested that 45–54 was the age group at which the average male would approach the peak of socioeconomic status. We learn from the data on impact, however, that, although the concerns of the male with purely economic matters may reach a peak among the 45–54-year age groups, these are not the ages during which an economic downturn will have the greatest potential impact on mental hospitalization. We must therefore look primarily to an explanation of the findings on impact that does not depend purely on considerations of economic loss. And actually, the fact that an economic downturn may prevent a male from assuming either the status of a qualified or that of a senior worker is not so much the result of the loss of potential income as it is of the loss of social status. By social status we mean here the generalized image, both public and private, of the importance, value, power, and prestige of a person's social role.

In this case, the individual in question may simply not regard himself as holding a dignified socioeconomic position commensurate with his age, manifest abilities, and training. This feeling of inadequacy may be particularly acute for the man who, in the first instance, has relatively high aspirations for his work career and whose wife, children, or friends may insist that he successfully measures up to the statuses of men of similar age and social background The possibility may also be entertained that, should the male fail to successfully bridge either of the two major transfer points in his work life, his status in the eyes of his family and friends may so diminish that they would be less likely to tolerate any substantial psychiatric disorder. Such intolerance might greatly increase the probability of his mental hospitalization.

Marital Status

Quite extensive variation occurs by virtue of categorizing the hospital-admissions data according to marital status. We go from the extreme of the divorced male, who in the case of only a 3-year change shows a 175-percent increase, to the single male, who in a similar 3-year period shows only a 30-percent increase (Table 23).

The data on the impact of economic change on the mental hospitalization of individuals of different marital status once again diverge from the findings based on directness of the basic relation. The relation between economic change and mental hospitalization was most direct for the married and the single, and considerably less direct for the separated, divorced, and widowed. These findings appear to support the position that individuals whose social roles were most concerned with maintaining or advancing family socioeconomic status would experience most immediately and directly the effects of an economic

Table 23. Percentage changes in the level of New York civil state mental-hospital admissions during periods of maximal change in the New York state employment index, 1914–1960, by marital status.

Marital status	Male				Female			
	3-year change		5-year change		3-year change		5-year change	
	Maximal increase	Maximal decrease	Maximal increase	Maximal decrease	Maximal increase	Maximal decrease	Maximal increase	Maximal decrease
Single	29.73	27.53	61.94	34.19	21.59	17.33	24.64	24.01
Married	43.14	20.81	58.97	26.41	16.56	14.21	12.50	14.06
Separated	67.43	44.77	115.18	57.10	28.94	26.44	32.72	35.24
Widowed	96.52	32.90	122.57	34.98	43.83	24.96	38.78	28.04
Divorced	175.45	46.61	284.93	54.07	49.29	41.07	62.43	40.49

downturn. The data on the impact of economic change clearly show, however, that it is the groups that are least involved in family life who experience the greatest ultimate impact of economic change in terms of proportionate change in mental hospitalization. In fact, there is a strong indication that among the five classifications of marital status investigated there is a highly precise inverse relation between involvement in family life and the impact of economic change.

For both sexes, the order of impact of economic change on mental hospitalization gradually increases from the status of married to divorced in the following order: (1) married, (2) single, (3) separated, (4) widowed, and (5) divorced. Among the marital statuses, the married group is clearly the most intensely involved in family life. The married group would be followed by the single category, assuming that the great majority of never-married patients not of marriageable age had chosen to live alone. The married and single should show greater involvement in family life than the separated and widowed, who presumably maintain a substantially reduced relation with some members of their families. The divorced, finally, should show the greatest reduction among these marital-status groupings in the extent of their involvement with their (formerly intact) families.

The inverse relation between the impact of economic change on mental hospitalization and closeness of family ties would seem to provide strong support for the argument that, once stress appears, group cohesiveness plays an important part in preventing mental hospitalization. The influence of family cohesiveness in preventing hospitalization could be channeled through the mechanism of greater nurturance or tolerance of psychiatric symptoms precipitated by economic stress. There are probably other mechanisms, perhaps including a sharing of financial responsibilities and burdens, that a cohesive family might adopt in support of a mentally ill member.

Ethnic Background

It is clear that when ethnicity is taken as the classification of data by which to measure variation in admissions patterns, the magnitude of variation is greater than with probably any other single classification. For the sake of keeping the relative size of the ethnic group from confounding the measure of relative proportionate change in hospital admissions, only the nine largest ethnic groups were examined in terms of the proportionate change in hospital admissions attributable to the impact of economic changes (Table 24).

Among the nine major ethnic categories, two stand out as showing relatively

Table 24. Percentage changes in the level of New York civil state mental-hospital admissions during periods of maximal change in the New York state employment index, 1914–1955, by major ethnic classification.

Major ethnic classifications	Male				Female			
	3-year change		5-year change		3-year change		5-year change	
	Maximal increase	Maximal decrease	Maximal increase	Maximal decrease	Maximal increase	Maximal decrease	Maximal increase	Maximal decrease
Scandinavian	171.43	−54.84	42.11	−60.00	109.52	−42.50	60.00	−51.79
English	146.15	−59.38	346.15	−54.84	100.00	−68.29	110.26	−49.18
Mixed	103.13	−28.85	127.11	−33.58	189.69	−84.85	322.22	−86.80
Negro	94.35	−47.53	149.99	−42.51	78.71	−37.39	68.16	−47.14
Irish	93.33	−39.42	172.29	−50.30	94.69	−26.31	100.67	−34.11
Slavic	84.51	−39.16	101.56	−47.78	36.36	−27.13	39.62	−26.12
German	68.52	−39.73	110.88	−47.12	62.39	−33.01	71.56	−35.60
Jewish	59.08	−38.30	57.88	−37.33	40.03	−26.68	54.39	−24.91
Italian	26.02	−23.45	50.55	−27.84	42.40	−22.86	45.70	−22.84

low levels of variation, namely, Italians and Jews. In fact, Italians and Jews of both sexes show approximately half the proportionate impact of economic change that is shown for any of the other groups, including Negro, English, German, Irish, Scandinavian, Slavic, and mixed. The greatest variation is shown by the English and Scandinavian groups; a high level of variation is shown by Irish, Negro, mixed, and Slavic groups, a moderate level by both sexes of the German group. These patterns of variation among the ethnic groups are well defined and generally consistent for both sexes. The similarities in patterns for the sexes in each ethnic group are frequently remarkable.

The estimate of the relation between economic change and mental hospitalization by ethnic groups is, once again, very different from that when the emphasis is on directness or on impact of the relation. Our earlier examination of directness of the relation indicates that when account is taken of both sexes in each of the ethnic groups studied the higher the socioeconomic status of the ethnic groups studied the more direct is the relation between economic change and mental hospitalization. The data on impact, however, reveal that all but two of the major ethnic groups appear to show similar levels of impact, regardless of economic status. In fact, the Italian and the Jewish ethnic groups of both sexes, which show approximately half the level of impact of the other ethnic groups, are themselves of grossly different socioeconomic status in relation to the other groups. Whereas the Jewish group ranks among the top socioeconomic status levels of ethnic groups, the Italian group would rank at a lower-middle level (see Chapter 7).[1]

What is it, then, despite considerable differences in socioeconomic and cultural backgrounds, that the Jewish and Italian groups have in common and that, moreover, distinguishes them from other major ethnic groups within New York State? The Jewish group is perhaps legendary among nationality and ethnic groups for its close family ties.[2] Whether this is a result of extended family ties, a strong nuclear family with relatively low rates of divorce, or a religious culture that takes the family as its basic unit of survival over the centuries, the available evidence overwhelmingly gives the impression of an unusually cohesive family structure. Not quite as much evidence is available on the relative cohesiveness of the Italian family. However, there are strong indications that the American-Italian family structure is distinguished by the extent of its family ties and the strong influence of Catholicism, which, intricately woven into the web of Italian cultural life, would tend to maintain a relatively low divorce rate.[3]

Among the various ethnic groups under study, there is evidence that the Jews and the Italians traditionally show the lowest divorce rates. The divorce rate is emphasized here because it is an obvious indicator of relative family instability, and presumably therefore an indicator of the lack of family cohesiveness. As has been suggested in our speculations on the interpretation of the impact of economic change on age and marital-status groups, it is possible that family cohesiveness operates via a relatively tolerant attitude toward psychiatric disturbance. It may be that the more cohesive and stable family has a greater willingness and capacity for tolerating the emotionally disturbed individual. Such emotional support may, in turn, result in the prevention of mental hospitalization despite the fact that severe economic stress falls on one or more persons in the family.

The different patterns revealed through different measures of the relation between economic change and mental hospitalization become especially sharp as one examines the different ethnic groups. Several very distinctive comparisons may be drawn. First, among the ethnic groups whose pattern of hospitalization was studied in terms of the impact of economic change, only the Jewish and the German groups (earlier) showed a very direct relation. Thus, although in the case of both Jews and Germans there are relatively few factors that intervene within the relation between economic change and mental hospitalization, the impact of the relation is severe in the case of the German and relatively mild in the case of the Jewish group. Second, although both the Italian group and the English, Irish, Scandinavian, and ethnically mixed groups show a moderately direct relation between economic change and mental hospitalization (the relation is slightly less direct for the Italian group), only the Italian group shows a relatively mild impact whereas the others show a very severe one.

Third, from the opposite viewpoint, although a severe impact of economic change is seen in the case of the German ethnic group on the one hand and the Slavic and Negro groups on the other, the German group shows a strongly direct relation whereas the Slavic and Negro groups show a strongly indirect relation. The implication is that, although the impact of economic change is severe for the mental hospitalization of the German, Slavic, and Negro groups, the probable mechanisms through which economic stress operates varies considerably between the German group on the one hand and the Slavic and Negro groups on the other. Whereas in the case of the German group the initial economic stress itself produces a severe impact, the occurrence of economic stress will result in mental hospitalization for Slavic and Negro groups only through a series of additional (and probably noneconomic) variables.

Economic Status

The difference in the extent of variation in patterns of mental-hospital admissions among the different economic classifications of the patient population are clearly distinguishable. Groups classified by the mental hospital as economically dependent and comfortable show substantially greater variability in proportional increases and decreases during both 3-year and 5-year spans than the group classified as marginal (Table 25). In addition, the dependent group usually shows a substantially greater variability in its admissions pattern during 3- and 5-year changes than does the comfortable group.

Together with the high degree of correlation between economic change and mental hospitalization found for all three economic classifications, these data allow us to ascertain the proportionate impact that economic change may have had upon the admissions pattern of these groups. It seems clear that the greatest impact has probably occurred among the dependent group, second among the comfortable group, and least among the marginal group. A different insight is provided by comparing the impact with the directness of the relation between economic change and mental hospitalization among economic-status categories. Our earlier observations of the differential directness of the basic relation among the classifications comfortable, marginal, and dependent supported the presumption that during economic downturns the mentally hospitalized population would be more likely to be classified as marginal and dependent than as comfortable. In other words, during economic downturns the marginal and dependent populations of the mental hospital would increase, whereas the population classified as economically comfortable would usually decrease.

Furthermore, when we re-examine the measure of directness of the relation between economic change and mental hospitalization, we find that the marginal group shows a far more direct relation than the dependent group. These findings appear on the surface to contrast sharply with those based on impact. The proportionate increase in mental hospitalization during an economic downturn is largest for the dependent classification, roughly twice that for the comfortable and marginal groups. It is therefore clear that, although admissions of the comfortable group do not regularly increase during economic downturns, they will frequently do so, and when the increases do occur, they are larger for the comfortable than for the marginal group. It is also apparent that although the inverse relation between employment and mental-hospital admissions is more clearly direct for the marginal classification than for the dependent, the impact is substantially greater for the dependent than for the marginal classification.

The implication of these last findings is that many patients who have arrived in the mental hospital during an economic downturn are likely to have suffered from the direct effects of a reduction in their economic status to a

Table 25. Percentage changes in the level of New York civil state mental-hospital admissions during periods of maximal change in the New York state employment index, 1914–1960, by officially recorded economic status.

Economic status	Male						Female					
	3-year change		5-year change				3-year change		5-year change			
	Maximal increase	Maximal decrease	Maximal increase	Maximal decrease			Maximal increase	Maximal decrease	Maximal increase	Maximal decrease		
Dependent	102.16	51.02	182.66	69.07			145.20	59.98	244.36	76.80		
Comfortable	69.26	50.36	59.01	53.01			55.79	41.84	115.15	35.53		
Marginal	43.67	25.87	60.16	29.18			20.12	16.50	26.76	18.17		

situation of marginality. However, the reduction of income during an economic downturn to the still lower status of dependency involves a number of substantial noneconomic implications, which are triggered by the initial economic loss but which do not appear to be suffered by the marginal group. The apparent result is that, although the marginal group suffers more directly from the effects of pure economic loss than does the dependent group, the ultimate impact of economic stress on the mental hospitalization of the dependent group is far greater than that on the marginal group.

The factors behind this difference in impact probably involve the far-reaching effects of the triggering mechanism of economic stress on noneconomic problems in the case of the dependent group. It would not be surprising, for example, to find that the stress on members of the marginal group during an economic downturn might consist almost entirely of losses of income and employment. On the other hand, stress on the dependent group might consist only minimally of economic loss and far more profoundly of the disorganization of family and social life. Data from other sources provide evidence that it is inappropriate to explain the differential impact of economic change on the economically dependent and marginal patients simply on the basis of socioeconomic differences. In other words, in examining the differential economic impact on the dependent and marginal groups, our observation of impact does not begin with groups whose economic status is originally marginal or dependent, but rather with groups who, by virtue of the economic downturn, *become* either marginal or dependent. Many of those who eventually become economically dependent rather than marginal might, prior to the economic downturn, actually have been of a considerably higher socioeconomic status than many members of the group who eventually would come to be classified as marginal.

Level of Educational Attainment

With this in mind, let us examine a socioeconomic classification of hospitalized patients that allows us to infer the economic situation of the patient prior to hospitalization. Among the data available on mental-hospital patients, the classification of socioeconomic status most appropriate for this purpose is that of differential levels of educational attainment. The absolute level of educational attainment is clearly related positively to socioeconomic status level. Furthermore, level of educational attainment would obviously not be altered downward in the course of an economic downturn.

We find that as level of educational attainment increases, the impact of economic change on mental hospitalization becomes increasingly severe. By contrast, as we have seen earlier, the differential losses experienced by these socioeconomic groups during an economic downturn apparently have the effect of producing the most direct relations between economic stress and mental hospitalization among the grammar-school and high-school educated, and the least direct effects among the high-school educated and patients with less than a high-school education. Integrating these two sets of data, we find the following:

(1) Among the college educated there is a very direct relation, as well as a very substantial impact, in comparison with other educational categories. In this unusual case, it appears that the more direct, purely economic effects of the downturn have a severe impact in terms of mental-hospital admissions.

(2) Economic change has a relatively indirect effect on mental hospitalization among the high-school educated, but it has a substantial impact on mental hospitalization of the grammar school educated, though not as substantial as in the case of the college educated. It is possible, therefore, that one major reason for the relative indirectness of the relation in the case of the high-school educated may be that this group loses comparatively less during economic downturns than the college or grammar-school educated. However, despite the indirectness of the relation among the high-school educated, initial economic stress appears sufficient to trigger additional noneconomic stresses that ultimately have a major impact on mental hospitalization.

(3) Despite the very direct and strong relation between economic change and mental hospitalization of the grammar-school educated, this relation results in a lower impact on hospital admissions for this group than for either the high-school or the college educated.

In contrast to the other groups, therefore, the grammar-school educated apparently tend to absorb the largest measure of the direct effects of economic loss. The over-all impact of such relatively pure economic loss is, however, relatively small. Finally, the relation between economic change and mental hospitalization for the groups with less than a grammar-school education is both largely indirect and of low impact. In this last case, although a number of factors apart from purely economic ones appear to be affecting mental hospitalization, the result of the full range of these factors in terms of ultimate impact is smaller than that for any group of higher educational attainment.

The scheme described above, which allows for an integration of the findings on the directness and the impact of the basic relations, may give the appearance of being contradictory. The general finding that the impact of economic change in terms of mental hospitalization increases as educational level increases would seem to be at odds with the earlier finding that the directness of the relation between economic change and mental hospitalization is highest for the grammar-school and college educated, and considerably lower for the high-school educated and those with less than a grammar-school education. However, there is really no basic contradiction between these two sets of findings. Rather, it is the interpretation that must take into account two different dimensions of the problem of estimating the relation between economic change and mental hospitalization. We sought to explain the finding that the relation between economic change and mental hospitalization was more direct for the college and grammar-school educated than for the high-school and less than grammar-school educated by reference to probable differences in the sheer magnitude of economic loss. Thus, it is likely that a greater fraction of persons among the college and grammar-school educated actually lose employment and income during economic downturns than is true for the other two groups.

This interpretation appeared to falsify the hypothesis of Henry and Short,[4] who argue that the higher the social status of a group, the greater should be their loss during an economic downturn, since they have more in the way of social and economic status to lose. It is entirely possible, however, that both the economic studies cited earlier and Henry and Short's hypothesis are useful in explaining the differential impact of the relation between economic change and mental hospitalization. In fact, there are possible grounds for integrating the two sets of findings in the following manner. Although a group of relatively low socioeconomic status may lose proportionately more income than a higher-status group, the higher-status group may suffer the greater impact of an economic downturn because the effect of income loss on this group may be to bring individuals closer to the level of lower-income groups. Thus, income loss among the higher-status groups may result in a decrease in relative socioeconomic status.

A clear, but perhaps extreme, example of such a situation might appear when, during an economic downturn, substantial economic losses occurred among all socioeconomic strata. In such a case it is possible that a significant fraction of persons falling within the highest economic strata would be reduced to the level of those in the lower socioeconomic strata. Although persons in the lower strata may have relatively little to lose in the way of income in order to become totally dependent economically, economic dependency might also result from substantial losses of income and savings among the highest strata. Such an example illustrates the potential of persons of high socioeconomic status for being reduced to the level of those of considerably smaller means.

Although the impact of economic change according to level of educational attainment is fundamentally similar for the two sexes, there is an indication that the lowest female socioeconomic status group suffers a greater impact than the two higher groups. It is difficult to interpret these data without knowing who those specific families are in terms of other socioeconomic characteristics than education. For instance, it might be that considerable numbers of those women who have less than a grammar-school education are divorced, separated, or aged and, in fact, might be much closer to a state of poverty than would be true of their male counterparts who have the same education. If it is true that the males at the lowest educational level find greater opportunities for employment and enjoy a higher level of income than similarly educated females, the females might well suffer a more severe setback during economic downturns. Even speculation is fraught with difficulty in this case, however, because we simply do not know the relevant socioeconomic characteristics of these particular women.

It is also interesting that although increases in educational level appear in general to be related to increases in the impact of economic change for both sexes, the impact of economic change on the college-educated woman is extraordinarily intense. In fact, the maximal impact of the economic downturn (within a 5-year period) is more than three times as great for college-educated women as for any other classification of females by level of educational attainment. In addition, the maximal impact of economic change on the mental hospitalization of college-educated females is almost twice as large as it is on hospitalization of college-educated males (the group that absorbs the greatest impact of the economic downturn among male educational-attainment groups).

It is entirely possible that we are merely observing the most exaggerated form of the generally direct relation between socioeconomic level and impact of economic change. Once again, however, in order to speculate knowledgably on the possible reason for the remarkably strong impact of economic change on college-educated females, we would need to know a good deal more about other characteristics of these women. For example, if these are women who had backgrounds of relatively low- or middle-level socioeconomic status, and who attempted to use their college experience and degree in order to advance their social status, then perhaps the outstandingly relevant attribute of these women would be upward mobility. It is clear that an economic downturn would be unusually damaging to the upwardly mobile person not only because past gains in socioeconomic level might be wiped out, but because the individual involved might well be reduced to a state of economic dependency in which there was little hope of ever retrieving the economic losses.

Social Stress and the Extent of Economic Loss

In this chapter, we shall examine the effect of economic change on the mental hospitalization of various socioeconomic groups and social roles. This examination is primarily an attempt to clarify the overall relation between economic change and mental hospitalization. Our general hypothesis is that the admissions of each of the subgroups of the population admitted to mental hospitals will show a systematic pattern, between 1910 and 1960, which can be best understood by reference to the unique pattern of economic changes each subgroup has encountered.

Thus, we again confront the question of whether those particular individuals who are hospitalized are also the ones who are suffering from severe economic stresses. In this chapter the question is dealt with by an examination of the effects of economic change on various socioeconomic statuses and social roles. Two specific hypotheses are tested: (1) the greater the economic loss sustained by a particular group during the economic downturn, the greater will be its sensitivity to the downturn in terms of mental hospitalization, and (2) the more directly and extensively a person's social role is concerned with maintaining or advancing socioeconomic status, the more sensitive he will be to economic changes in terms of his mental status (as indicated by mental hospitalization). We shall examine the first hypothesis in detail.

The Extent of Economic Loss: A Primary Predictive Model

Detailed Studies of the Great Depression

One predictor of the differential sensitivity of groups with varying socioeconomic statuses is offered in a study by Menderhausen on changes in income distribution during the Great Depression.[1] That study found that certain groups were economically disfavored and others were actually favored. Certain groups lost in income and employment whereas others gained in both. Of course, the very great majority necessarily lose, since majority economic loss is essential to the operational and theoretical definition of an economic downturn.

The model deriving from Menderhausen's study is that those particular socioeconomic groups that experience economic loss during the downturn ought to show a negative relation between the economic indicator and their mental hospitalization. The opposite should be true for those socioeconomic groups that are not among the great majority experiencing economic loss in the downturn period. These latter groups may either gain, or not change their economic status, during the depression. We would not expect the groups comprising this minority who either gain or experience no change in economic status to show an inverse relation between the economic indicator and their pattern of mental hospitalization.

The model based on Menderhausen's findings states that whereas the recipients of "moderately low" and "high" incomes sustain great economic loss during the downturn, the recipients of "very low" and "moderately high" incomes actually showed economic gains during the depression of the 1930's.

This model is based on Menderhausen's economic classification of families in 33 cities in the United States who are estimated to have gained or lost income during the depression period of 1929–1933. This study showed income change during 1929–1933 for eleven dollar-income categories as of 1929: (1) no income, (2) 1–249, (3) 250–499, (4) 500–749, (5) 750–999, (6) 1000–1499, (7) 1500–1999, (8) 2000–2999, (9) 3000–4499, (10) 4500–7499, and (11) 7500 and over. The reason that these 1929 income categories are arranged in increasing order of magnitude of range is (certainly) that the size of the earning population gradually decreases as one gets into the higher income brackets (above $2000).

The average 1929 income (based on a 50-week year) was $1534 for all male production workers, $1220 for unskilled male workers, and $1630 for skilled and semiskilled workers.[2]

Menderhausen found that the two lowest 1929 income groups (0 to $249) actually gained income in the depression, as did groups (8) and (9) ($2000–$4499), whereas groups (4), (5), and (6) ($500–1499) and group (11) ($7500 and over) showed substantial losses in this period. Groups (3), (7), and (10), located respectively between gaining and losing groups, did not show significant gains or losses.[3]

Menderhausen explains these findings in three steps. First he accounts for the absolute gain in income for the two lowest income groups by (a) the replacement of unskilled labor by still less well-paid labor ("the unemployed reserve army") and (*b*) the entry into the labor market of younger persons who initially earn little but show dramatic increases in income level within a few years despite the depression.

In the second step Menderhausen distinguishes those groups whose income depends primarily on their employment status (laborers, semiskilled and skilled workers, and certain managerial personnel) and who are employed. He argues that among these economic groups the more highly skilled the worker and the more valuable he is to management, the greater will be the stability of his employment status, and therefore the less likely he will be to lose income during an economic downturn.

The need for supervisory and skilled personnel tends to depend less on output than the need for unskilled labor. In many industries, workers of the first category are "fixed assets" to their employers, since their presence is necessary even for below-capacity production and they cannot be replaced as easily as unskilled workers. Therefore, skilled and supervisory workers are more firmly attached to their employers and retain their jobs longer than unskilled. It seems probable that the incidence of unemployment varies inversely with the level of skill and income of the working group and its rank in the production hierarchy.

Menderhausen goes on to show that the 1940 Census confirms this hypothesis in general:

The proportion of unemployed among nonfarm laborers was three times higher than among craftsmen, operatives, foremen, and service workers; four times higher than among clerical workers; and fifteen times higher than among proprietors, managers, and officials. Within each group, except male laborers, the percentage of unemployed was higher among negroes than among whites . . .
In addition, the upper strata of many occupations tend to be more firmly organized, wage reductions are likely to be relatively small where unions are strong.[4]

In further support of this general position, a study by Dunlop of hourly earnings in different occupations and industries is cited, indicating that in most occupations the lower quartile of the distribution of earnings fell by a greater percentage than the upper quartile during the Depression (1929–1932).[5] However, the study showed this tendency primarily among male workers.

In the third step the substantial income losses of the upper group are explained for the most part by losses in income from entrepreneurial work (profits minus losses from businesses and partnerships) and property loss (dividends, rents, royalties, interest, and capital gains minus capital losses). Menderhausen supports these explanations by citing studies which show that:

(1) the very high-income groups possibly hold larger shares in income from property than from work, and (2) income from property as a whole fluctuates cyclically more than income from work, especially among upper income groups.[6]

The general model derived from Menderhausen's (and Dunlop's) findings is that during the economic downturn, and primarily among males, the very lowest earners and the unemployed tend to gain, the employed unskilled and semiskilled laborer tends to lose substantially, the skilled and salaried worker may experience a mild decline or may actually benefit, and the individual whose income depends heavily on entrepreneurial profits or investments loses significantly.

Menderhausen's income-loss model gives rise to the primary predictive proposition of this chapter, namely, that the greater the economic loss experienced by a particular group during an economic downturn, the greater will be its sensitivity in terms of mental hospitalization.

This proposition, in turn, initiates two testable hypotheses: (A) the general model of income loss during the Great Depression is generally applicable to economic downturns occurring within the time scope of most of the present study (1910–1960), and (B) the general economic-loss model should enable us to predict the differential sensitivities to economic downturns of the mental hospitalization of groups classified according to that model.

The Relation Between Income Changes During 1929–1933 and During 1910–1960

Hypothesis (A) may be examined in the light of other empirical studies dealing with income and employment changes during specific economic cycles occurring after World War II.

One such study, by the U. S. Bureau of Labor Statistics,[7] examined changes in unemployment rates by major occupation groups during four post-World War II business cycles (1948–1950, 1953–1955, 1957–1958, and 1960–61) for the United States as a whole. It found that the sharpest impact of unemployment is felt by semiskilled operatives (mainly "production workers on factory assembly lines"). Less affected were occupational groups whose economic statuses are neither immediately below or above the semiskilled worker, namely, the unskilled laborer and the skilled craftsman and foreman. White-collar and service workers suffered least of all.

This study confirms hypothesis (A) for the postwar years 1948–1960. For if it is argued that the highest rate of unemployment is found among unskilled labor, then to be consistent with Menderhausen's 1929–1933 findings and explanation, the next higher economic status level of occupation, semiskilled labor, ought to suffer the most among workers whose income is closely intertwined with their employment status. Finally, we see that among these workers who depend on employment for their earnings, excluding unskilled laborers, the higher the economic status of the occupational level, the greater the stability of employment (and, inferentially, income) and the lower the sensitivity to an economic downturn. Thus, the craftsman and foreman suffer less in the downturn than the semiskilled, and white-collar workers suffer least of all of these.

A second post-World War II study, based directly on income loss during an economic downturn, also strongly supports the applicability of the 1929–1933 income-loss model to later economic downturns. This study[8] was made during 1957–1958 in a midwestern city, "one of the largest cities in the country," which "in retail sales per family in 1957 . . . ranked among the five largest cities in the nation."

The study reports:

The recession year of 1958 had a far greater impact on blue-collar than on white-collar workers in the city. During that year, because of lay-offs and reduced work weeks, the income of "operatives and service workers" declined $500 from the 1957 median. The income of "craftsmen and foremen" declined $200. At the same time, the incomes of "clerical and sales workers" *increased* by $400. The income of "professionals" and kindred occupations increased by the same amount.[9]

This study supports the position that during the downturn, among those who are usually employed and whose earnings are dependent on their employment status—that is, those who do not derive their major earnings from profits or investments—(1) the income loss of manual or "blue-collar" workers will be less, the higher the income level of the occupation, and (2) nonmanual or white-collar workers do not appear to suffer appreciable income loss, and they in fact gain.

We have examined the close similarities between differential income and employment loss by occupational and income categories during specific pre- and postwar economic downturns as reported in independent studies. But the most appropriate test of hypothesis (A) would require examination of the aggregate effects, during the entire last half-century, of economic cycles on income changes in specific groups.

A study dealing with this particular question was completed in 1956 under the sponsorship of the National Bureau of Economic Research.[10] In this study Creamer used the Burns-Mitchell technique[11] to describe the relation between business-cycle changes and changes in personal income.

Creamer estimated the relative amplitudes of income change during economic upturns and downturns (or "business expansions and contractions") for various classifications of earnings. On the basis of the business-cycle chronology of the NBER, Creamer finds that: (1) among persons receiving income from manufacturing enterprises (except for proprietors), the higher the income level of the employee, the lower the amplitude of income and employment fluctuations with the economic cycle; (2) the incomes of nonfarm proprietors, and their dividend disbursements, have larger relative upturns and downturns than those of any group of nonfarm laborer's earnings; and (3) farm proprietors' incomes show greater fluctuation during the economic cycle than those of nonfarm proprietors, and farm wages and salaries show greater fluctuation than nonfarm wages and salaries.

Findings (1) and (2) regarding differential income loss by employee classification and source of income directly corroborate hypothesis (A) and support our extension of Menderhausen's income-loss model for the years 1909 to 1951. Finding (3) on relative farm-nonfarm income fluctuation during the business cycle is relevant to the mental-hospitalization findings of the present study comparing urban and rural fluctuations. (The urban-rural differential sensitivity to economic change is discussed later in this chapter.)

Finding (1), that income fluctuations are greater among wage-earners than amony salary-earners during the cycle, is based on: (a) national personal income data compiled and adjusted to form continuous series running from 1909 to 1951 for wage and salary receipts (farms and manufacturing), of corporate officers' and proprietors' (farm and nonfarm) income and dividends, and compensation of corporate officers, 1920–1949 (Bureau of Internal Revenue) and "other salaried personnel," 1920–1949; (b) factory employment of wage earners and salaried personnel, Ohio manufacturing industries, 1919–1939, and employment and payrolls of wage and salary earners, Wisconsin manufacturing industries, 1920–1936.[12]

Finding (2), that the amplitudes of nonfarm proprietors' incomes and dividend disbursements are greater during the economic cycle, is based on national, NBER-assembled data, 1907–1951, and national data compiled by the Department of Commerce, 1929–1948.[13]

The Economic-Loss Model and Sensitivity of Mental Hospitalization to Economic Change

The strong empirical support for hypothesis (A) upholding the model proposed to explain the findings of this study on differential sensitivity according to socioeconomic level enables us to proceed with a close examination of hypothesis (B) that the greater the economic loss suffered during the economic downturn, the stronger will be the inverse relation between the indicator of economic change and mental hospitalization.

Hypothesis (B) may be examined by observing the sensitivity of various groups, classified according to the position they would occupy within the economic-loss model, to the economic downturn, in terms of their mental hospitalization. The following categories by which mental-hospital admissions in New York State have been grouped may be reclassified to fit into the economic-loss model: (1) level of educational attainment, (2) normal or subnormal intellectual capacity, (3) voluntary and court-committed admissions, (4) urban or rural place of residence, (5) length of residence of the foreign-born in the United States, and (6) ethnic group.

Level of Educational Attainment

The mental-hospitalization data show that when educational attainment is classified according to (1) less than grammar school (including "illiterate," "reads only," and "reads and writes"), (2) grammar school, (3) high school, and (4) college, it is comparable with Menderhausen's classification (and those of other economic studies) of findings for economic loss during the downturn.[14] Thus, low negative and frequently positive correlations between mental hospitalization and the economic indicator are found for the majority of both males and females in the lowest educational group—those with less than a grammar-school education. Furthermore, not a single one of the correlations shown by the two sets of less than grammar-school educated groups shows a higher correlation than that of a corresponding grammar-school educated group (Table 26). This is comparable to Menderhausen's findings (and those of other economic studies) that the majority of lowest- and no-income groups do not show great losses and tend actually to gain income during the downturn. It is also consistent with the explanation that this group tends generally to show high rates of unemployment even before the downturn.

In the case of the grammar-school educated, the reverse occurs—both males and females show extremely high negative correlations. This finding is consistent with the reversal in the data of the economic studies which show that the "moderately low" income groups lose heavily in the downturn, and certainly more heavily than the low or moderately high income groups. In addition, this is the group which, according to Menderhausen's findings, should lose most heavily during the downturn. Correspondingly, the present data indicate, in fact, that this group consistently shows the highest negative correlations of their mental hospitalization with the economic indicator (see Fig. 18).

Table 26. Multiple correlations[a] between employment and mental-hospital admissions during 1914–1960, by level of education and sex.[b]

	Education									
	Less than grammar school				Grammar school		High school		College	
	Illiterate or reads only		Reads and writes							
Psychosis	M	F	M	F	M	F	M	F	M	F
Total undifferentiated	−0.62	+0.65	+0.65	+0.79	−0.93	−0.90	−0.50	+0.68	−0.73	+0.56
Total functional	+ .48	+ .35	+ .61	+ .68	− .88	− .83	− .50	+ .75	− .71	− .62
Alcoholic	− .76	− .59	− .38	+ .22	− .90	− .57	+ .36	+ .37	− .70	+ .25
Paretic	+ .63	− .53	+ .47	+ .74	− .83	− .85	− .77	− .53	− .69	− .62
Epileptic	− .51	+ .42	+ .67	+ .68	.67	− .74	+ .56	+ .56	− .27	− .27
Cerebral arterio-sclerosis	− .69	− .68	− .47	+ .26	− .91	− .86	+ .40	+ .47	− .62	+ .51
Senile	+ .72	+ .74	+ .66	+ .76	+ .78	+ .82	+ .69	+ .76	+ .66	+ .69

[a] The sign of R depends on the signs of the beta weights.
[b] First admissions to New York civil state hospitals correlated, at 0–3-year lags, with New York State manufacturing employment index (secular trend subtracted from both series).

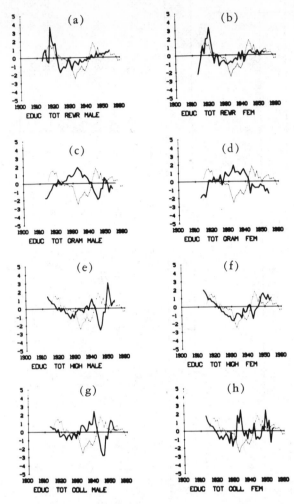

FIG. 18. Fluctuations in employment and in mental-hospital admissions during 1914–1960: first admissions with functional psychosis (schizophrenia, manic-depressive psychosis, and involutional psychosis), by level of education and sex. First admissions to New York civil state hospitals matched with New York State manufacturing employment index (secular trend subtracted from both series).

LEGEND:
...... New York State Manufacturing Employment Index
_____ First admissions with functional psychosis, by level of education:
     (a,b) reads and writes (c,d) grammar school (e,f) high school
     (g,h) college
SCALE: Deviations from secular trend in admissions and in the employment index are expressed in standardized normal scores. Scalar range describes relative magnitude of variation in each series.

The senile category shows no negative correlations regardless of educational attainment. This finding is consistent with and further supports those reported later in this chapter. There it is seen that the mental hospitalization of the aged responds not necessarily to economic depression and frequently to prosperity.

The high-school group appears to show, for both males and females, a mild, and usually insignificant, correlation, either negative or positive, depending on the diagnostic classification of psychosis. Again, this is consistent with the findings and explanations of the economic studies. The findings indicating that the "moderately high" income group either gained slightly or experienced a slight decline during the depression and the explanation that this income change occurred among skilled and salaried workers conform to our similar finding among high-school educated groups.

Finally, the mental-hospitalization data reverse themselves a third time for the college educated group as they do for the highest income group represented in the economic studies. Similarly, the mental hospitalization of the college educated males increases appreciably in the downturn just as the highest income groups lose severely according to the findings of the economic studies.

Thus, the broad patterns of the mental-hospitalization data accurately match the findings of the economic studies. These studies show that during the downturn the lowest income groups lose less than the moderately low income groups; the latter, in turn, lose appreciably more than the moderately high income groups; and the highest income groups experience greater economic loss than the moderately high. Correspondingly, the mental-hospitalization data show that, in general, the first admissions of the lowest socioeconomic groups, represented by the groups with less than a grammar-school education, show lower negative (and higher positive) correlations than those with immediately higher socioeconomic status, as indicated by grammar-school education. First admissions of the latter, in turn, show higher negative correlations than those of the high-school educated, for whom, finally, lower negative correlations are shown than for the college educated.

When age is not controlled, the college educated females do not show the complete reversal in the sign of the correlation coefficient that the males do, but their mental hospitalization is certainly increased in the downturn more heavily than the high-school educated females. In any case, Menderhausen's explanation that this upper income group represents mainly entrepreneurs and investors, and especially professionals in the case of males, is consistent with the classification of the highest educational-attainment group.

This strong similarity between the mental-hospitalization findings according to educational-attainment categories and Menderhausen's classification of findings on income loss becomes more striking still when age is controlled in the mental-hospitalization data. The major reason for controlling for the effect of age is that it may interfere with the well-documented relation between education and income.[15] Since there is an increasing trend over time toward higher educational attainment,[16] the presence of the older age groups who in general have less formal education may make the sensitivities of certain educational groups more an artifact of age than of income status.

Thus, the general principle that educational attainment is linearly related to income may be more nearly accurate at later points in the time trend. For example, in earlier periods a worker might obtain a great deal of apprenticeship training with little or no additional formal education. Similarly, it has become increasingly difficult to obtain managerial positions in industry without a college education. In the case of the females, an example would be the increasing tendency among middle and upper-middle income families to provide college education for them. It seems likely, for instance, that many women, especially those who are middle-aged or older, who had obtained only a high-school education were actually on as high an income level as the female college graduates.

We may partially control for the effects of the presence of the oldest group among the mental-hospital admissions by eliminating admissions with organically related illnesses (senile psychosis, psychosis with cerebral arteriosclerosis, and paresis, whose frequency continues to decrease at a precipitous rate) and concentrating on the functional psychoses (schizophrenia, manic-depressive psychosis, and involutional psychosis).

The correlations of first admissions with functional psychosis (classified by educational attainment) to the economic indicator shows an even closer parallel with the findings of the economic studies than was the case without the control for age (see Table 26). In the age-controlled data an even greater majority of the lowest educational group (less than grammar-school education) shows a positive correlation. Similarly, the college educated females show the same reversal of sign of the correlation coefficient as do the college educated males—also the highest income group in the economic studies.

The Mentally Normal and Mentally Defective

We may extend the economic-loss model to the differential behavior of mental defectives and nondefectives. An extensive review by Tizard and his associates[17] of research on the employability of mental defectives yielded a profile of the economic status of the mental defective. This review covered the research literature of the depression period between the World Wars and between World War II and 1949–1950. The general summary indicated that in times of full employment the defectives showed that they were not dependent to any great extent on the consideration and protection of their families. For the most part jobs were obtained without either family assistance or the help of social agencies; often as many as 80 percent of those employed were working for someone other than a member of the family or a family friend. Wages earned were comparatively high and a large fraction showed themselves capable of handling jobs requiring some skill or responsibility.

During periods of high unemployment, however, the studies are unanimous in showing a substantially higher unemployment and relief rate among the defectives.[18] Also, although the defective shows ability in fulfilling his tasks as a worker, in general he is slower than his fellow workers and is often discharged first in an emergency.[19]

According to our economic classifications, then, the noninstitutionalized defective may be thought of as being substantially more damaged by an economic downturn than his mentally normal counterpart in industry. The prediction follows that the mental hospitalization of the mentally subnormal should show a stronger inverse relation with the economic indicator. The data strongly support that prediction (Fig. 19) regardless of diagnostic category (except for psychosis with cerebral arteriosclerosis) or sex (see Table 27).

Table 27. Multiple correlations[a] between employment and mental-hospital admissions during 1915–1960, by intellectual capacity, sex, and diagnosis.[b]

Psychosis	Intellectual capacity			
	Normal		Subnormal	
	Male	Female	Male	Female
Total undifferentiated	−0.85	+0.59	−0.89	−0.77
Total functional	− .73	+ .38	− .84	− .75
Alcoholic	− .83	− .34	− .85	− .58
Senile	+ .79	+ .88	− .61	+ .63
Cerebral arterio- sclerosis	− .83	− .75	− .82	− .75
Paretic	− .82	− .76	− .90	− .85
Epileptic	− .55	− .42	− .73	− .62

[a]The sign of R depends on the signs of the beta weights.
[b]First admissions to New York civil state hospitals correlated, at 0–3-year lags, with New York State manufacturing employment index (secular trend subtracted from both series).

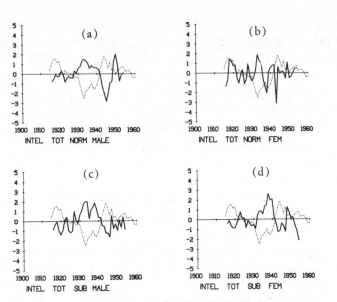

FIG. 19. Fluctuations in employment and in mental-hospital admissions during 1914–1960: first admissions with functional psychosis (schizophrenia, manic-depressive psychosis, and involutional psychosis), by intellectual capacity and sex. First admissions to New York civil state hospitals matched with New York State manufacturing employment index (secular trend subtracted from both series).

LEGEND:
...... New York State Manufacturing Employment Index
_____ First admissions with functional psychosis, by intellectual capacity;
(a,b) normal (c,d) subnormal
SCALE: Deviations from secular trend in admissions and in the employment index are expressed in standardized normal scores. Scalar range describes relative magnitude of variation in each series.

Voluntary and Court-Committed Admissions

Another opportunity for classification according to the scheme of the economic-loss model is provided by the breakdown of first admissions according to legal status of admission. Initially it was found in the data of this study that first admissions of the college educated showed a strong inverse relation to the economic indicator. This relation appeared to be explainable by the fact that the college educated, who have a high proportional representation among proprietors (especially self-employed professionals) and investors of all types, would show unusual economic vulnerability to the economic downturn.

In their study of the prevalence of treated mental illness in New Haven, Hollingshead and Redlich examined according to socioeconomic status the source of referral for psychotics entering treatment for the first time.[20] They found that only in the classes of highest educational and occupational rank were the patient himself or his family the two principal sources of referral. It was also found that patients from these classes were the least likely to use the court and police as the agents responsible for hospitalization. This study leads to the conclusion, then, that the groups making the greatest use of voluntary, or noncourt, admissions are probably to be found among persons of the highest educational attainment and occupational rank.

The classes of self- or family-referred voluntary admissions would be most nearly comparable among educational-attainment categories to the college educated, the highest educational category in the mental-hospitalization data. On the basis of the high sensitivity of the college educated to the economic downturn as compared to the general population of first admissions (see Table 26), we may argue that the voluntary first admissions should be more sensitive to the economic downturn than the court admissions. The prediction is, therefore, that voluntary first admissions should show a stronger inverse relation to the economic indicator than first admissions and readmissions generally—of which well over 80 percent have usually been court committed—since 1910.

In general, the data support this prediction. Stronger inverse relations are found among many of the diagnostic categories of voluntary first admissions (Fig. 20). In a few instances, however, the strength of the relations is not significantly greater for the voluntary first admissions (Table 28). In the case of readmissions, however, voluntary admissions consistently show higher negative correlations.

The legal classification of the admissions also enables us to check on the first-admissions–readmissions differentials for their consistency with findings reported later in this chapter. The data do show that even when voluntary admissions are examined, regardless of diagnosis or sex, stronger inverse relations are found for the first admissions.

Ethnic Background and the Response to Economic Stress

One of the difficulties in applying to the ethnic-group data the economic-loss model derived from the economic studies is that it presupposes the ability to classify these groups accurately by economic status. Most of the ethnic groups in this study probably contain a mixture of economic classifications, each of which, in turn, would more or less correspond to the average economic status of all ethnic groups. We therefore felt safest, in our understanding of the

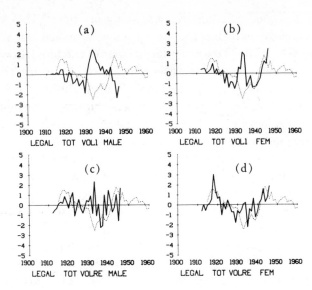

FIG. 20. Fluctuations in employment and in mental-hospital admissions during 1914–1948: voluntary admissions classified as first admissions or readmissions with functional psychosis (schizophrenia, manic-depressive psychosis, and involutional psychosis). Admissions to New York civil state hospitals matched with New York State manufacturing employment index (secular trend subtracted from both series).

LEGEND:
...... New York State Manufacturing Employment Index
——— Voluntary (legal status) first and readmissions with functional psychosis:
      (a,b) first admissions (c,d) readmissions
SCALE: Deviations from secular trend in admissions and in the employment index are expressed in standardized normal scores. Scalar range describes relative magnitude of variation in each series.

ethnic data, in focusing on those groups whose economic status is most easily discriminated from the average of the general population, namely, those that earn the very lowest and the very highest incomes.

The Low Socioeconomic Status Groups

Following the earlier evidence, we may argue that among the ethnic groups the lowest in socioeconomic status ought to be the least damaged by the economic downturn. The mental hospitalization of these groups, therefore, should show the lowest negative or highest positive correlations with the economic indicator.

Earlier in this chapter we saw that the diagnostic category of psychosis that best fitted the economic-loss predictions on the basis of the educational-attainment classification was functional psychosis. The possible reasons offered for this were (1) that the functional category includes the largest fraction

Table 28. Multiple correlations[a] between employment and mental-hospital
admissions during 1925–1960: voluntary and total admissions,
by diagnosis and sex.[b]

	Admissions			
Psychosis	Voluntary		Total	
	Male	Female	Male	Female
Total undifferentiated	−0.89	−0.48	−0.75	+0.33
Total functional	− .73	+ .44	− .66	+ .49
Alcoholic	− .79	− .64	− .78	− .30
Senile	− .32	− .26	+ .80	+ .80
Cerebral arterio- sclerosis	− .61	− .37	− .82	− .81
Paretic	− .84	− .50	− .79	− .77
Epileptic	− .44	+ .56	− .50	− .28

[a]The sign of R depends on the signs of the beta weights.
[b]First admissions to New York civil state hospitals correlated, at 0–3-year lags, with New
  York State manufacturing employment index (secular trend subtracted from both series).

of admissions and would therefore be the single most highly representative
category (thus, we may control the presence of groups whose economic
statuses are difficult to ascertain or complicated by their illness) and (2) that the
confounding effects (over time) of older age were substantially reduced, since
the senile, cerebral arteriosclerotic, and paretic categories are not present.
In attempting a necessarily limited application of the economic-loss model to
ethnic patterns of mental hospitalization, therefore, it is useful to restrict
ourselves to the functional category.

The prediction of lack of sensitivity for very low-income groups is strongly
borne out by the fact that the only ethnic groups showing significant positive
correlations ($R \geqq + 0.50$) for both sexes are the Negroes and Spanish
Americans (Table 29 and Fig. 21). In the 1950 Census the foreign stock and
racial groups are classified by income.[21] Among all of these groups the Negro
earns the very lowest incomes. Among first-generation (foreign-born)
groups, classified by country of nativity, the Mexicans and Puerto Ricans—or
ethnic "Spanish Americans"—have the lowest incomes. Among second-
generation (foreign- or mixed-parentage) groups, classified by country of
nativity of parents, the Mexican is still lowest, and the Puerto Rican remains
among the five lowest-income groups (including American Indian, Filipino,
Mexican, and Negro).

Since there is abundant material on Negro-white differences in socioeconomic

Table 29. Multiple correlations[a] between employment and mental-hospital admissions during 1914–1955: admissions with functional psychoses, by ethnic group and sex.

Ethnic group	Level of multiple correlation							
	$R \leq -0.60$		$R \leq -0.50$		$R \leq -0.40$		$R \leq -0.30$	
	M	F	M	F	M	F	M	F
Division I								
Jewish	−0.809	−0.779						
German	−.841	−.594						
Armenian	−.674	−.673						
Scotch	−.618	−.668						
Division II								
Irish	−.775			−0.549				
Mixed	−.634			−.569				
English	−.637					−0.463		
Dutch and Flemish	−.640					−.488		
Scandinavian			−0.567			−.454		
Finnish		−.631	−.516					
Division III								
French				−.530	−0.474			
Italian				−.501	−.450			
Slavic				−.509	−.458			
Magyar					−.464	−.239		
Division IV								
Greek							0.328	0.398
Negro							.553	.621
Spanish American							.563	.528

[a] The sign of R depends on the signs of the beta weights.

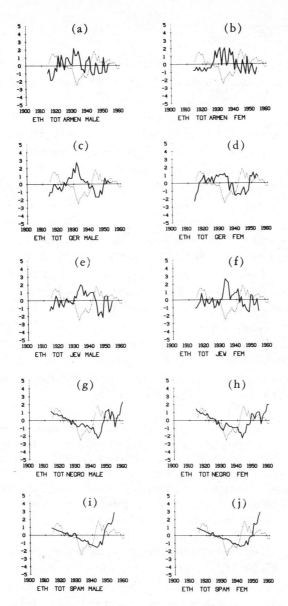

FIG. 21. Fluctuations in employment and in mental-hospital admissions during 1914–1955: admissions of selected ethnic groups with functional psychosis (schizophrenia, manic-depressive psychosis, and involutional psychosis), by sex. First admissions to New York civil state hospitals matched with New York State manufacturing employment index (secular trend subtracted from both series).

LEGEND:
...... New York State Manufacturing Employment Index
——— First admissions with functional psychosis, by ethnic group:
    (a,b) Armenian (c,d) German (e,f) Jewish (g,h) Negro
    (i,j) Spanish-American
SCALE: Deviations from secular trend in admissions and in the employment index are expressed in standardized normal scores. Scalar range describes relative magnitude of variation in each series.

status and differential employment fluctuations during the economic cycle, it would be useful to examine the Negro-white differential in greater detail. In the first place, it is quite clear that unemployment is far more common among the Negro population. Thus, for example, as late as the post-World War II period, from 1947 to 1957 inclusive, the rate of unemployment for nonwhite workers has been 90 percent higher than the rate for white workers.[22] On the basis of this fact, it might be argued that the Negro should suffer less during the downturn because a large part of this population earns little, and, if unemployed, has proportionately less to lose by a general economic downturn.

This argument is further supported by the fact that in all regions of the United States whites are better able to capitalize on their education than nonwhites. In the North and West as well as in the South, as late as 1950 the nonwhite who had invested 4 years in a college education earned less on the average than the white who had not completed high school.[23] Thus, within each category of technical or occupational skill (as described by educational attainment), the Negro is and has been at a very substantial disadvantage in earning power. Not only, therefore, has the Negro less to lose on the basis of employment status, but at every level of occupational skill the Negro will lose less income since he has less income to lose under conditions of high unemployment. As Henry and Short point out:

It may be argued that a person who loses all of a $10,000 yearly income during business contraction suffers a greater loss of status relative to others in his reference system than a person who loses all of $2,000 income during business contraction. A person with little income to begin with may suffer little or no frustration with its loss. Furthermore, if he compares his state with that of others higher in the status hierarchy, he may actually experience a gain in status relative to others when he sees that others who had much higher positions are now reduced to *his* state.[24]

On the other hand, it appears that Negro unemployment rates are not, in general, more or less acutely affected by the economic downturn than the white. Two independent studies of the effects of post-World War II recessions on employment status by race show that the downturn takes a similar toll among the white and Negro populations. The Bureau of Labor Statistics has found that, in four economic cycles which they measured between 1948 and 1961, "the data invariably show a larger absolute rise in the unemployment rate for Negroes as the economy *moves into a recession, but not necessarily a larger relative rise.*"[25] Similar conclusions are drawn by Bogue, who examined the nonwhite-white ratios of unemployment rates during periods of high, medium, and low general unemployment for the years 1947–1957. He found that "during periods of recession the unemployment rates for nonwhite workers increased by a larger (absolute) amount than the rates for white workers, although the percentage increase was about the same for the two groups."[26]

Thus, on the grounds that (1) during times of substantially higher unemployment rates under any conditions the Negro group is less likely to be affected by a change in the employment level, (2) at any level of occupational skill the Negro has less income to lose by the economic downturn, and (3) the Negro population does not suffer a relatively larger proportional increase in unemployment during the downturn, it is argued that in general the Negro who becomes unemployed should be less sensitive to the downturn than his white counterpart, and that mental hospitalization for Negroes should not show as strong an inverse relation to the economic indicator and might tend to show a positive relation.

Additional support for the validity of this prediction and these findings comes from an examination of the relation of homicide to the business cycle by race between 1910 and 1940. In this study Henry and Short found that although homicide by whites was inversely related to the business cycle, homicide by nonwhites was positively related to the business cycle.[27] If one accepts their interpretation that homicide is a manifestation of extreme frustration, then the homicide findings concur with the prediction and findings of this study, which argue that, because of their relatively low socioeconomic status, Negroes may have actually benefited by the economic downturns between 1910 and 1960.

High Socioeconomic Status Groups

The ethnic groups showing the highest negative correlations ($R \leqq -0.60$) for both sexes are the Armenians, Germans, and Jews (Table 29 and Fig. 21). According to the predictive model based on the economic studies, these particular groups should earn the very highest incomes.

Bogue's analysis of the 1950 Census materials shows that among the first generation (according to country of nativity, as discussed above), the Russian Jewish and Austrian (ethnic German) groups rank highest in socioeconomic status (by income, level of education, and occupation), and Germans emigrating from Germany proper are among the top five socioeconomic status-ranked groups. Among the second-generation groups, the Russian Jewish group is still highest, and the German (country of nativity) and Austrian groups rank sixth and seventh respectively.[28]

Unfortunately, the Armenian group was not classified as were the other groups above, and we must go elsewhere for data on their relative socioeconomic status. Warner and Srole[29] compared the occupational rankings of several "ethnic groups" with that of the "native" population of "Yankee City," a middle-sized city in New England, for the year 1933. The ethnic groups, in descending order of occupational status, were "native" Jewish, Armenian, Irish, Italian, French Canadian, Greek, Russian, and Polish. Similar indications of the relatively high socioeconomic status of Armenians among ethnic groups in the United States are given by other authors.[30]

The predictive model is therefore strongly supported by the fact that these very highest status groups, which, like the very lowest, are least likely to contain a mixture of economic classifications, are the most sensitive to the economic downturn. Additional support for the validity of these findings may be found in the predictive model of Henry and Short. Here, the very high income groups will certainly stand to lose the most (the opposite of the case of the very low status groups who have very little income to lose). Finally, the additional psychosocial factors of upward mobility aspirations and concern with social status may act to further sharpen the blow of great economic loss for these particular high-income ethnic groups.

First, it has been shown that groups that achieve some upward mobility tend to want more.[31] In addition, it has been observed that strong motivation for economic achievement is found more often in the subcultural role definitions of higher than in those of lower socioeconomic status groups. Rosen, for example, found that the mean age of independence training, achievement values, educational aspirations, and vocational aspirations all increased linearly with Hollingshead's scale of socioeconomic class.[32] Hyman reported similar findings in relation to high status educational and occupational "preferences" and "recommendations" according to socioeconomic class.[33] Again, in an examination of class and family dynamics in the mental illness of patients of Classes III and V (Hollingshead's Index), Myers and Roberts found the theme of frustrated achievement aspirations prevalent in the middle-class (Class III) but not in the lowest class (Class V).[34]

Finally, it has been shown that concern with social status was necessary in the first place in order to achieve such high socioeconomic status.[35]

Ethnicity and Socioeconomic Status: The Overall Relation

Our hypothesis of a relation between socioeconomic status of an ethnic group and sensitivity to economic change of its mental-hospital admissions was strongly supported by data that compared the highest and lowest socioeconomic status group. The findings led to the speculation that the original hypothesis might actually extend to a considerably larger number of ethnic groups.

We therefore attempted to include all of 17 major ethnic groups whose frequencies of admission were sufficiently high to permit such a comparative analysis in a study of relative sensitivity to, or directness of, the relation between economic change and mental hospitalization for functional psychosis.

In attempting to estimate the directness of our basic relation according to ethnic classifications, both sexes in each ethnic group were considered. In other words, an estimate of a strongly direct inverse relation between economic change and mental hospitalization was indicated if a high inverse multiple correlation was shown for *both* sexes of an ethnic group. When the 17 major ethnic groups were arranged by sex according to magnitude of direct relation, four major divisions appeared (see Table 29).

The first division consisted of four ethnic groups—Jews, Germans, Armenians, and Scotch—which, for both sexes, showed a multiple correlation coefficient of −0.60 or less. The second division, which demonstrated moderately direct inverse relations between economic change and mental hospitalization, showed multiple correlations of at most −0.50 (R lies between −0.50 and −1.00) for males and −0.40 for females (most of the multiple correlations in this group were actually less than −0.60 for males and −0.40 for females). This second division consisted of the Irish, mixed English, Dutch and Flemish, Scandinavian, and Finnish ethnic groups. The third division consists of four ethnic groups with relatively weak direct inverse relations between economic change and mental hospitalization, showing multiple correlations of less only than −0.50 for both sexes; these are the French, Magyar (Hungarian), Slavic, and Italian groups. The fourth division consists of three ethnic groups which show relations that are very weakly inverse or at least occasionally positive. The groups involved which show for both sexes multiple correlations of more than −0.40 or positivity are the Greek, Negro, and Spanish-American.

When these four major divisions are observed in terms of levels of socioeconomic status, we find that the higher the socioeconomic status, the more direct is the inverse relation between economic change and mental hospitalization. In other words, the higher the socioeconomic status of an ethnic group, the more exclusively does the mental hospitalization of its members depend on the purely economic factors associated with an economic downturn. The primary[36] sources for our estimate of comparative socioeconomic status among the various ethnic groups, over a 50-year period are Warner and Srole, *Status Systems of American Ethnic Groups,* and Bogue, *The Population of the United States.* Warner and Srole's material was collected in the New England community of "Yankee City" in the mid 1930's, and is based on commonly held judgments of the social standing of the members of several ethnic groups. Bogue's estimates of the socioeconomic status of various nationality categories of the foreign-born are based on indicators of assimilation into the American economy as measured by educational and income status. Thus, the original hypothesis is again supported, but we now have found it applicable to the 17 largest ethnic groups.

Apart from the issue of the influence of socioeconomic status on the basic relation, we notice that in many ethnic groups the males show a substantially more direct relation between economic change and mental hospitalization than do the females. This is of course the usual, or normal, pattern, as we have seen in all but a few areas of the present study. Among several other ethnic groups, however, we do not find the males showing a more direct relation than the females. Furthermore, the difference between the sexes in terms of the basic relation between economic change and mental hospitalization does not appear to be related to the socioeconomic status of the ethnic group. Specific ethnic groups of both relatively high and relatively low economic status show similarity (rather than divergence) between the sexes in the directness of the basic relation.

The question then is: for what types of ethnic groups do we see the usual pattern in which greater stress is placed on only the male during an economic downturn, rather than on both sexes? At this point, we can have only a preliminary impression of the distinguishing characteristics of these two groups. It appears that only those ethnic groups that are characterized either by unusually high or unusually low socioeconomic status show relative equality between the sexes in terms of an even distribution of the purely economic stress of an economic downturn on mental hospitalization. It is possible that ethnic groups which are distinguished by their relatively high or low socioeconomic status from the Anglo-American, or "native," population at large show similarity rather than divergence in the degree to which the sexes suffer purely economic loss.

Now, since the usual patterns for the females are not as sensitive to purely economic concerns as are those for the male, we may raise the question of why certain females behave more like male members of their own ethnic group than like females in the general population. One possible answer is that females who do not belong to an ethnic group that is considered, or considers itself, either of relatively high or relatively low social status are not intensely concerned either with losing their relatively high prestige or with the indignity of further assuring their relatively low position.

Specifically, the ethnic groups that have relatively high socioeconomic status and show great similarity between the sexes in terms of purely economic effects of economic loss are Jews, Armenians, and Scotch. The relatively low socioeconomic status groups showing distinctive similarities between the male and female responses to economic loss are French (especially French

Catholic and French Canadian), Italian, Slavic, Negro, and Spanish American. These two groupings are perhaps far more distinctive in their relatively high or low socioeconomic status than the "middle-American" set of ethnic groups that populate New York State, including the Irish, ethnically mixed, English, Dutch and Flemish, Scandinavian, Finnish, and Welsh. It is the "middle-American" ethnic groups that show the dominant pattern of greater sensitivity of males to the purely economic impact of the downturn.

The females of distinctive ethnic groups of relatively lower socioeconomic status, according to this hypothesis, behave more like the other (male) members of their own ethnic groups, whose ethnic background can be strongly identified by the native population, than like other females in the population at large. Their economic losses might therefore not be seen in terms of their specialized female roles but rather in terms of the socioeconomic status of other members of their ethnic group who, together, form a distinctive sociocultural unit. This might not be the case for those groups whose ethnicity is not a distinguishing feature of their personalities. In the case of females of the middle-American groups, whose socioeconomic status is not identifiable simply by virtue of their ethnicity, their identities as females might overshadow their identities as holders of a particular socioeconomic status. Thus, a woman of the middle-American group may not be expected to be of unusually high or low economic status.

Sensitivity to the Economic Downturn by Duration of Residence of the Foreign Born in the United States

Additional support for the argument that persons earning higher incomes tend to lose more because they have more to lose and therefore suffer greater emotional stress during the downturn than those earning lower incomes is found in the mental-hospitalization data. The scope of these data permits us to examine the effect of economic change on mental hospitalization in relation to duration of residence in the United States of the mentally hospitalized foreign born.

Fortunately, the data also permit a control for age. Data on age by themselves show the usual pattern—a hyperbolic arrangement of relations with the economic indicator, where the peak of inverse sensitivity occurs in middle age (Table 30).

The duration-of-residence categories are 0–5, 5–9, 9–14, and over 15 years. It is apparent that, in general, the longer the duration of residence, the stronger is the inverse relation between the economic indicator and mental hospitalization. After 15 years of residence, however, increased length of

Table 30. Multiple correlations[a] between employment and mental-hospital admissions, during 1926–1954: admissions of immigrants, by duration of residence in the United States, age, and sex.[b]

Age (years)	Duration of residence (years)							
	Male				Female			
	0–4	5–9	10–14	15+	0–4	5–9	10–14	15+
0–14	−0.39	+0.58	−0.28	+0.66	+0.45	−0.61	−0.45	—
15–19	+ .53	− .42	− .64	− .61	+ .53	+ .69	− .53	+ .52
20–24	+ .66	+ .57	− .62	− .58	− .71	− .72	− .50	+ .60
25–29	+ .65	− .64	− .78	− .62	+ .58	− .63	− .75	− .69
30–34	+ .67	− .61	− .71	− .55	+ .56	− .59	− .85	− .62
35–39	+ .55	− .79	− .81	− .49	+ .54	− .59	− .81	− .60
40–44	+ .55	− .50	− .82	− .77	− .40	− .67	− .91	− .65
45–49	+ .38	− .48	− .64	− .80	+ .38	− .53	− .77	− .76
50–54	+ .52	− .50	− .51	− .77	− .42	− .73	− .81	− .71
55–59	+ .49	− .46	− .38	− .76	− .28	− .73	− .62	− .72
60–64	+ .38	+ .33	− .54	− .71	− .43	− .59	− .62	− .76
65–69	+ .43	− .50	− .70	− .72	− .42	− .56	− .70	− .80
70+	+ .43	− .56	− .55	+ .67	+ .39	+ .59	− .65	+ .65
Total	+ .58	− .82	− .81	− .80	+ .48	− .85	− .86	+ .76
0–19	+0.49	−0.52	−0.65	−0.64	+0.50	−0.67	−0.55	+0.52
20–29	+ .66	− .68	− .75	− .59	+ .68	− .68	− .68	− .63
30–39	+ .63	− .71	− .79	− .57	+ .56	− .62	− .86	− .63
40–49	+ .52	− .65	− .79	− .81	− .29	− .65	− .60	− .72
50–59	+ .54	− .58	− .89	− .79	− .37	− .73	− .77	− .73
60–69	+ .40	− .48	− .70	− .80	− .37	− .62	− .68	− .86

[a]The sign of R depends on the signs of the beta weights.

[b]First admissions to New York civil state hospitals correlated, at 0–3-year lags, with New York State manufacturing employment index (secular trend subtracted from both series).

residence seems to affect only the hospitalization of the late middle-aged groups, 45–69 years (Fig. 22).

It is possible that this relation does not extend to the younger and oldest groups in the over-15-year duration-of-residence category because, despite the control for age, age must of necessity be interrelated with duration of residence. Thus, in the case of the over-70-year-old group, the effects of old age may begin to blunt the general relation within the over-15-years residence category.

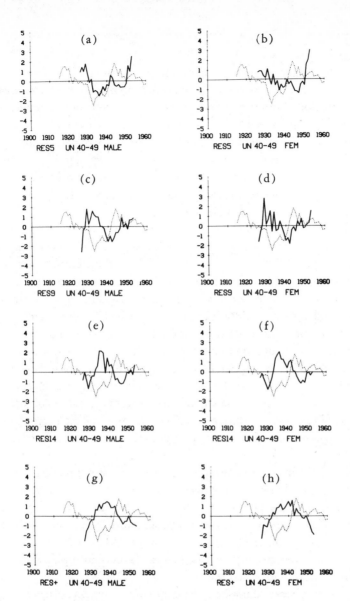

FIG. 22. Fluctuations in employment and in mental-hospital admissions during 1927–1953: admissions of immigrants, by duration of residence in the United States and sex. First admissions to New York civil state hospitals matched with New York State manufacturing employment index (secular trend subtracted from both series).

LEGEND:
...... New York State Manufacturing Employment Index
────── Total admissions of immigrants, ages 40–49, by duration of residence in the United States:
(a,b) under 5 years (c,d) 5–9 years (e,f) 10–14 years
(g,h) 15 years and over
SCALE: Deviations from secular trend in admissions and in the employment index are expressed in standardized normal scores. Scalar range describes relative magnitude of variation in each series.

In the case of the under-20 age group, the effects of having lived in the United States for over 15 years may be equivalent to having lived here since birth.

The explanation of this strong direct relation between length of residence of the mentally hospitalized foreign born and the economic indicator may be that the longer the duration of residence of the foreign-born person, the longer he has had to secure a high-paying job and to accumulate savings and property.[37] And, as in the case of the ethnic classification of sensitivity to economic change, the greater the income, savings, and property, the more there is to lose as a result of the economic downturn.

It is also significant that here again, in the duration-of-residence classification, we find that the category of lowest duration of residence (0–5 years) shows *positive* correlations with the economic indicator for all male and several female age categories. This pattern of positive relations strongly supports the predictive economic-loss model which states that those earning very little or no income tend either to lose mildly or even to gain in the downturn. The assumption, of course, is that a significant fraction of the foreign born— especially the most recent immigrants—tend to be unemployed or earners of very low income. This assumption is, in part, supported by Census data. As late as 1950, among white urban males 25–44 years old in the United States, the rates of unemployment for natives of native parentage, natives of foreign parentage, and foreign born were, respectively, 3.7, 4.7, and 6.0 percent. For white urban females of the same age groups they were 3.3, 4.0, and 4.6 percent.[38]

As in the case of the findings on ethnic groups, however, it is possible that there are factors in addition to the strict extent of income loss that affect the reaction of the foreign born to the economic downturn according to duration of residence. These additional factors may be substantially the same as those that affect the extraordinary sensitivity of ethnic groups of high socioeconomic status discussed earlier, namely, increase in upward mobility aspirations and greater concern with social status.

In the case of increased duration of residence of the foreign born, we may be encountering an additional factor that tends to elevate upward mobility aspirations and concern with social status. With increasing assimilation of the foreign born resulting from longer duration of residence, there is an increase in their identification with the majority of the population. This engenders feelings of inferiority over the continuous immigrant status, which add to the status discrepancy felt by the immigrant as he advances in assimilation. Such feelings progress with increased duration of residence until, in the following generation (the sociologically famous second generation), we find the full-blown identity crisis.[39]

8 Economic Change and Role Performance

We now examine the interacting effects of actual economic loss and role failure that result in the differential sensitivities to economic change of various categories of age, illness, sex, and marital status.

The Life Cycle and Economic Stress

Predictions Based on the Economic-Loss Model

As in the case of education, the economic-loss model permits us to predict the differential behavior of various age groups on the basis of an economic classification.

The economic-loss model indicated that persons outside the labor force by virtue of unemployment (or not earning income) would not be directly affected by an economic downturn. This is the case simply because, economically speaking, this group has nothing to lose. In fact, according to Menderhausen's findings, this group actually tends to gain. Applying this argument to mental-hospital first admissions classified by age, we would predict that age groups showing the highest unemployment rates would be least likely to increase and may actually decrease their admissions during the economic downturn.

Bogue[1] analyzed the Census unemployment data, by age group, from 1940 to 1958 (beginning with age 14). The data clearly show for both sexes that unemployment rates are highest for the age groups under 25 and over 60. This tendency for the middle-aged groups to show proportionately greater labor-force activity (by reason of lower unemployment levels) is increased by their much higher rates of labor-force participation. Bogue shows the age- and sex-specific labor-force participation rates for 1900–1955, starting with age 14. From 1900 to 1955, among males, the highest participation rates range between 25 and 54 years of age. Among females, there is greater variation between 1900 and 1955 but, in general, the highest age groups (54 and over) show the lowest participation rates.

A combination of the unemployment and labor-force participation data suggests that, for both sexes, those age groups under 25 and over 54 were the least active in earning income between 1910 and 1960. We would argue, therefore, that these younger and older age groups should suffer less unemployment and income loss during an economic downturn than the middle-aged groups.

This argument finds support in two independent analyses of age-specific loss of employment during economic downturns. Bogue examined age-specific unemployment rates for each year between 1948 and 1958 and for 1940; the last was included to permit examination of the age pattern under conditions of high employment. The rates for these years were indexed according to "high," "medium," or "low" unemployment.[2]

Bogue finds that

when unemployment is at a low ebb . . . everybody has a job except the very youngest and the very oldest people. The workers in these two age groups seem to have the greatest difficulty finding jobs even during times of full employment. Rising unemployment affects all age groups, but it causes the greatest percentage increase of unemployed among workers in the central age groups 25 to 54 years of age. Thus, when the overall rate of unemployment rises, all age groups are affected; however, the proportional increases in joblessness are greatest among adult workers, and the major breadwinners become much less secure.[3]

Similar findings were obtained in a Bureau of Labor Statistics analysis of age-specific unemployment rate changes in four business cycles, 1948–1961. This study compared changes in unemployment rates during years of higher and lower unemployment. The conclusions:

On the way into a recession, men between the ages of 20 and 54 are most severely affected by rising unemployment. Similarly, these workers tend to show the sharpest decline in unemployment rates during recovery periods. There are at least two reasons for this: (1) the men in the prime working ages are more heavily concentrated in durable goods manufacturing and other recession-affected industries than are other workers, and (2) these men are nearly all year-round labor force members (except for a few college students and some totally disabled persons) whereas many younger workers, older men, and women workers have the option of leaving the labor force upon losing a job. The unemployment rates in these other groups do show a strong cyclical response, but they are not as sensitive as the rates for men in the central age groups 20 to 54.[4]

The economic-loss model may be approached from still another direction. The case of age differentials in economic loss makes it particularly relevant to ask, regardless of the fraction of people in each age group who may lose *some* income and employment, what the actual differential income loss is during the downturn.

In 1935–1936, the United States Family Composition Study classified more than 400,000 single-family urban households by income, age of family head, and size of household. The survey showed, starting with the 20–24-year age group, that family income increased with the age of the family head up to the age group 40–54, and thereafter declined. The Census of 1940 obtained similar results for male wage or salary earners 25–64 years old for the United States. Here, the median income peak occurred in the 35–44 age group.[5]

Likewise, the 1950 Census was able to classify income of family head by type of family and age of head for the United States. Again the usual pattern prevailed, with the median in the 35–44 age group. The identical pattern was found for husband-wife families, all other families headed by males, and families headed by females.[6]

The same Census reported the identical age classification by income findings for both males and females of farm and nonfarm residence.[7] These data again support the prediction that middle-aged males and females lose the most income during a downturn because they earn the most and, under conditions of severe unemployment, have the most to lose.

Still another position supports the prediction that the middle-aged group is the hardest hit by the downturn. We may argue that, "other things equal," the age group whose family heads have the greatest number of family members to support is the group that requires the highest income and steadiest employment. Thus, should the family head in this age group become unemployed, his family suffers the most far-reaching income loss.

Woytinsky's analysis of the U. S. Family Composition Study of 1935–1936 shows that both the mean and the median numbers of persons per family are highest for the age groups with family heads between 40 and 49 years of age. From the 40–49-year age peak, family size gradually declines with both decreasing and increasing age.[8]

The same findings were obtained by the 1950 Census for New York State. In this case the number of children under 18 years of age was classified by age of family head and type of family. It was found that for husband-wife families, other male-headed families, and female-headed families the number of children in the family reaches a peak when the family head is between 35 and 44; below and above 35–44, the number gradually decreases.

The strict economic-loss prediction that, among the age groups 20–64, the middle aged ought to suffer most severely during the economic downturn in terms of their mental hospitalization is based, then, on four well-supported arguments: (1) the middle-aged groups are the most active in the labor force, (2) the middle-aged groups show the greatest increases in unemployment during the economic downturn, (3) since the middle-aged groups earn the highest incomes, they have the most to lose as a result of unemployment, and (4) the middle-aged family heads support the largest families, thus their families stand to suffer the most far-reaching income loss should the family head become unemployed.

The economic-loss model suggests, then, that for both both sexes the middle-aged groups ought to show the highest inverse correlations between the economic indicator and their mental hospitalization.

The data of the present study strongly support this prediction. For both sexes the age-differential magnitudes of the correlations between mental hospitalization and the economic indicator jointly resemble a nearly perfect hyperbola (Figures 23 and 24). In general, at the polar extremes of the age spectrum between 20 and 64, the correlations are low or insignificant, or even positive. In the case of the males, they gradually reach a peak of negativity between 35 and 54; in the case of the females, the peak occurs between 40 and 49 (Table 31).

Predictions Based on the Effects of Role Failure

There appears to be general agreement in the literature that stages of the life cycle serve as fundamental criteria for the allocation of social roles.[9] According to Eisenstadt, for example,

a cultural definition of an age grade or age span is always a broad definition of human potentialities and obligations at a given stage of life. It is not a prescription or expectation of a detailed role, but of general, basic role dispositions into which more specific roles may be built, and to which they may be ascribed. At the same time it is not merely a classificatory category as it is sometimes used in statistical censuses. However explicit its formulations, it always involves an evaluation of the meaning and importance of the given age for the individual and for the society . . . It contains certain definite expectations of future activities, and of relationships with other people at the same or at different stages of their life career. In terms of these definitions people map out, as it were, the broad contours of human life, of their own expectations and possibilities, and place themselves and their

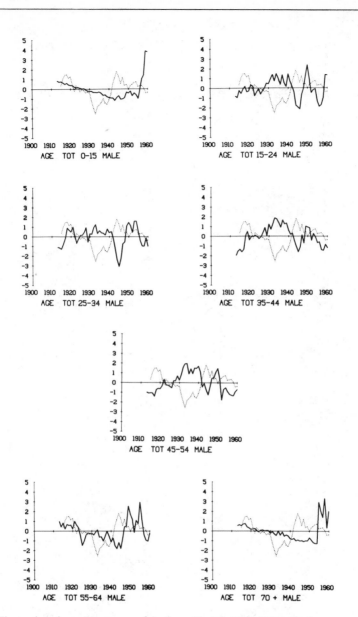

FIG. 23. Fluctuations in employment and in mental-hospital admissions during 1914–1960, male admissions with functional psychosis (schizophrenia, manic-depressive psychosis, and involutional psychosis), by age. First admissions to New York civil state hospitals matched with New York State manufacturing employment index (secular trend subtracted from both series).

LEGEND:
...... New York State Manufacturing Employment Index
———— Male first admissions with functional psychosis, by age group
SCALE: Deviations from secular trend in admissions and in the employment index are expressed in standardized normal scores. Scalar range describes relative magnitude of variation in each series.

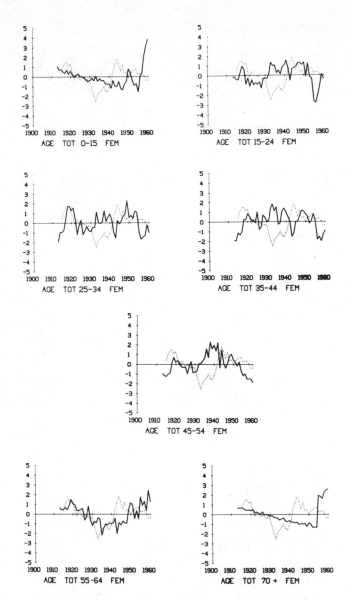

FIG. 24. Fluctuations in employment and in mental-hospital admissions during 1914–1960, female admissions with functional psychosis (schizophrenia, manic-depressive psychosis, and involutional psychosis), by age. First admissions to New York civil state hospitals matched with New York State manufacturing employment index (secular trend subtracted from both series).

LEGEND:
...... New York State Manufacturing Employment Index
———— Female first admissions with functional psychosis, by age group
SCALE: Deviations from secular trend in admissions and in the employment index are expressed in standardized normal scores. Scalar range describes relative magnitude of variation in each series.

Table 31. Multiple correlations[a] between employment and mental-hospital admissions during 1914–1960, by age, diagnosis, and sex.[b]

Psychosis	Age (years)												
	0–4	15–19	20–24	25–29	30–34	35–39	40–44	45–49	50–54	55–59	60–64	65–69	70+
Male													
Total undifferentiated	−0.35	−0.45	−0.61	−0.48	−0.75	−0.83	−0.90	−0.92	−0.85	−0.78	−0.76	+0.76	+0.50
Total functional	+.52	−.45	−.71	−.37	−.55	−.70	−.87	−.84	−.75	+.47	+.62	+.52	−.38
Alcoholic	.00	+.53	−.46	−.69	−.87	−.85	−.54	−.59	−.56	−.43	+.54	−.36	−.36
Senile									.	−.52	−.43	+.46	+.87
Cerebral arterio-sclerosis													
Paretic	−.71	−.54	−.62	−.65	−.79	−.80	−.77	−.67	−.77	−.64	−.64	−.61	−.57
Epileptic	−.44	−.41	+.23	−.48	+.38	−.43	−.42	−.52	−.54	−.33	+.53	+.41	+.36
Female													
Total undifferentiated	−.42	−.50	−.29	+.43	−.47	−.72	−.76	−.82	−.67	−.66	+.75	+.86	+.64
Total functional	+.39	−.49	+.20	+.47	+.54	−.76	−.66	−.71	+.32	+.70	−.54	+.52	−.40
Alcoholic	.00	−.46	−.25	+.74	+.29	−.44	+.35	−.46	−.49	−.42	−.47	−.49	−.34
Senile										−.40	−.53	+.49	+.83
Cerebral arterio-sclerosis													
Paretic	−.55	−.66	−.76	−.63	−.76	−.68	−.65	−.73	−.78	−.74	−.67	−.79	+.45
Epileptic	−.45	−.56	−.43	−.41	−.50	.29	−.45	+.42	+.62	+.55	+.19	+.55	−.49

[a]The sign of R depends on the signs of the beta weights.
[b]First admissions to New York civil state hospitals correlated, at 0–3-year lags, with New York State manufacturing employment index (secular trend subtracted from both series).

fellow-men in various positions, ascribing to each a given place within these contours [pp. 22–23].

It seems reasonable, then, to inquire whether particular age groups are more or less concerned with economic achievement. For, to the extent that they are concerned, we would argue that they must be sensitive to the loss of income or employment during the economic downturn.

Several attempts have been made to describe the set of social roles inherent in any given span of the life cycle. Buhler and Erikson, extending the work of earlier psychoanalytic ego psychologists, and Linden and Courtney provide examples of this approach.

Erikson's theory, extending the work of the psychoanalytic ego psychologists Freud, Hartmann, Hartmann and Kris, Lowenstein, and Kris,[10] outlines the sequence of phases of psychosocial development over almost the entire life cycle. Each phase of the life cycle is characterized by a phase-specific developmental task which must be solved in it, though this solution is prepared in the previous phases and is further worked out in subsequent ones. Among these theorists there appears to be general agreement that "late middle-age" (45–60) is the period during which the individual should theoretically show the greatest concern for economic achievement. This is the period during which the maintenance or advancement of socioeconomic status is the most central (or even the exclusive) problem of life.

Buhler writes that at about age 45

a new change takes place. One begins to test the *results* which have been accomplished up until now, namely, whether one has obtained all that one wanted, the position, the success, and the income for which one strove. For some reason or other, everyone is not satisfied with the results which he has achieved. There now comes a period in which the realization of the desired success is the main object in life. This period can be of varying duration. It is ended only through the new attitude of the aging person *who looks back on life* and begins to finish off with life. To this period, which to a certain extent lies after life, corresponds the period of childhood and youth.[11]

Erikson's period of greatest concern for economic achievement is that of "mature age." During this period integrity versus disgust and despair are the positive and negative alternatives to the individual as he seeks ego identity. These alternatives are partially described as follows:

(1) *Integrity*. Although aware of the relativity of all the various life styles which have given meaning to human striving the possessor of integrity is ready to

defend the dignity of his own life style against all physical and economic threats . . .
Ego integrity, therefore, implies an emotional integration which permits
participation by a fellowship as well as acceptance of the responsibility of leadership:
both must be learned and practiced in religion and in politics, in the
economic order . . .

(2) *Despair.* Despair expresses the feeling that the time is short, too short for
the attempt to start another life and to try out alternate roads to integrity. Such a
despair is often hidden behind a show of digust, a misanthropy, or a chronic
contemptuous displeasure with particular institutions and particular people—a
disgust and a displeasure which (where not allied with constructive ideas
and a life of cooperation) only signify the individual's contempt of himself.[12].

According to Linden and Courtney, this period encompasses the "social-
creative" and "state-creative" ages:

(1) *Social-creative.* Middle adulthood, or middle maturity, then appears as a
stage of widening social interest in which the family-society becomes increasingly
oriented within the framework of its responsibility toward a greater society.
This may be termed a *social-creative* period . . .

(2) *State-creative.* A ruling and protective sovereignty befalls the mature
adult at this level as he assumes the parental hierarchical leadership over his family
of families. Thus, the scope of interest here becomes wider and is concerned with the
creation, ordering, and maintenance of a larger society, or what may be called a state.
Thus, in a sense, the first segment of late adulthood may be called *state-creative.*[13]

Late middle age, then, represents the interval in the life span most
exclusively and prominently preoccupied with the problems of maintenance
and advancement of socioeconomic status. If serious socioeconomic status loss
occurs at this stage—the peak of social status and responsibility—then:
(1) the loss must be especially severe (the higher the social status, the more
there is to lose) and (2) the loss is irreparable, for there is no second chance to
fulfill the promise of that age; what would have been the culmination of
adulthood is not to be.

We might argue that, in general, adults (rather than the young or the aged),
and the late middle-aged in particular, should experience the greatest
stress as a result of loss of income or employment during the economic downturn.
It would follow, then, that economic loss would be a better predictor of the
mental hospitalization of adults than of the younger or older, and that it would
best predict the mental hospitalization of the late middle-aged.

The relative magnitude of the (multiple) correlation coefficient will
indicate the relative importance of the economic downturn for the mental
hospitalization of the various age groups. The mental-hospitalization data (see
Table 31) show, in support of the general argument above, that sensitivity

to the economic downturn is sharpest during adulthood for both sexes, and that this sensitivity rises to a peak in the 40's and 50's.

It is possible to relate these findings on differential age sensitivity to those of one of the rare attempts to assess the psychiatric effects of relative deprivation engendered by a major crisis.[14] Marks and Fritz,[15] in an analysis of affective and cognitive reactions and disturbances by "household role," found that "male heads without dependents" and "nonresponsibiles" were less likely than "male heads with dependents" and "females with dependents" to have shown "any strong affect" and more likely to have been "calm, unexcited" in the aftermath of a devastating tornado in Arkansas.

Two unexpected findings appear in the age data, however. First, the aged (over 70) in general and 25–29-year-old females appear to be hospitalized more frequently during economically prosperous than depressed periods. Second, male sensitivity to the downturn appears to reach a minor peak at 20–24, falls slightly at 25–29, and then rises to the major peak at 45–49.

The reason for the 25–29-year-old female sensitivity to the upturn would seem totally irrelevant to the reason for the similar sensitivity of the over-70-year-old males and females. Our explanations attempt to remain consistent with the initial argument that each sociologically identifiable age group encounters its own peculiar life stresses. The 25–29-year-old females are well within the high birth- and marriage-rate categories.[16] It is possible that the most important life stresses for these females revolve around early marriage and childbirth. It is well established, in turn, that marriage and birth rates tend to vary with the economic cycle and increase during economically prosperous periods.[17]

It remains, then, to explain why the 20–24-year-old females, who show even higher birth and marriage rates, do not also respond to economic upturns with increased mental hospitalization. It may be that at ages 20–24 both males and females face their first independence (especially financial) from their families of earlier orientation, and make their first strenuous efforts to acquire individual social status within the community. It is at this point in the life cycle that careers are begun in earnest and that the community (especially the employer) is making a first assessment of the individual's abilities. This initial evaluation will be a major determinant of the course of the career pattern—perhaps even whether this career is allowed to proceed at all. The outcome of these early years of independence will indicate to both the married and the unmarried man and woman the course that much of the rest of life is likely to take. Thus, for the males as well, we find a minor peak of sensitivity to the economic downturn at ages 20–24.

The next question concerns the sensitivity of the mental hospitalization of the aged (especially those over age 70) to the upturn. A partial answer may be, as we argued initially, that this group is not especially sensitive to the downturn because it does not have as much social status to lose as do the middle-aged groups. Some independent evidence that supports this argument is presented in an extensive review of the research on the differential effects of disaster situations on different age groups. In this review Friedsam distinguishes the "younger aged" from the "aged":

> Probably the one characteristic common to virtually all of the older people . . . discussed . . . is that they had something to lose. Several were obviously home owners, most were heads of households, several were still employed at the time that disaster struck, etc. In these respects they are "typical" of the aged, at least of the "young aged," a majority of whom do own their own homes, are heads of households, and many of whom are still employed. But these cases are not typical of the many aged persons who are living on minimal retirement incomes, who live alone or with relatives in a dependent relationship or who are in institutional situations, and who, in many cases are extremely isolated within their communities. These are the aged for whom a high degree of "absolute" deprivation exists before disaster strikes. With so little to lose, there is likely to be no difference between their pre- and post-disaster status. The interviews suggest that older persons so situated will be characterized not by feeling of deprivation but by feelings of resignation, by the feeling that nothing has really been changed—neither self nor situation.[18]

In addition to showing a lower sensitivity to the economic downturn, however, it is possible that the aged may be sensitive to isolation and rejection by their families—especially their children—which are perhaps far more likely to be shown in relatively prosperous than in depressed periods. For it is during prosperous periods that the opportunity for intergenerational mobility is greatest.[19] It is during prosperous times that the young man, woman, or couple is likely to be able to afford to establish an independent household.[20] It is also during this period of highest upward intergenerational mobility that the younger members of the family are probably least likely to spend time (since they are given alternatives),[21] or be associated by the community, with parents of lower socioeconomic status.[22] Thus, the most severe stresses of the senile aged period—isolation and rejection at the time when a person's great dependency needs are similar to those of young children[23]—are likely to be most in evidence at a time when upward mobility is greatest.

Economic Stress Among Persons Perceived and Treated as Mentally Ill

Research findings seem to be in general agreement that persons who have been in a mental hospital have considerably lower social status than those

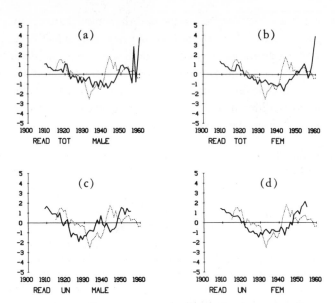

FIG. 25. Fluctuations in employment and in mental-hospital readmissions during 1914–1960: total readmissions and readmissions with functional psychosis (schizophrenia, manic-depressive psychosis, and involutional psychosis), by sex. Readmissions to New York civil state hospitals matched with New York State manufacturing employment index (secular trend subtracted from both series).

LEGEND:
...... New York State Manufacturing Employment Index
_____ (a,b) Readmissions with functional psychosis
         (c,d) Total readmissions
SCALE: Deviations from secular trend in admissions and in the employment index are expressed in standardized normal scores. Scalar range describes relative magnitude of variation in each series.

who have never been mental patients.[24] Since, then, by virtue of their lower social status, readmissions to the mental hospital have less to lose during an economic downturn than first admissions (they are already regarded as "social failures"), we would argue that the readmissions ought to be less sensitive to the economic downturn in terms of their mental hospitalization.

The data not only bear out these hypotheses (Table 32) for each diagnostic category of illness and for both sexes, but also reveal a tendency for the frequency of readmissions to increase during prosperous times (Fig. 25). One possible reason for this positive correlation of rehospitalization and economic change is related to the fact that those mental patients who are rehospitalized tend, in general, to be as financially dependent on their families as are the very young or the aged.

Freeman and Simmons, for example, reported on the posthospitalization

Table 32. Multiple correlations[a] between employment and mental-hospital admissions, during 1914-1960, by diagnosis and sex.[b]

Psychosis	Total admissions				Voluntary admissions			
	First admissions		Readmissions		First admissions		Readmissions	
	Male	Female	Male	Female	Male	Female	Male	Female
Total undifferentiated	−0.75	+0.33	+0.53	+0.59	−0.89	−0.48	−0.64	+0.59
Total Functional	−.66	+.49	+.58	+.66	−.73	+.44	+.65	+.67
Alcoholic	−.78	−.30	−.54	+.40	−.79	−.64	−.76	+.33
Senile	+.80	+.80	+.61	+.54	−.32	−.26	+.38	+.36
Cerebral Arteriosclerosis	−.82	−.81	+.52	+.66	−.61	−.37	−.67	+.59
Paretic	−.79	−.77	−.60	−.50	−.84	−.50	−.80	−.38
Epileptic	−.50	−.28	+.58	+.53	−.44	+.56	+.49	+.43

[a]The sign of R depends on the signs of the beta weights.
[b]First admissions to New York civil state hospitals correlated, at 0-3-year lags, with New York State manufacturing employment index (secular trend subtracted from both series).

work performance of former mental patients in Massachusetts in 1962.[25] They found that among former patients who were not rehospitalized within a year 50 percent failed to work more than half the time during the year after release. Among those who were rehospitalized within the year, the proportion who worked more than half the period between release and rehospitalization was significantly lower; only 30 percent were employed this amount of time. At the end of the year, about 60 percent of the males who were not rehospitalized were gainfully employed. By comparison, only 35 percent of those who were rehospitalized were employed at the time of their rehospitalization.

In the case of rehospitalized females, Freeman and Simmons reported that about 75 percent were never gainfully employed between hospitalizations, and less than 3 percent worked regularly. More striking still, about 45 percent regularly prepared morning and evening meals, about 53 percent did usual household cleaning, and about 21 percent did the grocery shopping.[26]

It may be that the downturn actually has a beneficial effect on the mental status of the former mental patient who continues to occupy the dependent sick role.[27] During economically depressed periods, this dependent "social failure," although a social and financial burden, is less likely to be regarded (or to regard himself) as an extreme deviant. He is more likely to be surrounded by other "failures" in responsibility, even among members of his own household. Thus, the threat to his already stigmatized self-image may be more severe during prosperous times when his role failure is much more likely to be conspicuous within his community of associates.

Sex Differentials in Sensitivity to the Downturn

With several notable exceptions, we have observed a marked tendency for male admissions to react far more sensitively to the economic downturn than female admissions. The major exceptions to this generalization (for example, among large educational and ethnic groups) indicate that sex role does not account for the difference in sensitivity.

It is possible, however, that a major explanatory factor lies in the degree of economic dependence of the female on the male household head. Thus, if the female's economic dependence on the male is complete, she should respond to the economic stresses of the cycle when he does. But a large fraction of the women on whom our data are based are employed outside the home. An average of 63 percent per year of female first admissions are not married—that is, they are single, divorced, separated, or widowed. And the 1940 and 1950 Censuses indicated that among single, widowed, divorced, and married women aged 16 years and older, by far the lowest percentage employed are married.[28]

An extensive review of the 1929–1936 depression literature by Stouffer and Lazarsfeld found consistently among all sources given statistical data that, economically, females fared better than males.[29] This conclusion was based on five sets of data which may be summarized as follows: (a) those industries in which women are ordinarily employed in largest numbers (consumer-goods industries) tend to be less seriously affected than the predominantly male industries (capital goods); (b) annual employment data compiled by five state labor departments for 1929–1934 indicate uniformly that index numbers of female employment showed less drop between 1929 and 1932 than index numbers of male employment; (c) the percentage of female gainful workers reported as unemployed was less than that of male gainful workers reported as unemployed in the Census of April 1, 1930; this was true in all broad industry groups, in all age groups, and in all sections of the country by Census geographical divisions; in 17 of the 19 cities enumerated in the unemployment Census of 1931 the female unemployment percentage is less than that of men; the Massachusetts Census of 1934 and the Michigan Census of 1935 produced similar findings; (d) among experienced workers on the public unemployment relief roles in the United States as of March 1935, females 16–34 years of age constituted a smaller fraction of all workers (18.9 percent) than did females among all gainful workers of the same age class in the 1930 Census (22.4 percent); (e) information from records of state (New York, Connecticut, Pennsylvania) and federal employment offices tend almost without exception to suggest that women were more successful in finding jobs during the depression than men.

Finally, two post-World War II studies of the effects of the economic downturn on male and female unemployment rates show consistently that the males were more adversely affected. Bogue reports that in the years 1947 to 1957, during periods of prosperity or generally low unemployment, the ratio of female to male unemployment rates is highest. During periods of high unemployment the reverse is true. Also, when jobs are plentiful, a disproportionately large share of women aged 25–54 are among the residual of unemployed; when the level of unemployment rises, however, and men of all ages are thrown into the unemployment category, the sex differential diminishes at ages 25–54.[30]

The Bureau of Labor Statistics reports similar findings for their four business cycles, 1948–1961. In each of the downturns, the male unemployment rate increases by a greater proportion than the female rate.[31]

Our own data on educational attainment and marital status similarly offer strong support to the position that female employment is a major explanatory factor in the lower sensitivity of female admissions to the economic cycle. Our data on educational attainment show that of the two major groups which, according to the economic model, should show strong sensitivity to the downturn—the grammar-school and college educated—the female college educated show substantially lower inverse correlation than the male (see Table 26). And again, among female marital statuses, the married—the group least likely to be employed—showed the highest inverse correlation (Table 33).

Table 33. Multiple correlations[a] between employment and mental-hospital admissions, during 1914–1960, by marital status and sex.[b]

Marital status	Males	Females
Married	−.85	−.65
Single	−.80	+.69
Separated	−.71	−.58
Divorced	+.40	+.61
Widowed	+.73	+.75

[a]The sign of R depends on the signs of the beta weights.

[b]First admissions to New York civil state hospitals correlated, at 0–3-year lags, with New York State manufacturing employment index (secular trend subtracted from both series).

Sensitivity to the Downturn by Marital Status

In the last section we presented data on differential sensitivity to the downturn for females by marital status. These data appeared to support our explanation of the difference between the sexes in sensitivity to the downturn. At this point we may add that a probable reason for the strong positive correlation between economic change and mental hospitalization for both widowed females and widowed males is that the widowed group contains a high percentage of the aged, who, as we have seen, respond to the economic upturn rather than the downturn. It remains for us, then, to try to account for the sharp difference between the strong inverse correlations of the single and married males, respectively, −0.85 and −0.80, on the one hand, and the substantially weaker correlations of the divorced and separated males, respectively, +0.40—not statistically significant—and −0.71 (Fig. 26, and see Table 33).

One explanation for these findings might involve responsibility for family support. Thus, the 1950 Census shows that, of the male population 14 years old and over, 74.3 and 98.5 percent respectively of the single and married

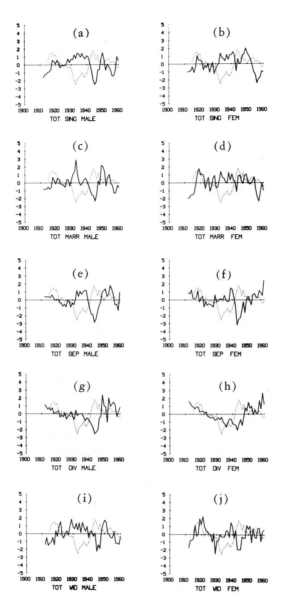

FIG. 26. Fluctuations in employment and in mental-hospital admissions during 1914–1960, by marital status and sex. First admissions to New York civil state hospitals matched with New York State manufacturing employment index (secular trend subtracted from both series).

LEGEND:

...... New York State Manufacturing Employment Index

———— First admissions with functional psychosis, by marital status:

     (a,b) single (c,d) married (e,f) separated (g,h) divorced (i,j) widowed

SCALE: Deviations from secular trend in admissions and in the employment index are expressed in standardized normal scores. Scalar range describes relative magnitude of variation in each series.

males were living in primary families, whereas the corresponding figures for the divorced and separated are 41.0 and 40.7. This explanation is in line with our previous suggestion that the groups whose roles are most exclusively concerned with the responsibility for maintaining or advancing family socioeconomic status should be most sensitive to the effects of the downturn.

Another possibility, however, is that women who are likely to be employed outside the home—and, especially, to be economically self-sufficient—may work in occupations or industries that have a somewhat different economic cycle than those in which males are predominantly employed. If this is the case, then a significant component of the difference between the responses of the economic downturn may be explainable on economic grounds alone. This possibility must await additional research.

Summary

In this chapter we examined the comparative sensitivities of various groups to economic changes in terms of their mental hospitalization. In so doing we attempted to identify the major factors that might influence such sensitivity. Two major factors were thought to be involved: (1) the absolute and relative extent of economic loss, and (2) the relative extent of loss of social status.

The extent of economic loss, in turn, depends on two factors: (a) the relative stability of employment during changes in the general economy and (b) the relative amount of income, savings, or property one has to lose. The relative extent of loss of social status, on the other hand, depends on the extent to which one's social role is exclusively concerned with the advancement and maintenance of family socioeconomic status. The latter factor, finally, is conditioned by cultural and subcultural definitions of role obligations.

9   Interpretations of the General Relation

Direction of the Relation

A primary issue in the causal analysis of the relation between economic change
and mental hospitalization is the direction of the relation. The problem of
ascertaining the causal direction of a relation is perhaps the most serious one
with which any study involving psychiatric epidemiology has had to grapple. The
basis of this problem (as it involves psychological variables) is in ascertaining
whether or not the variables under study are sufficiently distinguishable
to be treated as independent and dependent phenomena in a causal system.
Traditionally, the problem has been nearly insoluble in nonexperimental
investigations of the relation between stress factors and the distribution of
mental disorders.

The essential methodological difficulty consists in distinguishing the behavior
or attitudinal attributes of the persons under study from the allegedly
independent components of social interaction in which they may be involved.
The question is raised as to what distinguishable factors, within the
interaction situation, bring about changes in the thinking or behavior of the
population under study. If one wishes, for example, to test the hypothesis that
any one of several environmental stress factors is necessary or even important in
the development of mental illness, one may simply compare a random sample of
those who develop psychiatric symptoms and those who do not with respect
to the presence of the specific stress factor. Several stress factors, however,
especially if shown to be correlated with the occurrence of mental illness, could
be understood conceptually not as independent causal factors in the development
of symptoms, but merely as additional evidence of symptoms.[1] Many
"physiological" illnesses are thought to be characteristically psychophysiological,

in part or in whole, and are themselves indicators or symptoms of mental disorder (as are neurosis and psychosis) rather than possible causes of mental disorder.

Similarly, early traumatic family or peer-group experiences are believed to be important in personality development, and are possibly a factor in predisposition toward mental illness. Such experiences themselves, however, if found to be correlated with an indicator of mental illness, might well be suggested as early evidence of the manifestation of mental illness rather than as its cause.[2] Again, worries and feelings of deprivation concerning such varied areas as finances, employment, work, physical health, marriage, childhood, and parent-child relations, although found to be correlated with the development of psychiatric symptoms, may be regarded as additional symptoms of the pervasive character of mental illness.[3]

The difference between achievement and aspiration levels is another psychosocial factor that has been the subject of much speculation[4] and research as to its possible relation to mental disorder. This attitudinal factor has been ascertained directly by interview[5] and indirectly through the use of indices of "status-inconsistency"[6] or "status-discrepancy."[7] In either case, the situation of low achievement or downward mobility,[8] relative to subjectively or objectively expected achievement, may be regarded as a symptom as much as a cause of mental illness. Likewise, in studies where the possibility of downward socioeconomic mobility has not been specifically controlled,[9] the relation between socioeconomic status and the incidence of mental illness has been suggested as possible evidence of the relatively low social competence of the mentally ill rather than as causative of mental disorder.[10]

Even the association of upward socioeconomic mobility with neurosis or psychosis[11] may be challenged on this issue. It can be argued that the upwardly mobile are compulsively neurotic or psychotic, and therefore their upward mobility is indicative of underlying personality disorder. Moreover, if the problem exists for downward as well as upward social mobility, it certainly exists for any absolute change in social position. In this case, disorientation might be postulated as being the critical intervening factor.[12] Finally, even the most concrete and easily observed situations, such as those referred to in research dealing with specific occupations,[13] social isolation,[14] marital status[15] and migration,[16] when correlated with indicators of psychiatric symptoms, provide the same methodological difficulty in distinguishing independent and dependent variables.

In summary, it is extremely difficult to distinguish the occurrence of the stress situation from the occurrence of mental illness in an individual or aggregate, especially when both the stress situation and the symptoms are likely to have appeared at nearly the same time. Thus, it is easy to argue that the reason for the occurrence of any of a broad range of stress situations may be that the mentally ill person brings the stress upon himself because of his mental disorder. Viewed from the perspective of our problem of causal direction of the relation, the question becomes: is mental illness a cause or a result of low achievement, movement in socioeconomic position, problems of interpersonal relations, feelings of deprivation in childhood or adulthood, physical illness, or migration?

Methodological problems revolving around the issue of direction of the relation have been a continual source of frustration to researchers in psychiatric epidemiology and have been discussed in research literature as problems of questionable causation. It is certainly true that if the direction of a statistical relation cannot be determined, one may well question whether there is indeed a causal relation.

The present study treats this issue as its methodological point of departure and as its rationale for comparing changes in aggregate economic activity with changes in the level of mental-hospital admissions. The economic variable operates on the macro- or large-scale social system level, whereas mental hospitalization occurs on the micro-system level. Though economic change or aggregate economic activity represent changes in the entire economic system, each individual case of mental hospitalization represents the interaction of, at most, a small group of individuals. Thus, the unit of analysis of the economic variable includes the majority of the entire population; that of mental hospitalization includes, in each case, the particular small group involved. The great difference in unit levels of analysis of the independent and dependent variables makes it relatively easy to distinguish them conceptually and empirically, and therefore to avoid the problem of questionable causation. More precisely, because of the sharp differences among unit levels of analysis, the higher-order variable (the operation of the total economic system) can in no way be controlled by the actions of the mentally hospitalized person and his associates. Therefore, in the relation between economic change and mental hospitalization, the direction of causation necessarily proceeds from economic change to mental hospitalization rather than the reverse.

The fact that we can determine the necessary causal direction of our major relation does not, however, obviate the necessity of explaining the mechanism by which aggregate economic activity has an impact on the lives of a great many small groups and individuals. The difficulty created by attempting to intercorrelate aggregate units through statistical analysis has been referred to as the problem of the "ecological fallacy."[17] This problem, which is inherent in statistical analyses of ecological data, has been the most serious methodological obstacle encountered by those studies that have attempted to correlate broad economic conditions with mental-hospital admissions.

The Question of Spuriousness

One of the major problems raised in attempts to correlate large-scale social phenomena with individual or small-group behavior is the difficulty of ascertaining precisely which of many social changes is causally responsible for the relation. This problem of research into "social ecology" introduces the possibility that there may be *no* causal relation between the social change and the individual and small-group behaviors under study; the actual causal sequence may involve an external social change that may bring about both the social change and the individual and small-group reactions being investigated. In this case, the association under analysis would technically be referred to as a spurious correlation, and we would attempt to identify the mechanisms whereby the newly introduced social change causes both the large- and the small-scale changes.

In terms of the present study, it might be imagined that the relation between economic change and mental hospitalization is spuriously due to the influence of a second type of social change. The question might be raised, for example, whether, during the First or Second World Wars, the decreases in mental-hospital admissions were not due to increases in employment and income levels rather than to the influence of socially integrative aspects of the wars themselves. We might speculate that there was some lessening of competitive attitudes toward economic and social positions during these wars, with a greater concentration on national unity and contribution to the survival and national identity of the United States. Thus, it is possible that the social esteem of the people involved might have been more nearly related to their identity as Americans than as individuals competitively engaged in economic and social enterprises.

A second example of a possibly spurious relation has been raised by earlier studies of the relation between economic change and mental hospitalization in New York State. These studies, concentrating their analysis on the Great Depression period, examine three times for both economic change and mental hospitalization—before, during, and after the depression. They suggested that mental-hospital admissions may have increased in the middle period. However, it was thought preferable to attribute even the possibility of increased admissions during this period to the increased capacity of mental hospitals to accommodate large numbers of the mentally ill.

The fact that these types of short-term factors, such as wars and possible changes in admissions policies, occupy only a small number of years, relative to the very lengthy period for which we find the relation between economic change and mental hospitalization (1841–1967), does not raise the issue of spuriousness for the entire relation. Moreover, intensive analysis of the periods of the First and Second World Wars, as well as the early years of the depression of the 30's, indicates that there was no significant change in the character of the overall relation between economic change and mental hospitalization during these periods. It is possible to conclude, therefore, that such allegedly spurious short-term changes not only are not responsible for the major relation, but probably do not even exert an appreciable influence on their own on mental-hospital admissions that is independent of the influence of economic change.

One way to explore the question of spuriousness in the relation between economic change and mental hospitalization would be to investigate each of several factors that have been suggested as possibly having an influence on mental-hospital admissions during some period of time. Thus, as in the case of war and possible changes in admissions policies, the possibility that such factors might be responsible for both economic change and mental hospitalization should be investigated. Although it can be shown that political changes such as wars may have a substantial impact on the economy, mental-hospital admissions policies would not similarly influence the state of the aggregate economy. Thus, hospital admissions policies could not reasonably be raised as a factor that might be responsible for a spurious relation between economic change and mental hospitalization.

Similarly, one might speculate that such factors as changes in treatment procedures, changes in definitions of mental illness, or a sudden increase in the willingness of psychiatrists to hospitalize certain groups of mentally ill patients might be responsible for some change in mental-hospital admissions patterns. However, none of these factors would in turn have any substantial effect upon changes in the aggregate economy. There are certain long-term factors that do have an influence on both secular changes in the economy and long-term changes in patterns of mental hospitalization; these are factors in population change, including long-term increases (or decreases) in the population at risk, changes in immigration and emigration patterns, and changes in the age and socieconomic structure of the population at risk. It is precisely because of such possible influences on the very long-term relation between economic change and mental hospitalization that several different statistical procedures were employed in order to control for secular trends. In other words, given our statistical controls, the relation between economic change and mental hospitalization represents precisely a group of short-term relations although these relations cover the entire span from 1841 to 1967. We have therefore not been investigating the possibility that long-term changes in the economy may influence long-term changes in mental hospitalization. This does not mean that we have omitted an investigation of long-term changes in rates of mental hospitalization themselves; indeed, among various age groups, for example, we find that the most significant long-term changes in mental-hospitalization levels—in terms of a continuous trend—can probably be attributed to population growth.

A second approach to the problem of spuriousness would examine the possibility that there is some type of social or environmental change which is responsible for a continuous short-term and intermediate range of economic changes. Such changes, traditionally referred to as business cycles, have been the subject of a great deal of speculation and a large literature of empirical research.

Economic theorists and statisticians, who have studied this problem for more than a century, have not been able to suggest any single social or environmental factor (or even any group of such factors) that would consistently account for the great variety of economic cycles.[18] Moreover, three major classifications of economic cycles have been identified:[19] "long-wave" or Kondratieff cycles,[20] of approximately 50–60 years' duration; "major" or Juglar cycles,[21] of less than 10 years' duration; and "intercession" or Kitchin cycles, of approximately 40 months' duration.[22] Factors that operate from within the economic system, which have been suggested as possible producers or modifiers of economic cycles, include innovation in the form of new products, machines, or techniques,[23] accelerated demand for goods and services,[24] monetary expansion or contraction,[25] overinvestment,[26] underconsumption,[27] and improper distribution of purchasing power.[28]

Financial Considerations

The evidence on the question of whether financial destitution is the sole factor in the relation between economic change and mental hospitalization provides a generally negative answer, although it may be one of several major causes. The most direct evidence that destitution per se is not necessarily a factor in this relation comes from three sources. First, the data on admissions are categorized by economic status of the patient on admission to the hospital. Three categories are used: "comfortable," "marginal," and "dependent." The definitions of these categories have been maintained fairly consistently from 1916 to 1955. "Comfortable" refers to a patient who is earning money and has sufficient savings that, if the source of income were cut off, the family could maintain itself for 4 months. "Marginal" refers to the category of individuals who do not have savings sufficient for 4 months, but who are not dependent on persons outside the immediate family for financial support. The "dependent" patients are those who are not earning a living, and either are dependent for financial maintenance on persons or agencies outside the family or lack the necessities of life. If we hypothesize that financial destitution is responsible for mental hospitalization during the economic downturn, then it is largely the economically dependent patients who should be admitted during that period. Among both economically marginal patients, who comprise from 60 to 70 percent of the total patient population, and comfortable patients, sharp increases are found during downturns. Moreover, for the marginal population, a significantly more direct relation to economic change is found than for the dependent population.

Second, we find that admissions to private hospitals similarly increase during economic downturns and decrease during upturns. The cost per day of a private hospital can frequently be greater than that of a moderately expensive hotel. Thus, we have the ironic situation of the greatest amount of money being spent for psychiatric care at a time when people have the least amount of money to spend. The third piece of direct evidence is based upon data on hospitalization of the criminally insane, who have been hospitalized on the grounds that they committed a crime which was subsequently thought to be psychopathological in origin. It is clear that these legally defined criminals did not move into a relatively room-and-board-free state institution because it provided a roof over their heads, but rather because they committed crimes. Furthermore, it was probably the pathological crime itself, rather than any artifact of the hospitalization process, that originated during the economic downturn.

Finally, it is apparent that, despite substantial changes in welfare policies and the availability of public funds during much of the present century, the relation between economic change and mental hospitalization has continued to be relatively constant. In fact, the impact of the economic downturn on mental hospitalization has tended to become increasingly severe while economic services generally, and welfare services in particular, have been provided at increasingly greater rates.

Taking a more indirect approach to this problem, we find very considerable differences in the degree of sensitivity among different social and demographic groupings of the patient population to economic changes in terms of mental hospitalization. In particular, we must ask why, if financial considerations are dominant, is hospitalization among the aged and the young, who are the greatest financial burden on the family, less directly related to economic change than is that of the middle-aged of both sexes? Why, in general, are the admissions of women of most age groups less dependent on economic changes than are those of men of the same age groups? And finally, why is there such great diversity among ethnic groups in the degree to which the hospitalization of both sexes is sensitive to economic changes? (Why, for instance, is the pattern of Jewish and Scotch sensitivity strikingly similar between the sexes and so dissimilar for the Irish and the Italians?)

Intolerance of the Mentally Ill

A major factor thought to be related to determining whether a mentally ill person is brought to treatment is relative intolerance of mental illness by the family and community.[29] It is argued that mentally ill persons are perceived or dealt with differently in different settings.[30] This argument might be applied in partial explanation of our finding of a general inverse relation between economic change and mental hospitalization. Thus, it might be argued that (1) the incidence of mental illness is really constant over time and (2) the stress of an economic downturn acts not on the mentally ill person but on his family (or other close role associates) to decrease their level of tolerance for his behavior.

Intolerance of mental illness may be thought to take either a passive or an active (overt) form. Passive rejection may be understood as especially involving the withholding of needed psychosocial resources. Thus, Tyhurst, for example, writes:

> Some persons in turmoil, under circumstances we do not understand at all well, come to the attention of the social institution called "psychiatry." When they do, they are usually defined as "ill"; and that they are so defined appears more often largely a matter of social convention. *Turning to the psychiatrist may represent an impoverishment of resources in the relevant social environment* as much as an indication of the type or severity of disorder.[31]

Passive rejection may have a particularly damaging effect on the severely neurotic or psychotic person who, often alienated from much of his society, may require an unusual amount of tolerance—even nurturance—from the few persons with whom he may still identify. An example of this overwhelming requirement of nurturance of the mentally ill is well documented in a recent study:

> As Schwartz points out, the mentally ill tend to require other people to adjust *to them* at every point in their illness from onset to recovery. They resist change for the better, often, and are difficult to work with in a systematic, efficient manner. Psychiatrists, learning in training full well that schizophrenics constitute the most

challenging problem in their field, have set out in practice to devote their attention to psychotics only to find that they cannot take them, at least not as a steady practice; the patients prove to be too wearing, too trying, too tiring. Thus, even the most conscientious and devoted doctor may turn his back on them.[32]

On the other hand, persons who are overtly dealt with as mentally ill may be injured in at least two ways: (1) indirectly, through social stigma,[33] and (2) directly, by "severing the closest bonds that hold human beings together,"[34] that is, by deprivation of liberty, forcible detention, removal from the community, and imprisonment—not to speak of the destruction of the individual's chances for an economically and socially gratifying career. Thus, the Joint Commission on Mental Illness and Health, in its final recommendation to Congress, has written:

The mentally ill lack appeal. They eventually become a nuisance to other people and are generally treated as such . . . People do seem to feel sorry for them; but in the balance, *they do not feel as sorry as they do relieved to have out of the way persons whose behavior disturbs and offends them.*
Rejection, as practiced against the psychotic patient, takes many forms; some tantamount to complete denial of his right to human existence.[35]

At least two theoretical traditions may be drawn upon in support of the intolerance argument: (1) "balance theory" (of attitudes and perception) and (2) the "frustration-aggression" hypothesis. In the case of balance theory, role failure—through loss of job, for example—on the part of an already mentally ill person may lead to his becoming defined as mentally ill.[36] Similarly, rejection of the mentally ill may perhaps be most simply related to the frustration-aggression hypothesis through the mechanism of injury to the repulsed individual.[37]

Examination of the Hypothesis: Logic and Empirical Evidence

We have discussed two possible forms of the mechanism of hospitalization through intolerance of mental illness—passive and active rejection. In the case of passive rejection it might be argued that, although the incidence of mental illness is constant over time, during the downturn economic stress acts on the family, for example, so as to emotionally wear out the members. The family members, in turn, are then unable to nurture the mentally ill person, and he is hospitalized.

The clear implication, however, is that nurturance is of some therapeutic value; otherwise, the individual would not require hospitalization for lack of it.

It must follow, then, that, in the absence of such nurturance, that is, with passive rejection, psychiatric symptoms must increase, particularly during economic downturns. Hence, the argument based on passive rejection is inconsistent with its own initial premise that the incidence of psychiatric disorder is constant over time.

In fact, this argument actually supports our major hypothesis by demonstrating an important mechanism for its operation. Clausen provides a typical example:

Tolerance (or any other response to forms of deviant behavior) may in the last analysis determine not only who is brought to treatment, but whether or not the person needs to be hospitalized. In our own research on the families of mental patients, we have encountered instances in which an accepting and nurturant wife has been able to sustain a schizophrenic spouse for five to ten years before symptomatic manifestations in the work situation caused him to be brought to treatment. In other instances, we have seen the utter rejection of a husband within a few days or even hours of his manifesting far less deviant symptomatology. *The latter instances are often followed by a period of acting out which brings the patient to the hospital.*[38]

The argument that overt, hostile rejection of the mentally ill is precipitated by the economic stress of the economic downturn again turns out to support our major hypothesis rather than act as a probable alternative. Once again, the assumption is that the incidence of psychiatric symptoms is constant over time. The argument is that hostile, agitated behavior occurs in the normal population as a reaction to economic stress but does not occur among the mentally ill (that is, persons who are ultimately hospitalized). But if we truly expect overt rejection of the mentally ill by their families under economic stress, would we not at least expect a similar reaction by the mentally ill themselves—who allegedly have poorer adaptive capacities—expressed through accentuation or increase of symptoms (hostility, agitation, withdrawal)?

Test of Assumptions

Moreover, if intolerance were indeed the pre-eminent explanation of the general relation between economic change and mental hospitalization, then we should be able to use it in order to explain why hospital admissions of some population groups are far less dependent on economic change than are those of other groups. We now subject the intolerance argument to the latter test and require it to explain differential sensitivity to economic change.

In terms of our discussion in Chapter 2 of the difference between directness (or consistency) and impact of the relation, our use of the term sensitivity in the present chapter refers to directness (and consistency). The tolerance argument would, therefore, assume one of the following three generalizations regarding the individuals who became hospitalized (with control for economic position): (1) all such persons must be equally sensitive to the economic downturn; (2) in general, the more intolerable the individual, the more sensitive he must be; and (3) the more responsible he is held to be for the family's economic stress, the more sensitive he must be. Let us examine each of these possible assumptions in detail.

The first assumption would be premised on the notion that it is the entire family that is experiencing economic stress and, as a consequence, rejecting the mentally ill member in its midst. It matters not, therefore, what role this member occupies. The argument is that *whoever* is mentally ill is rejected by the family under conditions of economic stress.

This argument, of course, is not at all in accord with the data. The age groupings, for example, show a strong hyperbola-shaped pattern of sensitivity which reaches a peak at late middle age and in which children and the aged are barely sensitive. This assumption would also lead to the prediction that females, in general, would be as sensitive to the downturn as males. We have seen that this is frequently not the case, and that those females who are least sensitive are most likely to be employed.

The tolerance argument assumes, above all, that severe mental illness—certainly of the type that usually leads to hospitalization—occurs as frequently in prosperous as in depressed periods. If this is true, then these females should be unemployed, by virtue of their severe illness, as frequently in prosperous as in depressed periods. As a result, these mentally ill females should be economic dependents, as are the young, the aged, and most married women. Their hospitalization should therefore be as sensitive to the downturn as that of the males who support them.

The second possible assumption of the tolerance argument is that the hospitalization of persons who are more difficult to tolerate should be more sensitive to the economic downturn. A mentally ill person's tolerability might depend upon such things as (1) his contribution to the maintenance and advancement of the family's present and future socioeconomic status, (2) the degree of stigma that would be inflicted on both the family and the potentially hospitalized person if he were to be hospitalized, (3) the degree of the potential damage to the family's organization (role structure) which would be caused by his hospitalization, and (4) the chronicity or potential for remission of the illness—that is, whether or not the family felt that continued nurturance would lead to significant positive changes.

Judging from these kinds of criteria, it is certainly the very young and the aged rather than the middle-aged, females rather than males, and readmissions (persons who have had a history of mental illness and are not usually employed) rather than first admissions who are most intolerable. It is these same likely intolerables whose hospitalization should most completely depend on family intolerance. Our data, however, run contrary to this assumption. They show that (1) the middle-aged are far more sensitive than the young or the aged, (2) first admissions are far more sensitive than readmissions, and (3) with control for economic status and likelihood of employment, males and females appear to show similar sensitivity.

The second assumption of greater sensitivity for the lower-status family member, is also contradicted by findings that are independent of this study. A study in New York City, for example, found that the more critical the social position of a patient, the more rapidly he was hospitalized. In this study, the criterion of "critical" referred to the task of providing regular financial contributions to or care of a household or children in a family (more precisely, "in a unit involving at least one other adult"). This relation was explained as follows:

Since the existing organization of the social unit in question requires the performances defining the critical position, there must be rapid reaction to violation of structural norms by the occupant of a critical position. Furthermore, permanent reorganization without such a position-occupant is difficult, so that rapid hospitalization [for the purpose of therapy, rather than for the purpose of severance of ties with the individual] is a likely reaction.[39]

The third possible assumption is that those persons who are most likely to be held responsible for the family's economic stress are most likely to be hospitalized. Thus, one might argue that role failure (loss of job) on the par of the already mentally ill breadwinner would further demonstrate to the family that he was incompetent, and that he was certainly unable to function in the society.

Again, our data contradict this assumption. First, with control for economic and employment status, hospitalization of females is as sensitive as that of males. Second, the central argument of the tolerance position itself, that the incidence of mental illness sufficiently severe to require hospitalization is constant over time, runs against this assumption. If severe mental illness were constant over time, then so would be economic failure (the severely ill would allegedly not be competent to hold a job); if economic role failure is critical for intolerance to be operative, then mental hospitalization should similarly be constant over time.

Another set of assumptions that may be drawn from the tolerance argument concerns the willingness of the groups in question (families and groups of friends) to hospitalize the mentally ill. One such assumption, for instance, might be that the greater the concern of the group over possible loss of status, the less frequently they would hospitalize their mentally ill for reasons of intolerance. Thus, groups having relatively high socioeconomic status (which have a great deal to lose), and groups that show relatively high aspirations toward upward mobility, should hospitalize their mentally ill because of intolerance relatively less frequently. We find, however, that it is precisely such groups—ethnic groups of the highest socioeconomic status and the foreign-born of longest residence in the United States—whose members show the strongest tendency to become hospitalized during the economic downturn.[40]

In fact, one of the more interesting examples of high cohesiveness coexisting with high sensitivity to economic change is that of the Jewish ethnic group.[41] In addition to the Jews having one of the highest levels of socioeconomic status among the separately identifiable ethnic groups, Jewish family cohesiveness is legendary in historical studies and axiomatic in sociological literature. A reason frequently offered for this cohesion is the Jews' lengthy history as a persecuted minority.[42]

The findings for marital status, as we have seen in Chapter 8, similarly show the most cohesive groups to be the most sensitive. Thus, of the five marital statuses (single, married, divorced, separated, and widowed) the married group —presumably the most cohesive—is most sensitive to the economic downturn in terms of mental hospitalization.

Possible Effects of Intolerance and Mental Disorder on Different
Populations of Patients

Broadly speaking, we find a relatively low impact of economic change on groups whose admissions most consistently reflect economic changes—the middle-aged, married males, and females. However, those groups that tend to show the least consistent (or stable) relations to economic change also tend to show the strongest impact, in terms of proportionate increases and decreases, in mental-hospital admissions.

We suggested earlier that relations of relatively low consistency and stability that also showed relatively great impact of economic change indicated a relatively indirect relation, or one in which there was probably substantial interference of additional mechanisms other than the effects of pure economic loss. These additional mechanisms might involve breakdown in family structure or disorganization of groups of friends and fellow workers. Such social disruption may further result in intolerance, and eventual hospitalization, of mentally disturbed persons.

Thus, there may be two characteristically different populations of hospital admissions, each subjected to a somewhat different mechanism in response to economic change. Group I would consist of persons who have relatively high social responsibility, high socioeconomic status, strong aspirations for achievement, and little if any history of mental disorder. This group would be most likely to be emotionally injured, and to respond to economic loss with psychiatric symptoms, simply because it has the most to lose. Also, Group I consists of those individuals who are among the most highly integrated within economic and social organizations, are most likely to be found in cohesive groups, and are least likely to experience very great increases in mental-hospital admissions because of intolerance. Rather, for this group, the avenue of hospitalization would probably be trod cautiously even during economic downturns, and only on the rationale that the illness—not the person —is intolerable. For Group I patients, we would find a desperate wish on the part of family and friends for recovery from the illness, even to the point of allowing hospitalization, so that they might return home and resume their usual roles as rapidly as possible.

On the other hand, Group II patients seem to be characterized by relatively low responsibility for performance of important functions in society, relatively low socioeconomic status and aspirations, and a prior history of mental hospitalization. Patients in this group would be hurt least during the economic downturn (from a social and psychological standpoint), and would be least likely to respond to economic stress through increased mental disorder. They are also characterized by relatively poor integration in large or small social organizations, and are least likely to be found in highly cohesive groups. The chief mechanism for hospitalization of Group II individuals is therefore likely to be based on social disorganization, which for the mentally ill might result in relative absence of nurturance and perhaps even overt rejection and abandonment.

Finally, mental disorder would play a larger role in the case of Group I and a smaller role, relative to intolerance, for Group II (although perhaps for both Groups I and II intolerance and mental disorder are both necessary for mental hospitalization).

The Evidence of Independent Studies

Perhaps the most explicit and careful test of the tolerance hypothesis is found in the study by Freeman and Simmons of psychopathological and social factors in mental *re*hospitalization. By using differential tolerance of deviance as their point of departure, they were able to focus their investigation on the problem of the continued acceptance of the former patient by his community associates despite his failure to perform according to the community's basic prescriptions for age and sex role.[43] The authors cite Lemert (1951) and La Pierre[44] as the theoretical sources of their research problem.

Their prediction, in line with the tolerance argument, was that rehospitalization would be determined primarily by the characteristics of families and family members rather than by the patient's instrumental role performance or bizarre symptoms. Their data, however, were inconsistent with the tolerance argument, and instead showed that evidence of bizarre behavior was the primary reason for rehospitalization.

Freeman and Simmons's finding that instrumental role performance was (similarly) not critical for rehospitalization again supports our conclusions. Following our hypothesis that (1) the rehospitalized assume the dependent role of the young or aged, and that therefore (2) poor instrumental role performance would be a relatively weak stress factor, we found that rehospitalization was only moderately correlated with economic changes.

Likewise, in a second study, it was found that the closer the patient's relation to the members of his family (or other social unit representing his major primary group), the more likely he is to be hospitalized or to undergo therapy. The author reasons, therefore, that the dominant purpose of hospitalization must be for purposes of therapy, and specifically not as a means of rejection.[45]

A third important study appears at first glance to support the tolerance argument. Gibbs argued that mental hospitalization represents, sociologically, the isolation of the inmate from the general society. Assuming, then, that hospitalization is only a special case of societal reaction to deviant behavior, he argued further that hospitalization is a function of two variables: (1) the incidence of deviant acts that are viewed as "psychopathological," and (2) the extent to which the agents of social control are prone to isolate persons considered to be mentally ill.[46]

Gibbs's findings of a positive correlation between the fraction of foreign born and the rate of mental hospitalization (among the 48 states) seemed to confirm his hypotheses that: (1) the more socially and culturally alien a person is, the more likely he is to be isolated for committing a deviant act, and therefore (2) the larger the fraction of sociocultural aliens, the higher the ratio of the rate of isolation to the rate of deviant behavior.

Gibbs's underlying, but unstated, assumption, however, is that it is the society outside the allegedly "*isolated* sociocultural aliens" that is responsible for hospitalizing the mentally ill rather than the family or other major primary group. Needless to say, the bulk of research on hospitalization is firmly at odds with this assumption.

Moreover, as we argued earlier, the families of immigrants who maintain their original ethnic ties are probably more cohesive than those of the United States population at large. In fact, alternative hypotheses explaining the high concentration of the foreign-born in mental hospitals may be advanced on the basis of a simple stress argument (see Chapter 11).

Most interesting is the fact that the percentage of nonwhites (especially when added to the percentage of foreign-born) and the percentage of the population in lower-class agricultural and industrial occupations are also correlated with the percentage hospitalized in Gibbs's data. We would suggest a somewhat time-worn explanation of these data, namely, that they once again corroborate the essential inverse relation between socioeconomic status and mental illness.

The major problem posed by the tolerance argument brings out the question of the closeness of the relation between mental hospitalization and clinical indicators of mental illness.[47] Therefore, to demonstrate the essential validity of mental hospitalization as an indicator of psychosis would be to compare its behavior, over time, with another indicator, such as suicide.

Henry and Short offer the hypothesis that persons in "high status categories suffer greater frustrations during downswings in business and fewer frustrations during upswings in business than persons in the subordinate status categories with which they are compared."[48] They attempt to test this hypothesis by comparing this reaction to the business cycle with suicide of males and females, of whites and Negroes, of the young and the old, and of high and low income groups. They use four of Parsons' six criteria in their hierarchical ranking of these status categories.[49] They then argue that these criteria— achievement, possession, authority, and power—rank males above females, whites above Negroes, the young (starting with the age group 15–24) and middle aged above the aged, and the higher income groups above the lower income groups.[50]

In all four test cases (sex, age, race, and income), the higher status categories show higher negative correlations with the "business cycle" (as estimated by *Ayres' Index*) than the lower. Henry and Short's interpretation of these findings is that (1) suicide is an extreme reaction to frustration, and (2) the upper status categories experience greater frustration in terms of loss of status position relative to others in the same reference system during the economic downturn. This interpretation is related by the authors specifically to the findings for socioeconomic status categories (race and income)[51] but not to those for the social role categories (sex and age), although it is assumed that their general interpretation applies to both of these categories.

Following Henry and Short's hypothesis and findings, we may compare the findings of this study with those for suicide. We may argue that:

(1) Males have higher status than females;

(2) Middle-aged persons have higher status than the very young or the aged;

(3) Whites have higher status than Negroes;

(4) First admissions to the mental hospital (that is, persons without a public record of mental illness and hospitalization) have higher status than readmissions;

(5) Manic-depressives have higher socioeconomic status than schizophrenics;[52]

(6) The longer an immigrant resides in the United States, the higher his socioeconomic status;

(7) Voluntary admissions to the mental hospital have higher socioeconomic status than those who are committed by the courts;

(8) The higher the level of educational attainment, the higher the socioeconomic status; and

(9) Persons with normal intellectual capacity have higher status than those with subnormal intellectual capacity;

In groups (1) through (7) the proposition is supported by the mental-hospitalization data that higher status categories are more sensitive to the economic downturn (see Tables 1, 2, and 26–33). In these seven groups the higher status categories show higher inverse correlations with the employment index. Thus, in general, the patterns of suicide and mental-hospital admissions, over time, react in a similar way to the effects of economic change.

Incomplete matching of the suicide and mental-hospitalization data is found in three areas:

(a) There is a curvilinear relation between level of education and sensitivity of hospitalization to the economic downturn;

(b) Admissions of subnormal intelligence are more sensitive to the economic downturn than those of normal intelligence;

(c) In the suicide–business-cycle findings there are no positive correlations (that is, in no case does suicide occur more frequently during periods of economic prosperity). In the present findings, however, the mental-hospital admissions of several low status groups appear to be somewhat positively correlated with the employment index (for example, the senile aged, Negroes, readmissions, persons having less than grammar-school education, immigrants with less than 5 years' residence in the United States).

Although in seven out of nine observations a high level of predictive accuracy is achieved, it is possible that in predicting the behavior of mental-hospital admissions from suicides we may be biasing the predictions to a significant extent in favor of the dominance of factors associated with higher status. Thus, there is a good deal of evidence to show that suicide predominates in higher status groups.[53] This possible bias toward factors associated with high status may obscure the important effects of the economic downturn on persons of very low socioeconomic status or subnormal intelligence who have relatively poor adaptive resources.

The argument may be restated in propositional form as follows: (1) given the same degree of stress, suicide is a more typical reaction among higher status groups; (2) different status groups are likely to have different sources of stress; and (3) therefore, patterns of suicide (a higher status reaction) will more accurately portray those stress factors that more typically affect higher status groups.

One method of testing this interpretation, and controlling for the effects of high status in the indicator of stress (suicide), is to compare it with the reactions of a segment of the mentally hospitalized population in which higher status groups are also predominant. A higher status segment of the mentally hospitalized population is the category admitted with manic-depressive psychosis, a category of the affective psychiatric reactions. From the earliest ecological studies of the distribution of psychosis in Chicago to the more recent findings of Hollingshead and Redlich, the affective reactions (manic-depressive psychosis in particular) have been found to be far more prevalent among higher socioeconomic status categories.[54]

The nine categories of status rank (as in the test above) were used in a test for matching patterns of sensitivity to the economic downturn again with the suicide findings. In all nine categories of social status rank, the patterns of sensitivity of manic-depressives to the economic downturn were virtually identical to those of Henry and Short's findings on suicide. In every case, a positive linear relation was found between status-rank and degree of sensitivity (magnitude of the negative correlation) to the economic indicator.

Furthermore, as in the suicide findings, there was no observable pattern of positive correlation between the economic indicator and manic-depressive psychosis. These findings attest to the highest accuracy of prediction between patterns of suicide as a stress reaction and patterns of mental-hospital admissions where the effects of higher status have been controlled. They strongly support an initial proposition of this study that mental hospitalization is often a stress reaction to economic change, accurately matching the behavior of suicide in response to the same stress factor.

Possible Decrease of Intolerance During Downturns

There is a real question whether intolerance of mental illness would actually be more frequent during economic downturns or upturns. There seem to be at least four major difficulties in assuming an increase in intolerance during the downturns: (1) the stresses of upward mobility may bring greater intolerance, (2) the mentally ill, who may assume little in the way of a functional role, may be less visible as deviants during downturns, (3) there may be greater sympathy for, and less intolerance of, a person who fails in his economic role during the downturn, (4) one might not wish to confront the stress of breaking up the family under additional conditions of acute stress, and (5) our data indicate that the socially and economically least tolerable group is, to some degree, likely to be hospitalized during the upturn.

(1) During the upturn, the period of greater opportunity for upward mobility, economic failure becomes a threat and a fear rather than a reality. In contrast to the feelings of economic hopelessness engendered by the downturn, we share increased aspirations and, actually, higher upward mobility. During the downturn, then, there may well be more available time and spare emotional energy to nurture a mentally ill family member.

Then, too, as was pointed out in Chapter 1, upward mobility is characterized by a movement away from one's previous associates, including one's family (intergenerational mobility), and toward a higher status group, which itself may pose obstacles to acceptance.[55] Thus, the upturn may well be a period of lower social cohesion.

Finally, families may find it economically necessary to share living space during a period of joblessness of the household head.[56]

(2) Role failure (in this case, loss of job) is least unusual during the downturn. A person who loses his job during the downturn because he becomes mentally ill will be less visible as a social deviant since the rate of joblessness is highest for the rest of the population. In fact, during a period when the dominant family figure is most likely to be unemployed, the family would find it difficult to justify hospitalizing a mentally ill member on the grounds of being an economic (and perhaps an emotional) burden.

(3) Moreover, should mental disorder occur during a period of joblessness (or any other period of substantial stress), the behavior of the mentally ill would be much easier to define in nonmedical or even nonpathological terms. Agitated or depressed behavior is *expected* of a person undergoing unusual stress. Thus there would, if anything, be greater willingness and ability to understand and provide emotional support for the mentally ill during the downturn. And again, this should be all the more true of persons who

become sufficiently ill to be hospitalized. For if the incidence of such severe mental illness is argued to be constant over time, then job loss among the severely ill should be as frequent in upturns as in downturns; they should be too ill to work at either time. And if psychopathology is easier to sympathize with and is even expected during the downturn, then mental hospitalization should be highly correlated with economic upturns.

(4) Since family members are under unusual stress during the economic downturn, and require a high level of emotional support from one another, would they bring upon themselves the additional stress of breaking up the family by rejecting (actively or passively) and hospitalizing another family member? In fact, family relations are more apt to be reactivated in times of stress than at other times, when the family "comes into its own" as the emotionally supportive institution.[57] Thus, would not the unusual need for family cohesiveness and solidarity make rejection of a member—and resulting breakup of the family—less likely?

(5) As we pointed out earlier, the groups whose hospitalization is most likely to be a result of intolerance are least likely to be hospitalized during the economic downturn. Moreover, the group whose hospitalization most reliably corresponds to the economic upturn is that of the senile aged—perhaps the least tolerable of the groups we have studied. Actually, the fact that this group is hospitalized most frequently during upturns lends support to the position that intolerance increases during upturns. (We maintain, however, that such intolerance of the senile aged would also increase the likelihood of their developing psychiatric symptoms.)

Place of Intolerance as a Component in the Indicator of Mental Illness

In the previous section it was argued that the data of this study do not support the argument that intolerance of mental illness is the major explanation of the general relation between economic downturns and mental hospitalization. This not to say, however, that such intolerance is not a contributing factor. In fact, given the hypothesis that economic stress precipitates psychiatric symptoms, we may suggest that intolerance may operate as either a necessary component of hospitalization or an occasional contributor. Thus, once the stress factor precipitating severe or mild symptoms has done its work, it is clear that the degree to which the illness is tolerated will affect the rapidity with which the patient is brought to the hospital.

But does the fact that intolerance is a necessary component of mental hospitalization prejudice its effectiveness? The necessity for including the tolerance component as an indicator of mental illness arises from the problem of defining mental illness. Redlich and Wegrocki, for example, describe the problem of definition as follows:

In summary, we do not possess any general definition of normality and mental health from either a statistical or a clinical viewpoint. Actually, at this time clinicians can barely agree on satisfactory criteria. There is agreement only about extremes, not about the areas of transition or the "cut-off point."[58]
Should, for example, a paranoid trait, such as the conviction of persecution, be measured by judges with respect to the degree in which it causes personal unhappiness, or with respect to the degree in which it interferes with an adequate adjustment to the social group and creates opposition within the environment? Should the frequency with which it manifests itself in life situations be the determining criterion, or the intensity with which it is adhered to? Finally, should the degree of insight a person has into it be the standard? The bases for judging the "more" or "less" of a paranoid trait are, as is obvious, very divergent. No single criterion is any more justifiable than any other. A "paranoid scale" would, therefore, be of slight operational significance.[59]

Much of the difficulty surrounding the conceptual definition of mental illness has arisen from the questions (1) how it should be used as a clinical term, especially in relation to the concepts psychosis and neurosis in psychiatry, and (2) what its relation should be to characterizations of individual malfunctioning or maladaptation in the social environment; that is, in what sense is a man ill? (These two concepts are to be distinguished from a statistical concept of "normality" which is simply defined as relative frequency, or usualness, of certain behavior, and is unrelated to the concept of pathology or *illness*.[60] Thus, in discussions of the adequacy of definitions of mental illness, three general positions have been taken. The first two positions compete directly, and the third attempts to be eclectic.

A traditional position, as stated by Kubie, for example, takes a definite stance on the psychodynamics of abnormality. Here, the fundamental distinction between normal and neurotic lies in the relative distribution of conscious, preconscious, and unconscious forces that determine a single act. Acts motivated by conscious forces are more healthy than those motivated by the unconscious.[61] A similar position, for example, is taken by Wegrocki:

We could state the quintessence of abnormality as the tendency to choose a type of reaction which represents an escape from a conflict-producing situation instead of a facing of the problem. An essential element in this type of problem-resolution is that the conflict does not seem to be on a conscious level, so that the strange bit of resulting behavior is looked upon as an abnormal intruder and, at least in its incipient state, is felt as something which is not ego-determined.[62]

The most important problem is that similar behavior in different cultures and subcultures may vary in the degree to which they communicate a particular attitude or mental syndrome. Also, it is possible that the interviewer's value orientation might lead him to regard behavior that is not normal for his own culture or subculture as "abnormal" or "sick," even though the behavior might be normal or healthy in another culture or subculture, such as a middle-class psychiatrist interviewing a lower-class subject. It has been shown, for example, that psychologists' use of projective tests standardized on the middle class is subject to this kind of bias.[63]

Then there are those who point out that this traditional approach to abnormality is culture- or subculture-bound, and therefore not universally applicable. Benedict, for example, argues that "the concept of the normal is properly a variant of the concept of the good. It is that which society has approved. A normal reaction is that which falls within the limits of expected behavior for a particular society."[64] Here, the conceptual emphasis is on social functioning. Dunham states the case somewhat differently:

One can argue . . . that who is counted as sick in any social milieu is the result of a social judgement made by family members, friends, or neighbors and the judgement that the person must accept in some fashion by taking action or having some action taken upon him by others. This means that judgements about who is mentally disturbed or can be regarded as a mental case will vary in different social milieus, communities and subcultures.[65]

The third or eclectic position finds merit in both of the two competing arguments and refuses to choose between them. Instead, it takes each argument (or position) as focusing on another dimension of a more general concept. Redlich and Jahoda exemplify this position. Redlich feels that both clinical and normative elements must be included in a conception of mental illness.[66] Clinically, the wall separating the "normal" from the "abnormal" began to distintegrate with Freud, who showed that aberrant phenomena were not limited to the abnormal.

Redlich argues that a valid clinical statement about the quality of normality as opposed to abnormality must be preceded by consideration of at least the following points: (*a*) motivation—is the action compulsive (unconsciously motivated) or apparently rational, (*b*) context—the logic of the act under the circumstances, and (*c*) who is judging—experts or the public—and what is the extent of agreement.

In the normative approach, on the other hand, Redlich stresses social functioning, and attempts to take into consideration social structural influences and judgments. He writes:

The problem of normality . . . can be put in the form of the question "normal for what?" and "normal for whom?" A moderately inadequate person working in a position of little responsibility in an industrial plant may be a very small problem to anyone except himself. The situation is entirely different if the man with "problems" is an important executive. . . The self-perception of the person with the problem and the role-assignment of all actors involved will determine subsequent labeling (normal or abnormal with reference to certain tasks) and subsequent action.[67]

Jahoda, in an analysis of the extensive literature bearing on positive concepts of mental health,[68] finds six general conceptual orientations: (1) attitudes of the individual toward himself, (2) the degree to which the person realizes his potentialities through action, (3) unification of function in the individual's personality, (4) the individual's degree of independence of social influences, (5) how the individual sees the world around him, and (6) ability to take life as it comes and master it. Except for factor (3), a clinical criterion, all the factors include both normative (social functioning) and clinical components.

In terms of research application of these definitions, in both of the major population surveys of the total prevalence of mental illness, for example, the effort is made to construct an index that would measure both dimensions. In the Midtown Manhattan survey the conceptual definition standing behind the indicators of mental health was based on the following rationale:

The individual human being was regarded as a functional unit, with adaptation to life's circumstances as an important theme in his existence. The notion of function and malfunction deserves some discussion, and a comparison can be made between psychological and physical functioning. Both in physical and mental health, there is an extended gradation from health to severe morbidity. But whereas physical illness may be precisely defined by structural and functional impairments related to the body mental illness involves a particular function which relates the individual to his social environment. Society emphasizes the individual's ability to maintain socially acceptable behavior, to care for himself, and to refrain from interfering with others. Mental health might accordingly be defined as the freedom from psychiatric symptomatology and the optimal functioning of the individual in his social setting. It could hardly be otherwise assessed.[69]

The resulting index of mental health utilized two different ratings, of mental psychobiological functioning and social functioning.[70]

In the Stirling County Survey, similarly, three measures of mental status were used. The ABCD rating, a measure of the extent to which a person could be judged by a psychiatrist to be a "psychiatric case," and items from the Health Opinion Survey were used to indicate the severity of psychiatric symptoms.

Extent of impairment was used to indicate the degree of social malfunction. Impairment was defined as "a way of stating a crude estimate as to how much of the person's life had been displaced by illness during the time of his symptoms. For the most part, such 'displacement' meant interference with work, although sometimes it was possible to take into account matters of failure and ineffectiveness in family and in community."[71] Having established that tolerance by the social environment is necessary to an adequate definition of mental illness, what would be the ideal index of a composite definition of mental illness? Specifically, would we select a population survey of true incidence (assuming this were feasible) instead of first contact with treatment agencies?

Three major difficulties confront researchers who choose the population-survey method. (1) The data obtained from interviews and tests of a population sample do not generally permit the use of standard psychiatric classifications.[72] Consequently, severity of disturbance (degree of impairment, number of symptoms, need for treatment) may be differently gauged by different teams of clinical interviewers, who may proceed from varying theoretical positions on the definition and measurement of pathology.[73] (2) Diagnoses are usually made on the basis of brief clinical interviews and do not allow for a sufficiently long period of observation in which to systematically verify consistency of development of symptoms in the subject's behavior. The fact that changes are made in initial (or provisional) diagnoses in a large number of cases upon admission to the mental hospital testifies to the need for a period of observation of the course of the illness.[74] (3) In the population survey, the extent of social malfunction is not judged by the individual's "significant others," as it is in mental hospitalization, but by objective interviewers and psychiatrists. The difficulty here is that the true estimate of social malfunctioning is, to some degree, a subjective phenomenon which varies with the individual's subculture (including family "culture") and depends heavily on the relative tolerance the individual's role associates have for his deviant behavior. In other words, in the dimension of mental illness concerned with social malfunction, the process of becoming mentally ill is a social process by which the individual is increasingly dealt with and defined by his society of role associates as nonresponsible for, or unable to control, his behavior and socially irresponsible or not accountable for nonfulfillment of his social obligations. This process of becoming mentally ill, then, is the process of acquiring a social label or designation by the "significant others" in the individual's life space.[75]

In mental hospitalization, we have an index of how both the professional psychiatrists, focusing on psychiatric symptoms, and the individual's other relevant associates, focusing on social functioning, regard the individual's behavior. If the individual's total community, including the relevant psychiatric professionals, the individual himself, and his role associates, regards him as so severely disturbed that he cannot function, for his own sake or the community's, within the community, it is assumed that he will be hospitalized. Thus, mental hospitalization is the usual method by which society labels a person "severely mentally ill," or so mentally ill that his remaining in the community would involve inordinate psychological or social cost.

A classic description of this labeling process through mental hospitalization is given by Enid Mills:

Richard Swallow is one of the 120 men and women from this borough who entered Long Grove Hospital in 1956 and 1957. As he entered the gates of the hospital he became, for the first time, a mental patient—someone whose behavior, in the eyes of society, is not merely strange, but diseased. It is a hard truth to accept, of yourself, or of someone you love. For to call someone mentally ill is to put in question his competence in every social relationship. Once he is admitted to hospital, his behavior receives an interpretation from which no amount of protest can extricate him, since little he may say or do will be accepted at its face value. He is no longer regarded as his own master, but as mastered by the sickness of his mind.

Few people, therefore, dare acknowledge that they are mentally ill. Most will search for other explanations of their difficulties, and other ways of solving them. To enter a mental hospital is an admission that they have failed, and whatever the circumstances which led to it, the event is crucial to their relationship with the society in which they hope for a cure, they may lose the right to be considered responsible for their own affairs. They are recognized as a special group within society.[76]

Sequence of Causation

To summarize, then, the data provide evidence that neither the need for the financial wherewithal for subsistence, nor intolerance of psychiatric symptoms, nor even actual psychiatric symptoms are by themselves sufficient to explain the entire relation between economic change and mental hospitalization. The implication here is that each of these three factors may play some part in a multicausal sequence whereby an economic downturn serves to increase hospital admissions, whereas an upturn decreases them. It is also possible that any one or a combination of any two may be sufficient for the hospitalization of any one individual.

Moreover, the question of the meaning of "mental illness" or "psychiatric symptoms," as they influence the level of hospitalization, is not without problems. Definitions of mental disturbance vary all the way from discussions of psychochemical changes to changes in social performance. One possibility, for example, is that a schizophrenic might attempt to escape his environment during a period of economic stress through the mechanism of demonstrating more highly agitated or disturbed behavior. This behavior might be observed as constituting psychiatric symptoms, perhaps even as "unconscious" and "irrational" behavior, but does it represent an increase or exacerbation of schizophrenic symptoms? The definition of "intolerance" is perhaps just as complex. Most important, is intolerance to be understood as an aggressive, rejective posture toward the mentally disturbed, or is it directed not toward the person but toward his illness? In the latter case, the intolerance signifies that, for the sake of the person, treatment is brought about as rapidly as possible to deal with the illness. In the former case, by contrast, the patient is rejected and purposely abandoned, perhaps to a life of isolation in the mental hospital. These problems of definition are in reality problems of accurate description of the dynamic mechanisms that actually operate in the process of mental hospitalization.

Finally, it is possible that two or even three of these factors (such as financial difficulties, symptoms, intolerance) may link economic change to mental hospitalization. Thus, problems of economic necessity and stress may exacerbate psychiatric symptoms which in turn may bring about intolerance of the deviant behavior; or the economic stress may first bring about intolerance of a mildly disturbed individual, and the rejection of this person may then, in turn, initiate symptoms.

Thus, at its best, the intolerance of precipitating stress is a vague concept when used in an attempt to understand causal sequences. In a sense, each short-term link in the casual chain is a precipitant. This issue of the meaning of precipitation raises a related set of questions with regard to factors that may intervene between economic change and mental hospitalization. If we understand the concept of the precipitating stress to mean the factor, or set of factors, that is most closely related in time to mental hospitalization, then it is quite likely that economic stress itself may not be the precipitant in a large fraction of the cases involved in the relation between economic change and hospitalization. For example, economic stress may initially bring about some degree of breakdown in family or other close social relations, which may in turn engender various intolerable social stresses resulting in hospitalization.

Consideration of the manifold pathways through which initial economic stress may lead to mental hospitalization forces us to question even more strongly the meaning of the terms precipitation and predisposition— precipitation of exactly what, and predisposition of a weakness for what specific type of stress? Although the character of the data used in this study does not lend itself to giving definitive answers to these questions, its findings do provide a concrete empirical framework within which these questions themselves take on meaning. It is also entirely possible that there is no typical sequence of causation. In other words, the kinds of factors that are intrinsic to the process by which economic change brings about mental hospitalization may vary so considerably from one individual case to another that it may not be useful to speak even of major patterns of causation. This position should not really surprise anyone who is familiar with the literature on social stratification or social mobility. A great variety of socially disruptive behavior has been found to be associated with both the socioeconomic structure of society and changes in it. Finally, it should be pointed out that the data presented here do not appear to falsify or to verify any specific theory that has a bearing on the psychology of mental illness, simply because the aggregate classifications of patients cannot provide evidence on internal mental dynamics or processes. This is not to say, however, that these data cannot be interpreted from a sociological standpoint. On a purely factual level, for example, it is clear that families and other normally cohesive social groups are, in the aggregate, experiencing some disintegration by virtue of the physical separation of members through mental hospitalization. Similarly (and obviously) relations between a substantial number of individuals and their society (and other persons who are formally or informally associated with them) are being considerably altered, if not, in many cases, destroyed through mental hospitalization.

On a simple factual level, mental hospitalization of an individual implies that he is no longer able to function adequately within his society. From a sociological viewpoint, then, adverse economic changes usually bring about severe social and personality disorganization for a considerable number of persons in the society. This process of disintegration is so marked and thorough that, as a result, individuals are defined and treated by society as being mentally ill—a label that prevents the use of common-sense understanding and ordinary supportive mechanisms for reintegrating the displaced individual.

The Impact of Changes in Employment Levels

Quite independent of the meaning of mental hospitalization is the problem of interpreting the concept of economic change. Our statistical analysis utilizes fluctuations in employment as the indicator of economic change. Employment changes were deliberately selected as a means of measuring changes in the extent of economic activity or, more properly, of the expansion and contraction of the economy.

On a low empirical level, then, our basic relation indicates that changes in the level and rate of mental hospitalization conform inversely to economic changes in general rather than to changes in employment specifically. Thus, a large fraction of those persons who are hospitalized during economic downturns may not necessarily have lost their jobs, but rather have decreased their earnings. This is particularly true of persons who either are self-employed, earn much of their livelihood on a commission basis, or derive much of their income as a result of returns on investments. It is precisely for this reason that we desire our indicator of economic change to be representative of changes in both employment per se and personal income. We are taking fluctuations in the level of employment, then, to indicate, in addition, the extent of changes in (1) the level of unemployment (inversely), (2) the level of personal income, and (3) the level of advancement or demotion in occupational status.

The viewpoint of this study is that any one or a combination of these three economic factors may be responsible for the major stress that, through various processes, leads to mental hospitalization. The over-all array of findings indicated by this research emphasizes two factors that underlie the degree of consistency of the basic relation. Consistency is taken to mean the degree to which the pattern of response of mental hospitalization to economic change is similar in magnitude from one economic downturn to another and from one upturn to another. The two sets of factors involved are (1) the extent of economic stress and (2) the extent of role failure.

The first set of variables is derived from the concept of economic stress. The question is: who is economically hurt during an economic downturn? The answer to this question is found in the analysis of the relation between the individual and the economic system, namely, the specific position occupied by the individual within the system. Groups of individuals having different levels of income, different types of occupation, different levels of job skill, different levels of employment and unemployment, and located in different industries and regions within the economic system are all somewhat differently affected. Our major source of information on the economic impact of downturns on different economic classifications of the population is the traditional research of economists in the areas of business cycles, economic history, and labor economics. The rich and extensive economic literature in these areas is drawn upon for basic information in the present study. It is also true, however, that persons who have different social backgrounds will exhibit different economic behavior and reactions to changes in the economy. This is true, for example, of all age groups, both sexes, major ethnic groups, groups having different average levels of intelligence, groups having different psychiatric histories, and immigrant groups (who have different lengths of tenure in the United States).

Apart from the question of who is involved in specific economic-system changes is the question of who, by virtue of a second set of factors, will respond to these stresses in such a way as to bring about mental hospitalization.

Here we become involved in the derivative problem of the degree to which social role is affected by economic loss. Among other things, this issue of the extent of role failure will be influenced by relative social status, the importance to the individual's social group of maintaining a particular life style, and the importance of achievement in general and of economic achievement in particular. Here the impact of the value system is dominant. It is a question of the definition of a dignified way of life.

10   Economic Change and the Structure of Psychiatric Care

Hospital Capacity and the Impact of Economic Change

A very persuasive group of arguments has traditionally played a major role in discouraging detailed studies in psychiatric epidemiology from using mental-hospital admissions data arrayed over time. The substance of these arguments has been that, since mental hospitals were imagined to be nearly always overcrowded, any actual change in the incidence or prevalence of mental illness could not be reflected in increased mental-hospital admissions because there would be no place to hospitalize the newly mentally ill. A corollary of this argument further assumed that the only major increase in mental-hospital admissions that might occur would be the result of increases in hospital capacity.

Finally, a tradition has grown up within the health-planning field around the theme that, when an inpatient facility is constructed, it will be filled fairly rapidly with patients, regardless of whether or not true need of the population for such new facilities has dramatically increased.[1] This group of traditional arguments has had particular relevance to, and impact upon, the early studies of economic change and mental hospitalization that utilized New York State data.[2]

Studies of the question of whether there was an increase in mental-hospital admissions as a result of stresses during the Great Depression discuss the fact that there were substantial increases in New York State's mental-hospital capacity during the 1930's. The general question was then raised whether consideration of the period of the 1930's is altogether valid within this type of study, since the increase in hospital capacity might somehow have been instrumental in causing increases in admissions.

Despite arguments that have had the effect of making a relation between economic change and mental-hospital admissions theoretically impossible, the facts are that this relation obviously exists, has existed at least since 1841, and has continued until at least 1967. This relation occurs at least on a "cyclical" (3–5- and 8–10-year-change) basis, and normally on a 1–2-year-change basis. For certain population groups, in addition, it is normally reliable on a year-to-year change basis.

The relation between economic change and mental hospitalization is continuous and highly reliable for 127 years, despite the impact of historical factors of noneconomic character, including changes in hospital capacity. Mental-hospital admissions increased proportionately less during the economic downturn of the early 1930's, despite the fact of significant increases in hospital capacity, than during any other downturn between 1915 and 1967.

The precise inverse correlations, on a *year-to-year basis,* with control for autocorrelation within the time series and the residuals, between economic change and mental-hospital admissions are highest during the 20-year period 1925–1945, the very period within which the capacity of the New York State mental-hospital system experienced its greatest increase.

In the early phases of this project, methods of detrending were used to eliminate the problem of the possible effects of large-scale increases in hospital capacity that might produce long-term changes in the resident population. Later in the project, additional data transformations were used to pinpoint the time range in which the relation between economic change and mental hospitalization could be found. The data transformations included changes of 1, 2, 3, ... years, and variable polynominal and Fourier curve fits to these changes. Regardless of the specific technique employed, it was found that the inverse relations between economic changes and admissions is consistent for short-term measurement (1- or 2-year changes) as well as for long-term measurement (8–10-year changes). The point is that, if changes in hospital capacity, for example, did bring about changes in admissions patterns, then the consistency of the inverse relation between economic change and admissions should break down at some level of change, if not at several levels. We do not find, however, that any specific level, or set of levels, shows a breakdown in the general relation.

The group of arguments that ultimately declare that the major, if not the only, source of changed mental-hospital admissions levels is changed capacity are grounded on several basic assumptions. These inferred assumptions may be stated as follows:

(1) Mental hospitals are always overcrowded, and they cannot be filled beyond a certain fixed capacity.

(2) Policy restricts the number of admissions to a quota, made necessary

by the attempt to maintain a specific maximal level of overcrowding. Such policy may be executed through either of the two following methods: (a) major pronouncements are occasionally made as to the over-all quota of patients, or types of patients, who will be granted admissions or (b) general policy dictates that admissions levels will change only according to the extent of decreases in (i) the size of the resident population or (ii) the magnitude of overcrowding.

(3) There is a strict relation—perhaps one-to-one—between admissions and the number of patients in the hospital at any given time. This statement further implies that the turnover rate per admission is constant, that is, (a) the discharge rate is constant and (b) the duration of residence of new patients is constant.

(4) Given assumptions (1), (2), and (3), therefore, the only way to increase admissions is through (a) increasing the size of facilities *and* (b) changing policy in order to allow a larger quota of admissions.

Let us now examine these assumptions in terms of both their own internal logic and the empirical evidence.

The first assumption, that hospitals are nearly always overcrowded, presupposes either a constant rate of overcrowding (at least within narrow limits) or that hospitals cannot be filled beyond a fixed capacity. The facts, however, are at odds with this assumption. In the first place, there is actually very great variability in overcrowding. Traditionally, overcrowding of nearly 40 to 60 percent was not at all uncommon within ten of the New York State civil hospitals during the period 1912–1960 (Table 34). Thus, under the pressure of increased admissions, the mental hospital traditionally responds by overcrowding itself even further. In fact, even if it wished to remain conservative in its admissions procedure, it could overcrowd up to at least 60 percent.

The second assumption, that there have generally been policy restrictions on the level of admissions, is expressly contradicted by Patton and Weinstein of the New York State Department of Mental Hygiene. These authors indicate that there were no policy changes on admissions during the 1930's that might have tended to increase admissions in accordance with increases in capacity within certain hospitals; specifically:

The most pronounced movement in first admission rates [to the New York State mental hospital system] was the prolonged rise which began in the middle 1920's and lasted through the 1930's. As far as is known now, it has been department policy throughout the present century to admit all individuals requiring care for mental illness. Nevertheless, it is clear that without the marked expansion in hospital capacity during the early 1930's, it might not have been possible for the concomitant expansion in admissions to occur.[3]

Table 34. Overcrowding[a] (percent) in New York civil state hospitals of over 37 percent, 1923–1933 and 1948–1960.

Year	Hospital					
	Brooklyn	Gowanda	Central Islip	Kings Park	Rochester	St. Lawrence
1923	40.1					
1924	40.5					
1925	48.7	44.0				41.1
1926	50.4	49.4		41.2		39.4
1927	49.8	48.3	42.1	47.5		39.4
1928	60.8	48.0	50.1	45.5	43.5	40.2
1929	40.3		43.1	43.5	45.9	
1930	37.3		50.4	54.4	50.2	38.1
1931	39.3		48.7	43.6		

Year	Hospital						
	Brooklyn	Gowanda	Buffalo	Creedmore	Marcy	Rockland	Utica
1948			41.0				
1949			40.5				
1950			42.4				
1951			44.7				43.0
1952		38.9	49.2				44.2
1953	45.4	42.9		40.3	40.8		44.9
1954	47.0	41.4		45.6	44.5		45.4
1955	46.9		45.2	43.8	43.7	43.8	42.0
1956	46.3		40.2	43.7	40.6	40.6	
1957	47.6		43.2			40.7	
1958	53.2		41.4				
1959	47.3						
1960	47.5						

[a]Excess of resident patient population over official capacity level (in specified numbers of beds) for each hospital.

Evidence from the present study also gives strong support to the Patton and Weinstein statement. We find that there is indeed an increase in admissions within the downturn of the first half of the 1929–1936 cycle during which overall hospital capacity also increased. However, hospital capacity continued to increase for the following 4 years, during which, nevertheless, hospital admissions fell sharply, in precise inverse relation to the sharp economic upturn during the second half of the 1929–1936 cycle.

These data support Patton and Weinstein's historical analysis, and especially the statement that there was no new policy that might tend to increase admissions while capacity increased. The point is that under such an alleged change in policy mental-hospital admissions should have continued to increase for the 4 years following 1932, the absolute bottom year of the Great Depression.

Although Patton and Weinstein state categorically that admissions policy did not change during the Great Depression, regardless of increases in capacity, they further feel that the increase in admissions might not have occurred without concomitant increases in capacity. The latter statement does not, of course, conflict with the factual relation found in this study between economic change and mental-hospital admissions. Rather, it would tend to argue that it could only be the increase in capacity that *allowed* economic change to produce greater numbers of admissions by permitting those increased admissions to be channeled into the mental-hospital system. The increase in capacity would thus become a necessary component in the equation that in the first instance links economic change to mental hospitalization.

Although Patton and Weinstein's statement does not conflict with the findings linking economic change to mental hospitalization, there is substantial evidence indicating that increases in capacity probably did not even bring about more admissions than would have occurred by virtue of the 1929–1932 economic downturn. In fact, as was indicated earlier, the increase in admissions during the Great Depression was proportionately less than during any other economic downturn in the 20th century. On the other hand, it may well be true that the increases in hospital capacity which occurred in the 1930's were in general necessary in order to accommodate expanded rates of admissions over the long term.

An examination of long- and short-term changes in rates of admission indicates that, though the hospital system would have been able to accommodate the expanded short-run, or cyclical, increase in admissions during the downturn of the early 1930's, which was followed by a sharp decrease in admissions during the last half of the cycle, without expanded facilities it would have had considerably greater difficulty in adjusting to the generally upward trend in admissions beginning in 1909 and extending at least through 1950. More generally, then, though the mental-hospital system has clearly been able to deal with cyclical increases in the admissions rate without expanding facilities, it was apparently necessary to expand facilities in order to accommodate secular increases in admissions.

The fundamental evidence that the mental-hospital system has been able to keep pace with cyclical change without major expansions in facilities is that such expansions are not correlated over time with cyclical increases in admission rates. However, there are sharp rate increases and decreases of a cyclical nature corresponding inversely to changes in the economy. On the other hand, an examination of admission rates by age shows that all age groups (except those under 15 and over 65 years) show no secular increase in rates during the period 1910–1960. It seems relatively clear, therefore, that the hospital system has been able to keep pace with long-term population change. Furthermore, since there is no general increase in the middle-range (approximately 10-year) trend of admission rates during the entire period of the 1930's (the cycles of admissions move around a flat trend), it appears clear that the rapidity with which the newly constructed or greatly expanded facilities were filled does not indicate any change in either admissions policy or medical-care organization, but rather that the mental-hospital system was keeping up with long-term population change.

Another approach to the question of whether policy changes on admissions influence admissions rates is based upon evidence from rates of discharge. (Analysis of the relation between discharges and economic change is discussed in greater detail later in the present chapter.) If there were a policy change by which mental-hospital admissions were allowed to increase, especially because of an increase in capacity, then why did it become necessary during the Great Depression to discharge patients at a much higher rate? This rhetorical question argues that the increase in capacity had no observable effect on the usual increase in discharge rates which historically has followed greatly increased admission levels; such capacity increases would therefore hardly lead to increases in admissions. One would surely not expect hospital policy to call for increased admissions while discharges increased enormously under the pressure of sharp initial upturns in admissions.

It seems clear then that alleged major shifts in policy on admissions were in fact not responsible for short-term or middle-range (cyclical) changes in admission rates during the entire period 1914–1967, or even for 1929–1932. However, another possible technique by which hospital policy might control admission levels is that of allowing increases in admissions only under the condition that there are decreases (1) in the size of the resident population or (2) in the magnitude of overcrowding. If this theoretical avenue of policy control actually corresponded to reality, then we should find an inverse relation between changes in admission rates and changes in (1) the size of the resident population and (2) the extent of overcrowding.

The facts, however, run precisely counter to these hypotheses, that is, we find strong positive correlations between changes in admission rates and the size of both the resident population and the magnitude of overcrowding. Explanations for these relations would not be hard to find. It seems logical that as admissions increase, so should the size of the population channeled into the mental-hospital system, namely, the resident patient population. Second, it is entirely reasonable that, once mental hospitals accept the notion that they will receive all patients who require psychiatric care, they will probably need to overcrowd their facilities beyond earlier levels in order to increase the size of their resident populations.

A third assumption in the argument that increases in hospital capacity are essential for increases in admission levels is that the rate of patient turnover is relatively constant. This assumption underlies the idea that there is a one-to-one relation between changes in the level of admissions and changes in the level of the resident population. This presupposes, at least, that the rate of discharge is constant. The findings of this study indicate, however, that changes in the rates of discharge are inversely related to economic change and, in addition, are dependent upon the extent of recovery from psychiatric illness.

Table 35. Number of years, 1914–1960, during which the correlation between employment and mental-hospital discharges $\leqq$ −0.65,[a] by level of recovery, diagnosis, and sex.[b]

Mental disorder	Recovered		Much improved		Improved		Un-improved	
	M	F	M	F	M	F	M	F
Total	38	24	7	8	33	44	41	46
With functional psychosis	7	7	7	7	24	37	38	41
Schizophrenia	0	6	13	7	30	31	41	40
Manic-depressive	29	16	11	25	15	39	18	41
Involutional	13	29	21	8	24	31	16	28
Alcoholic	38	38	16	13	20	20	32	20
Paresis	29	28	29	9	27	25	20	14
Convulsive	26	28	7	18	10	21	22	15
Mental deficiency	35	27	16	6	11	22	15	27
With cerebral arteriosclerosis	15	22	13	28	6	13	15	22
Senility	33	19	13	14	13	28	22	37

[a] r between −0.65 and −1.00. Only correlations not significantly affected by autocorrelation of residuals, as measured by the Durbin-Watson statistic, are included.
[b] First discharges from New York civil state hospitals correlated with New York State manufacturing employment index (secular trend subtracted from both series).

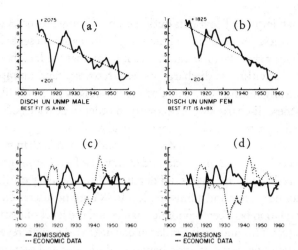

FIG. 27. Fluctuations in employment and in mental-hospital discharges during 1914–1960: discharges classified as unimproved. Discharges from New York civil state hospitals matched with New York State manufacturing employment index (secular trend subtracted from both series).

LEGEND:
(a,b) ———— Discharges, unimproved ...... Best estimate of trend
(c,d) ———— Discharges, unimproved ...... New York State Employment Index
SCALE:
(a,b) Numbers of discharges are expressed as fractions of the highest number, which is set equal to 1.0, for each population group.
(c,d) Deviations from trend are expressed as fractions of the largest absolute value which is set equal to 1.0, if positive, or −1.0 if negative.

Two specific findings are particularly relevant in this context. The first is that patients classified by the hospital as "recovered" are likely to be discharged during economic downturns; the second is that patients who show little recovery (that is, those who are classified as "improved," rather than as "much improved"), as well as the altogether "unimproved," are also extremely likely to be discharged during economic downturns (Table 35). Now, it may not surprise us to find that patients regarded as being recovered tend to be discharged close to the time when hospital admissions also tend to increase, namely, during economic downturns.

In this case it can be comfortably argued that a certain fraction of new admissions tend to recover fairly rapidly, so that we find, over time, a relatively consistent positive relation between changes in admission levels and changes in discharge levels of "recovered" patients. However, the hospital system has also traditionally been discharging "unimproved" patients, those showing very low levels of recovery or indeed complete lack of recovery, during economic downturns. On the other hand, there has been very little tendency to discharge "much improved" patients during economic downturns. A detailed examination of these phenomena and their implications are presented later in this chapter. For the moment, suffice it to say that the fact that the hospital system is willing to discharge its least-recovered and unimproved patients specifically during economic downturns (Fig. 27) in all likelihood indicates that these discharges were necessary in order to provide beds to accommodate the pressure of greatly increased admissions.

The data on the relation between discharges and economic change demonstrate once again, but in a backhanded way, the fact that programs of expansion of facilities in the 1930's did not alter the consistency of the relation between economic change and admission levels. We see no alteration in the inverse relation between economic change and the level of discharge during the 1930's. This finding is similar to one discussed earlier, revealing that there was no alteration in the relation between admissions and economic change during the 1930's. It is clear that both of these relations remain relatively constant during the 19th and 20th centuries. Thus, we observe no slackening whatever in the hospital system's apparent willingness to use increased discharges as the principal mode of accommodation of increased admissions, even during a period of substantially increased hospital capacity.

In fact, increases in discharges appear to be the mechanism most consistently used by the mental hospital to compensate for sharp increases in admissions during economic downturns. The most prominent evidence bearing on this issue is that, although during the 1930's there was a sharp increase in newly constructed capacity, which took place before, during, and after the major economic downturn, there was also a sharp increase in the rate of discharges during this downturn. Thus, despite the fact that far greater bed space was allegedly available, the hospital system probably continued to use increased discharges as its principal method of compensating for admissions (as it had done since at least 1850 and until at least 1960).

It appears, then, that the major implication of greatly increased hospital capacity during the 1930's was certainly not to alter the pattern of admissions, but rather to increase the physical space available in the hospital for resident patients, thus obviously decreasing overcrowding very substantially. Apart from increased discharges, further overcrowding and short-run increased capacity (probably through the increase in number of beds per hospital unit) have been the traditional mechanisms whereby the hospital has compensated for increased admissions during economic downturns. During the downturn of the early 30's, however, for the hospital system as a whole there were great increases in capacity due to building programs that were not synchronous with the economic downturn but that did have the effect of decreasing overcrowding. Nevertheless, several individual hospitals

(Binghampton, Brooklyn, Harlem Valley, and Hudson River State Hospitals) did not undergo large-scale expansion programs during the period 1929–1932, and these hospitals continued to resort at least to increased overcrowding.

The fourth and final assumption in the argument that links increases in admissions to increases in hospital capacity is that capacity increases are necessary to accommodate new admissions. Direct evidence may be brought to bear in an examination of this assumption. In the first place, there have been substantial increases in mental-hospital admissions during periods in which there was no indication of significant increases in hospital capacity, as we have seen throughout this volume. These periods of sharp increase in admissions from 1841 to 1967 occurred almost entirely during economic downturns.

Second, the increase in capacity that occurred during the years 1932–1938 (and the construction during this later period of Rockland and Pilgrim State Hospitals and the Psychiatric Institute) would, of course, make possible the accommodation of a substantially increased flow of admissions during the later 1930's. In fact (Table 36), there was a larger absolute increase in the

Table 36. Total number of beds available in New York civil state hospitals, 1929–1938.

Year	Number	Year	Number	Year	Number
1929	34,783	1933	48,623	1936	56,185
1930	35,146	1934	52,328	1937	58,935
1931	39,366	1935	52,915	1938	60,153
1932	46,243				

number of available beds in all of the New York civil state hospitals during 1932–1938 (13,910) than during 1929–1932 (11,560).

If it were true that simply through the enlargement of hospital capacity there would somehow come into existence a substantially larger patient population, then the downturn of 1936–1938 would have resulted in a greater increase in admissions than occurred during the disastrous downturn of 1929–1932. In fact, however, for the largest fraction of patient groups whose admissions were at all sensitive to the changes in the economy, the reverse actually occurred.

The Impact of Economic Change on Patient Care

The foregoing material provides clear evidence of sharp increases in both discharges and hospital overcrowding during economic downturns. What, then, are the implications for patient care resulting from the influence of economic change on these two phenomena? Although an increase in discharges would result in both benefits and disadvantages in terms of psychiatric care, an increase in overcrowding would appear to have only deleterious implications.

An increase in discharges would, first of all, result in a reduction in the duration of custodial care, which involves little in the way of therapy and may well significantly hamper the recovery of many patients.[4] However, discharging patients who have not recovered, as was discussed earlier, may result in increased illness to the patient or disruption of the life circumstances of the family to whom the patient has returned. Moreover, since the increase in discharges occurs during a period in which families of patients may be in reduced financial circumstances, the former patients and their families may be thrown into a very difficult financial situation, one that might even result in rehospitalization of the patient. There is evidence, furthermore, that the attitude of a former patient's relatives is important in influencing whether or not he will make a reasonably good recovery in the community.[5]

An increase in overcrowding, on the other hand, would seem to have no redeeming features for the cause of patient care. Perhaps most important, it might bring an increase in the regimentation of the lives of the patients. The reason is that an increase in overcrowding would necessitate a more highly bureaucratized structure in order to deal effectively with the basic needs of a considerably larger number of patients. One would then need to manage patients in groups rather than as individuals, and to increase the ratios of custodial care to individualized therapy and of group activities to individual activities. This issue of bureaucratization or institutionalism has inspired a good many writers, including Goffmann[6] and Wing,[7] who feel that this administrative scheme is, in any case, a fundamentally unsatisfactory feature in the lives of perhaps the majority of mental patients.

Third, a substantial increase in the hospitalized patient population might destroy many of the therapeutic relations that occur among individual staff members and individual patients. Such increases in the number of patients may even tend to destroy the therapeutic benefits inherent in the interaction of small groups of patients by altering the cohesion and basic character of these groups.[8]

The Impact of Economic Change on Discharges

Earlier in this chapter, three methods used by the mental-hospital system to accommodate increased admissions during economic downturns were discussed. It was found that the most readily used method involved a considerable increase in discharges. But the extent to which the hospital system is prepared to discharge patients during the downturn depends largely on the degree to which the patient is thought to have recovered. The patient's level of recovery, in turn, is substantially influenced by the specific diagnosis given him. We will now examine these generalized findings in detail.

The most basic pattern of relation of discharges to economic change is shown among the population of discharges as a whole, that is, without regard to diagnosis. The data show that during economic downturns the groups classified as "recovered" and "unimproved" are the most likely to be discharged, the "improved" are nearly as likely to be discharged as the previous two groups, but the population classified as "much improved" are least likely to be discharged.

Examination of the total functional psychotic categories (hereafter TOT), including schizophrenic, manic-depressive, and involutional psychotics, indicates that the unimproved and the improved groups are highly likely to be discharged during economic downturns, whereas the recovered and much improved are not. In other words, the TOT category follows the general pattern of high sensitivity of the least improved (that is, improved and unimproved) groups to the downturn. In contrast to the overall pattern, however, the TOT recovered group is not likely to be discharged during the downturn.

Discharges of alcoholics, paretics, epileptics, and mental defectives, on the other hand, present a pattern of relations to economic change that to a large extent resembles those for the entire population unclassified by illness. However, in this case the inverse relation to economic change is particularly strong among patients categorized as recovered. This is in sharp contrast to the functional psychotics and especially to the schizophrenics, among whom the recovered show little tendency to be discharged during the economic downturn. These data furnish the explanation of why, among total discharges, the recovered group is so very sensitive to the economic downturn; they are sensitive only because of the sizable impact of four illness categories—alcoholic, paretic, epileptic, and mentally defective. On the other hand, the functional psychotic group appears to provide the basis for the extreme sensitivity to the economic downturn of the improved and unimproved categories among the general patient population.

In the case of seniles, sex difference plays a major part in their relative tendency to be discharged during economic downturns. The males show a major tendency to be discharged, which increases sharply as psychiatric condition improves, whereas the female discharges increase sharply as psychiatric condition fails to improve. The seniles may give us a clue to understanding the over-all distribution of discharges during the economic downturn for the total population of discharges. This clue may explain why total female discharges are somewhat less responsive to the economic downturn than male discharges among the recovered group and are somewhat more responsive than are male discharges for the improved and unimproved group. In other words, the senile discharges may help us to understand the sex difference in the response of discharges to economic change.

Possible Explanations of the Inverse Relation of Discharges to Economic Change: The Overall Pattern

A first question is why the "much improved," as distinguished from other categories of discharges, do not appear to be sensitive to economic downturns. Let us offer the following speculation. In the first instance it may not be thought entirely respectable to discharge patients solely on the grounds of providing needed bed space for new patients who enter the hospital during an economic downturn. But under the pressure of greatly increased admissions and insufficient space and staff to accommodate an expanded resident population, there is substantial need to reduce that increased population. The issue becomes one of deciding who can be most appropriately discharged, or who has the least legitimate reason for continued residence in the hospital.

It may be seen as most legitimate to discharge the most and the least improved on the following grounds: the most improved (that is, the "recovered"), probably have the least legitimate reasons for remaining in the mental hospital. The sole rationale might be that the outside community, especially the family, is unable or unwilling to receive the returned mental patient despite the fact that he may be recovered according to the official hospital classification. Thus, in the mind of the official responsible, under the pressure of overcrowding and the need for bed space to accommodate new patients, discharging the recovered patient would be least illegitimate.

There is also a strong legitimating factor attached to discharge of the least improved ("improved" and "unimproved") cases under the pressure of need for bed space. If we consider that the least improved among all patients have been the least responsive to treatment (by the time of discharge), then a major legitimate reason for continued hospitalization is nullified. In addition, persons who are not responding to treatment provide poor role models to both staff and patients in terms of optimistic expectations of treatment and possible recovery. Patients and staff may be greatly discouraged if the unimproved patient becomes an example of what is expected by the hospital. It is also possible that patients will not recover as rapidly if they must continue to interact with severely ill patients. The individual patient may derive less emotional support and sense of structure among a population that is highly disorganized and overtly symptomatic.

Thus, in tending to eliminate the patient population that is unresponsive to treatment, the hospital may ultimately be providing a healthier and more encouraging atmosphere for recovery of the majority of patients. Then, too, it is entirely possible that the specific treatments or environment of a given mental hospital are inappropriate to the care of certain patients, and this may be the reason that they are unresponsive to treatment. Under such conditions it may be more fruitful to discharge these patients and allow for the possibility that ordinary social processes, or such alternative modes of therapy as are available in the community, might be more promising avenues for their recovery.

It is not very difficult to imagine that, despite the possible rationales offered above, one might consider it outrageous that many severely ill hospitalized patients are released into the community—not to speak of the fact that these releases occur largely under conditions of hospital overcrowding. Reasons for public and professional concern over release of such patients might be the possibility (1) that the patient's condition will deteriorate, (2) that the patient will be unable to support himself financially, (3) that he might break the law or become the victim of illegal activities, (4) that he might do physical or emotional harm to members of the society, including his family, (5) that he might do harm to himself, and (6) that he might be irresponsible in such ways as to damage economic or social endeavors. It seems, then, that some rationale can be mustered on both sides of the argument whether to retain in a state mental hospital patients showing little significant recovery after a reasonable time. The very fact of questionable legitimacy of maintaining an unimproved patient in the hospital, under the conditions in which bed space is at a high priority, may make the unimproved patient the best candidate for discharge in a situation of critically reduced resources.

Discharges of Patients with Functional Versus Certain Organic Disorders

A second question concerns the fact that discharges of functional psychotics are most sensitive to economic downturns among the least improved category, whereas discharges of alcoholics, paretics, epileptics, and mental defectives show greatest sensitivity to the economic downturn among the recovered. These facts indicate that the overall pattern of discharges is somewhat complicated by the specific illness categories. It was initially observed that, among the total population of discharges, the recovered as well as the least improved categories showed the greatest tendency to be discharged during the economic downturn. Subsequently, it was found that it is largely discharges with functional psychosis that are responsible for the extreme sensitivity to the economic downturn of the least improved groups among total discharges; and it is the alcoholic, epileptic, paretic, and mentally defective discharges that are responsible for the very high sensitivity of discharges classified as recovered.

With regard to the total population of discharges, the speculation was offered that persons labeled as recovered or relatively unimproved would have the least legitimate reason for continuing to be maintained in a hospital under conditions of scarcity of beds; therefore, these groups would be most likely to experience discharge in response to an economic downturn. The functional psychotic and especially the schizophrenic discharges are responsible for the extreme sensitivity of the least improved group of discharges to the economic downturn. It is possible that, in general, among the functional psychotic population, it is felt either that a patient is capable of significant improvement within a reasonable period, or that his illness is continuous, chronic, possibly genetically based, and thus not effectively treated within the context of a mental hospital.

The population that is thought to be improvable through hospital treatment may not be discharged during an economic downturn, and it may be that such a population is never considered to be "recovered," but rather to require continued care regardless of its level of recovery. The population requiring continued care will improve under treatment, but only up to a point, because its affliction is deemed to be based on a fundamental personality disorder (schizophrenic, cyclothymic, or compulsive). Therefore the effects of treatment may be viewed as merely temporary. The implication would then be that among the functional psychotic group, and particularly the schizophrenic subgroup, the category of discharges called "recovered" would be felt, on a practical basis, not to be truly recovered as compared with the recovered among other illness groups, but rather closer, in a practical sense, to the "much improved" category. Finally, the patients who are not readily responding to treatment (the "unimproved" and "improved") would have the least legitimate place in the mental hospital.

This argument would then leave the problem of why the alcoholics, paretics, epileptics, and mental defectives show especially high sensitivity to the economic downturn among the recovered group. Let us note, first of all, that in these four illnesses recovery by some definition is thought possible among a substantial fraction of cases. In fact, for the acute brain syndromes associated with alcohol intoxication and convulsive disorders, high probability of recovery is the principle condition for the diagnostic concept of acuteness.

Similarly, in the case of paresis, though diagnostically listed as a chronic brain disorder (with central-nervous-system syphilis), "the underlying pathological process may partially subside" under chemotherapy to the point where "the loss of function may be almost imperceptible clinically."[9]

Even for the mental defective, there are grounds for assuming that the notion of "degree of recovery" refers to the effectiveness of hospital treatment in improving his ability to function outside of the hospital. Thus the American Psychiatric Association manual indicates, in its definition of degree of severity of mental deficiency, that a number of physiological and social factors beyond I.Q. measurement are important in assessing the degree of impairment. This formulation suggests that hospital treatment of the mentally defective may rely upon similar criteria of adjustment to the social environment as an indication of the degree of "recovery." The question for the mental hospital in terms of rehabilitation is whether the mentally defective require protective custodial care or whether they can be trained to function reasonably adequately in a relatively nonthreatening environment outside the hospital.

Finally, there would be a possibility that additional emotional or intellectual impairment beyond the mental deficiency due to psychiatric, neurotic, or behavioral reactions (as the APA manual puts it) can, in many cases, be largely eliminated. Among mental defectives, therefore, those labeled as "recovered" are probably a group for whom mental hospitalization is no longer useful on a practical basis. To summarize, then, the functional psychoses or "disorders of psychogenic origin or without clearly defined physical cause or structural change in the brain"[10] are distinguished from certain brain disorders (psychosis with alcoholism, epilepsy, and paresis) and from mental deficiency by the fact that the underlying pathologic condition relates in the first case to personality structure, and in the second case to fundamental structural or intellectual brain incapacity.

The suggestion is being offered at this point that, in a crisis over hospital space, the functional psychotic will be retained in hospital so long as he gives reasonable evidence of improvement, whereas the alcoholic, epileptic, paretic, and mental defective will be discharged under the same conditions. The difference is that "recovered" will signify "improving under hospital regimen" for the functional psychotic and "improved as far as is possible under hospital regimen" for the alcoholic, epileptic, paretic, and mental defective. The corollary of this argument is that the least improved ("improved" and "unimproved") functional psychotic will be discharged in a crisis of hospital space since he has little chance of improving in the hospital, whereas the less improved alcoholic, epileptic, paretic, and mental defective will be retained on the grounds that improvement is possible.

Discharges of Seniles by Sex

A third question concerns the fact that male seniles tend to be discharged during economic downturns—a tendency that increases as psychiatric condition improves—whereas the relation of female senile discharges to economic downturns is closest among the least improved.

The answer to this question may be based on arguments similar to those suggested earlier in explanation of the difference between discharges of functional psychotics versus discharges of patients having certain brain disorders and mental defectives. The argument proposed was that diagnostic groups for which "recovery" is possible are discharged, in a period of scarcity of hospital beds, when recovery has occurred or is imminent. Diagnostic groups for which recovery is improbable, on the other hand, are discharged when little or no improvement is seen (that is, when the patient does not adjust to the hospital regimen or benefit from it).

It is entirely possible that, as in the society at large, males are treated far more attentively than females, who occupy social positions of lower status. This situation might apply particularly pointedly to the seniles, who, in any case, are discouraging as patients since their condition is seen as progressively deteriorating. A high premium would then be placed upon even minimal therapeutic attention, which is a relatively scarce resource in state-hospital psychiatry. If it is true that the male senile is more likely to be favored with some form of therapy than the female senile, then it is more likely that male rather than female seniles would be viewed as capable of at least a minimal level of "recovery," or readjustment to community living.

If male seniles were more likely than female seniles to be treated as "improvable," then it is possible that male seniles in general would be retained in the hospital, with the hope of some improvement in their condition. In that case, only those male seniles who managed to show the minimal degree of improvement that signified "recovery" would be legitimately discharged under the pressure of reduced hospital space. By contrast, female seniles would not in general be treated as "improvable," and only those whose condition improved despite the lack of therapeutic attention would be retained in the hospital when the need for beds sharply increased.

Discharges of Senile Patients Versus Those Having Psychosis with Cerebral Arteriosclerosis

A fourth question is concerned with the fact that the seniles show a pattern of discharge in relation to economic change that is similar to the pattern of the total population, whereas patients diagnosed as having psychosis with cerebral arteriosclerosis (CER), a somewhat younger group of older persons, do not show unusually high sensitivity among either the recovered or the (slightly) improved or unimproved.

An examination of the total pattern of CER discharges according to designated level of recovery indicates that the most improved and least improved CER's, who are usually the most sensitive to the economic downturn, are nearly always considerably less likely to be discharged during the downturn than the seniles of the same discharge categories.

Once again we may offer a speculation as to the reason for the lower general sensitivity among the CER's. It is possible that the seniles, by the very definition of their illness, represent cases with more severe symptoms than the CER's. This may be largely due to the fact that, given the progressiveness of these illnesses, the seniles are simply older and therefore their symptoms will be more advanced and less amenable to recovery. That the seniles might therefore be more severely ill than the CER's suggests the possibility that totally unimproved seniles would present more of a burden to the mental hospitals than the unimproved CER's. Now if, on the other hand, the seniles had "recovered," at least in some dimension of their illness, the hospital might be more willing to release them on the ground that little more actual improvement could be expected of these patients (especially if part of their illness is thought to be related to the degenerative aging process).

The Relation of Discharge to Family Economic Status

There appears to be considerable agreement among writers familiar with hospital psychiatry that an important factor in the decision whether or not to discharge a psychiatric patient is the relative willingness of the patient's community to accept him once again. This acceptance (or lack of it) is viewed chiefly as depending on the relation of the patient's family to him. The patient must once again adjust behaviorally and emotionally to a definite position in the household that is different from that of his former status as a mental patient.

Clearly, the family will be in a better position to accept a newly discharged patient if, in the short run at least, it is able to support him financially without seriously compromising the economic stability of the rest of the family. This condition of financial readiness to accept the returning mental patient would become particularly important when the patient is the former male head of the household, whose hospitalization, in the first instance, probably resulted in serious damage to his family's financial situation. A family that has experienced the loss of its chief breadwinner and that would therefore encounter great difficulty even in maintaining a stable economic situation would probably need to make substantial sacrifice in order to support an additional (especially an adult) family member. Thus one would imagine that under a relatively stable economy the financial position of the family would play an important part in its willingness and ability to receive a newly discharged mental patient.

Examination of the data on discharges nevertheless indicates that the largest fraction of discharges, regardless of level of recovery, occurs during periods of economic adversity. This means not only that the economic status of families actually receiving discharged mental patients is likely to be significantly lower than it usually is, but that the possibilities of employment for the newly discharged mental patient are unusually poor. Among several implications of this situation is that, above all, the patient is returning to a situation which may be economically more difficult than the one that led to his hospitalization in the first place. We have seen that the economic downturn is a primary factor in a very large number of mental-hospital admissions. There is therefore a reasonable probability that a patient who was hospitalized during an economic downturn was also discharged during the same or another economic downturn. But his chances of surviving the second downturn may be far poorer than his ability to cope with the downturn that led to his admission to the hospital.

With a background of mental hospitalization behind him, the former patient will find it difficult to gain employment,[11] not only because of a peculiar employment history, but because of the stigma of "irresponsibility" attached to mental hospitalization. He may, furthermore, find it extremely difficult to adjust to a new employment situation both because he has not been at work for some time and because the internal setting of the mental hospital may be completely unrelated, if not actually alien, to that of his new work situation. These considerations may provide a clue to explaining the very large number of readmissions that are also strongly related to downturns in the economy.

The problem of discharge during the economic downturn is particularly acute in the case of a former head of household. The former household head will be returning to a family that probably lost considerable income because of his hospitalization, and whose income is even further diminished because of an economic downturn. The impact of discharging a mental patient during an economic downturn may not be as severe for an economically dependent member of a household (the spouse or a child of the household head) but will nevertheless create additional, and perhaps severe, economic strains.

Implications of Economic Change for Institutions that Deal with Deviance

We have examined some of the effects of economic change as related to changes in the pattern of psychiatric care in a continuously crowded mental-hospital system. Some of the probable implications of discharge during an economic downturn for the possibilities of rehabilitation of the mental patient were also discussed. Up to this point we have been concerned only with the population of mentally hospitalized patients in New York State. Recent evidence suggests, however, that a considerable fraction of even the severely mentally ill are not hospitalized.[12]

We might imagine that the general implications of economic change for mental-hospital admission and patient care would increase greatly if the general population of severely mentally ill persons tended to become hospitalized during an economic downturn; we might anticipate a substantially larger fraction of patients discharged for reasons that have little to do with their actual state of recovery or the ability of their families to receive them.

Similarly, we might expect far greater shift and flux in the composition and structure of the hospitalized-patient population which, as we have seen, has further major implications for the quality and effectiveness of psychiatric care. There does, moreover, seem to be a concerted effort to bring the general population of the mentally ill within the psychiatric-care system. The public-health approach to psychiatry, which focuses upon the epidemiological facts of mental illness, involves broad coverage of patients within the population who can be psychiatrically defined as mentally ill whether or not they had received care in the past.[13]

This tendency within the community mental-health movement has also spilled over into the area of criminal behavior. Frequently, furthermore, we find that criminals—particularly those who have committed violent crimes against persons—are discussed in psychiatric terms as requiring treatment rather than in criminological terms as requiring punishment. The data of this study on hospitalization of the criminally insane show a very similar pattern of relation to economic change to that shown for mental hospitalization generally. One of the implications of this finding is that the tendency to define such criminal behavior in terms of a psychiatric classification, which then results in hospitalization, probably brings about the same dynamic problems of change in the mental-hospital system that we see occurring in the mental hospitalization of noncriminals.

A further implication is that the economic downturn may have similar effects upon the treatment of criminals in prisons and other correctional institutions. If during an economic downturn only a minority of psychiatrically disturbed criminals are mentally hospitalized, then a far larger group would presumably be entering a prison. Thus, while their psychiatrically defined counterparts were causing changes in mental-hospital administrative procedures, an untold number of criminally defined mentally ill persons would presumably exert a similar impact upon prison administrations.

Data presented in the present study also indicate that admissions to private hospitals follow a very similar pattern of relation to economic change to that of state hospital admissions. And although the private hospital may not initially be as overcrowded as the state facility, it may be that the effect of greatly increased admissions during the economic downturn has significant consequences for psychiatric care in private institutions. In fact, it is possible that the impact of such a change in admissions may be far more serious for the private patient, since the private hospital would presumably provide considerably higher quality of care and closer attention to the needs of individual patients. In other words, since so much of psychiatric care in the state hospital is custodial, it may be that the state-hospital patients lose far less in terms of an untimely discharge and the experience of instability in their relations with staff and other patients than they would if they were receiving intensive therapy in a private facility.

Finally, and perhaps most important, we should consider the implications of two long-range trends that appear to be converging in hospital psychiatry. One is the increasing sensitivity of the population to economic change in terms of psychiatric hospitalization, and the other is the continued impact of the mental-health movement in bringing increasingly larger numbers of socially defined deviants within the spectrum of psychiatric care. The present study would suggest that the interaction of these two trends would exacerbate the impact of economic change upon patient care and, ultimately, upon the resumption of a normal life style by persons who become involved in the psychiatric-care system. Perhaps the logical extension of the tendency inherent in the convergence of these two trends would be that certain social correlates of economic change eventually come to dominate patterns of psychiatric care and rehabilitation. Such social forces would operate with little regard to the requirements of individual patients or the capabilities of the administrative staff.

Thus far we have been considering the effect of economic change upon the institutional care of mentally disturbed persons. It was suggested that social deviance of the sort that is viewed as irrational may result in arrest and imprisonment if the acts involve transgressing a specific law. Similar behavior may result in psychiatric care if the deviant acts are thought not to be under the control of the individual involved. However, we have not as yet considered the relation between economic change and psychiatric illness that may have substantial physiological involvement. Some of the illnesses traditionally thought to be affected by mental stress are heart disease, ulcers of the stomach and duodenum, ulcerative colitis, asthma, and allergic reactions.[14] Furthermore, it is entirely possible that an even larger number of illnesses are precipitated, or exacerbated, by mental stresses. The implication is that economic downturns may be related to increased utilization not only of psychiatric services and perhaps imprisonment, but also of general inpatient and outpatient hospital services.

The present study has also indicated that psychiatric hospitalization of persons diagnosed as having psychosis with alcoholism increases sharply during economic downturns and decreases during upturns. One possible inference is that the incidence of alcoholic addiction similarly increases sharply during downturns and decreases during upturns. It is also possible that the incidence of addiction in general, perhaps even of narcotics addiction, is inversely related to changes in the economy. If, in general, addiction were inversely related to economic change, then admissions to treatment centers that serve alcoholic and narcotic addicts, as well as the imprisonment of addicts, might increase sharply during economic downturns and decrease during upturns.

In summary, then, one major implication of economic instability may be increase in many different types of social deviance as well as physical illness and it may thereby stimulate the development and expansion of corrective and rehabilitative industries and organizations. Thus, from the perspective of the society as a whole, the decline of economic institutions may in turn be responsible for the growth of industries and institutions that are designed to deal with a wide variety of related social problems.

11 Conclusions and Implications

In Chapter 9 we proposed and examined various mechanisms whereby mental hospitalization could be increased through economic change. These mechanisms included possible increases in (1) intolerance of mental illness, (2) development of psychiatric symptoms, and (3) the use of the mental hospital as an almshouse. At that point it was concluded that any or all of these mechanisms might in some way be responsible for mental hospitalization. It was found, however, that for many population groups probably neither intolerance of mental illness nor the need for the material necessities of life was the *primary* factor intervening between economic change and mental hospitalization. It was therefore suggested that fluctuations in pathological behavior in the population at risk might in many cases be a major, if not *the* major, intervening variable. In any case, it appears that both the presence of psychiatric symptoms and intolerance of these symptoms are necessary components in hospitalization, and both of these inferences are consistent with prevailing theory and research evidence bearing on mental illness and psychiatric hospitalization.

Social and Personality Disorganization During Economic Change

At this juncture, it might be useful to speculate on the implications of various interpretations of the findings. Two interpretations of the data that do not require great imagination are simply that economic change has a substantial impact on psychiatry as an institution and on the lives of persons who eventually become mentally hospitalized. The data of this study consistently indicate that, historically, the role of psychiatry as an institution has been intimately tied to dislocations in the economic system.

This is a very different perspective on psychiatry from the one that is frequently seen in popular and even in professional literature. A common image is that of a face-to-face relation between a clinician and a distraught individual whose emotional and intellectual personality development is largely responsible for his mental disorder. This study, by contrast, emphasizes the institutional aspect of psychiatry and offers the view that psychiatry is an arm of the social system which has been called upon largely to assist in patching up ruptures resulting from poor economic and social integration. In this sense, psychiatry is seen as having a large-scale structure analogous to that of the economy itself.

Such a structure is, of course, an abstraction, asis the concept of the national economy as a system. Much as the economy is highly organized in terms of industries and occupations, the mentally ill have historically been cared for (for the most part) in large-scale organizations and with the participation of psychiatrists and other clinicians loosely allied to such organizations. Moreover, psychiatry is organized through professional associations and through the training of professionals in schools of medicine and allied clinical institutions and settings.

It is interesting, however, that the clinicians who are involved in psychiatric care, in the United States in particular, operate under a set of values and beliefs that are probably antithetical to the perspective of this study. The data shown here clearly portray psychiatry historically as an agent of social repair, whereas traditionally the strategies of psychiatric care have, theoretically, been largely irrelevant to large-scale societal disequilibria.

Moreover, psychiatric care has traditionally not been focused even on major *individual* problems other than the disorder itself. The underlying theory is that the source of mental disorder lies not within the network of an individual's relations, but within the individual himself. We thus find responsibility for the disorder placed on the irrational and largely unconscious activities of the individual in whom it is observed. This assumption, that it is reasonable as well as possible to treat the individual's disorder apart from becoming involved in the social context in which it is enmeshed, may be debated on the ground that the disorder itself may largely depend on *continuing* interactions in which the individual is involved.

However, there is now a substantial accumulation of research evidence which indicates that the development of psychotic patterns of behavior and schizophrenic patterns in particular, may occur through familial patterns of interaction.[1] Presented with a dynamic model of this sort, it becomes difficult for the independent observer to ascertain which of several family members may be most "sick." In fact, it might require an unusually severe set of precipitating stresses to bring about the classical pattern of disturbed intellectual or emotional functioning in any one of these family members.

Given data such as those found in this study, questions may be raised as to the relative effectiveness and appropriateness of much of traditional psychiatric practice. It appears from this study that many of the major reasons for psychiatric hospitalization—the most prominent modality of psychiatric treatment of severe mental illness—have to do with disruption of the social ties of individuals; furthermore, these disruptions are not initially under the control of, or in any way due to, the behavior of the individuals in question. The probability is quite strong that the person who becomes psychiatrically hospitalized is reacting to social changes affecting not only his own immediate style of life, but those of many other people as well. The needs of such persons probably encompass far more than has been traditionally considered the province of psychiatric care.

It is even possible that, in a substantial fraction of cases, psychiatric care may not be necessary in order to alleviate what were initially problems related to large- or small-scale social change. This possibility may present itself in at least two ways. First, once the problems of social disruption are dealt with, it is possible either that the individual will cease to react symptomatically or that the family might be better able emotionally to cope with his disorder. Second, it is possible that once the major social stresses have been moderated the individual may be better able to tolerate his own disorder and therefore, in fact, *be* less sick, that is, feel less uncomfortable with his own feelings and thoughts.

This view of the social processes by which mental illness may become more or less of a severe problem points to the potential importance of the clinician's ability to affect the social situation in which he finds his patient. It also suggests that the clinician ideally ought to be able to exert some control over the flow of social stresses that continuously disrupt his patients' social relations. The traditional psychiatric approach, however, does not focus on problems of social interaction or on the implications of social or economic change.

The fact that the psychiatric professions have traditionally not been able to deal with the major stresses which lead to mental hospitalization may simply be one way of referring to mental hospitalization as a social problem. However, hospitalization is not only a psychiatrically inappropriate response to economic stress; it actually compounds the social impact of economic stress enormously. Under conditions of economic stress, mental hospitalization represents the culmination of a process of disruption and disintegration of family and other close relations. It closes off and isolates an individual from his normal social context, placing him in a situation in which the focus of his life consists of adaptation to the routine of a highly bureaucratic organization.

The needs of the hospital as an organization, in turn, frequently bear little relation to the needs of the hospitalized patient in terms of his adjustment to social life. The image of the mental hospital as a place of confinement, rather than of readjustment, of the patient is partly responsible for the development of the community mental-health-center model which includes forms of psychiatric treatment that are fundamentally integrated with community life.

Within the scheme of mental hospitalization, the patient's economic and social careers can be very seriously damaged. There is not only immediate disruption of his career itself, which removes the patient from his usual socioeconomic matrix, but, more important, there may be a lasting impression of the former patient as a relatively high risk for potentially severe mental disorder, which may disqualify him from a position that has even a modest level of responsibility attached to it. In addition, there is evidence that removal of an individual from a specific social group, such as friends or family, changes the structure and functioning of the group so that it may be quite difficult to reintegrate him into such a group.[2] The overall economic and social disruption brought about by economic stress may thus be greatly compounded by the intervention of hospitalization or another isolating experience.

Aside from examining the implications of economic change for the operation of psychiatry as a therapeutic endeavor, or for hospitalization in particular, we are interested in exploring some of the rather diffuse, but more socially pervasive, implications of economic stress. Two somewhat related concepts that describe disruptive characteristics of mental hospitalization are "pathology" and "social disintegration." Pathology refers especially to individual personality disorganization, whereas social disintegration implies breakdown in the functioning of the structure of social groups. It is entirely possible that personality disorganization rarely occurs except under conditions of social disorganization. The reverse may also be true, that is, there may be social structural decay only under conditions of personality disorganization. The two phenomena can, however, be separately investigated, and they have somewhat different implications.

For example, in the intensive examination of violent crimes among specific individuals, we may discover patterns of individual psychopathology or a disturbance in personality integration. If, on the other hand, we compare *rates* of violent crimes among various populations, we would probably not say that the population showing the highest rates was necessarily the most pathological, although we might wish to describe it as the least well integrated. In common parlance, "pathological" is a term that is most closely identified with unusual and probably severe social disruption, especially behavior for which a person may be criminally liable. Social disintegration, on the other hand, ordinarily refers to the more commonplace, and less precipitous, breakdown in cultural, political, institutional, or family systems.

The findings of this study raise the possibility that, for a substantial portion of the mentally hospitalized population, a primary reaction to economic stress occurs in the form of psychiatric symptoms. If this inference is correct, then it is probably true that other indicators of psychopathology would increase in the population at large during periods of economic stress. The data of this study on hospitalization of the criminally insane appear to substantiate this speculation. Admissions to hospitals for the criminally insane are as closely related (inversely) to economic change as are admissions to state or private psychiatric hospitals. Is is only recently, however, that we have routinely begun to define and treat as psychiatrically ill a considerable number of persons judged to have committed crimes.

Nevertheless, the implication is that criminal behavior generally, and crimes against persons in particular, may respond as sharply to economic change as does mental hospitalization. There does appear to be some evidence supporting this hypothesis among scattered reports published during the last century.[3] Realistically, then, both the mental hospital and the prison might be considered agents of social control that are brought into play particularly during periods of economic disruption. On an institutional level, in fact, we might expect to see that the administration of the prison behaves very much like that of the mental hospital during economic changes.

Again, there is considerable evidence of an inverse relation between mortality from suicide and economic change.[4] Suicide is another example of an act that is frequently thought to be fundamentally psychopathological or, at least, to be a symptom of an underlying pathological condition. Moreover, in the case of suicide there are some studies that show very similar relations with economic change (in terms of age and sex) to the ones found in the present study of mental-hospital admissions. In fact, one of the major hypotheses of the present study—that the pattern of hospital admissions of higher socioeconomic groups would be more directly related to economic changes than those of lower socioeconomic groups—is drawn from studies of suicide in the United States.

Although we may consider relatively high rates of criminal behavior or suicide as unusually strong evidence of the lack of social integration, the concept of social integration is perhaps more directly understood as the overall cohesiveness of social ties. Similarly, whereas mental hospitalization provides a strong inferential indication of disruption in social relations, we do not have first-hand evidence of dramatic changes in the structure of families or friendships that might be assumed to have preceded hospitalization. In fact, it may be true that economic change can bring about mental hospitalization only as the conclusion of a lengthy causal chain of breakdowns in social relations.

Yet for most of the population that experiences economic stress, mental hospitalization is not an outcome. The implication may be that large-scale social disintegration nearly always produces some mental hospitalization. And finally, in speaking of mental hospitalization as one indicator of social disintegration, we imply that there are probably a number of such indicators of breakdown in family and other social relations that are the consequences of economic stress.

Implications of the Empirical Relation

Social Class and Mental Illness

Despite the fact that this study deals largely with relatively short-term (1–10-year) economic changes, for a large fraction of the patient population mental hospitalization is related to such economic change. This suggests that the most disruptive of economic changes—especially those that tend to be associated with mental hospitalization—occur at relatively short intervals. The significant losses in jobs or income on the part of persons who soon thereafter become mentally hospitalized is, for the most part, attributable to short-term changes in the economic structure rather than to long-term technological changes, or to individual crises, which may result in decreased effectiveness on the job.

This inference may shed some light on a long-standing controversy in the field of psychiatric epidemiology. Perhaps the most consistent finding in this field is that the prevalence of mental disorder (treated or untreated) is inversely related to socioeconomic status. Two alternative theories have attempted to explain these findings. The life-stress theory argues that more stressful life circumstances are to be found as one approaches the lower end of the social structure, and that therefore the greatest prevalence of mental illness is found among the lower socioeconomic levels of the population.[5] On the other hand, the downward-drift hypothesis argues that the mentally ill (1) are less effective workers, (2) drift downward in social position as a consequence of their relative incompetence, and (3) finally accumulate over time at the lower end of the social structure.[6]

Although there is some factual support for these apparently contradictory positions, evidence from this study suggests that both points of view may be partially correct. First of all, it is probably not true that persons who become mentally hospitalized as a result of downward economic mobility usually do so because of their own incompetence. The present study indicates that large-scale economic changes are, mainly, responsible for such downward mobility. It is also a fact that economic instability, in terms of exposure to disruptive changes in the economic system, is much more a fact of life among lower socioeconomic groups.

Thus, stresses brought about by large-scale economic change are likely to fall most heavily on those in lower socioeconomic strata. The lowest socioeconomic groups may, for this reason, show the highest rates of mental hospitalization (and perhaps of mental disorder as well). On the other hand, it is entirely possible that persons with a history of psychiatric disturbance may, because of lower effectiveness as workers, find that they become the first victims of an economic downturn. These people, along with those whose job skills are not in great demand, may be among the first groups to lose employment from firms experiencing an economic slump.

Continuity of the Relation for 127 Years

The relation between economic change and mental hospitalization has been observed to occur for longer than a century and a quarter despite significant long- and short-term social changes in the lives of the population at risk. Some of the large-scale social changes that may have affected the relative impact of economic change on mental hospitalization are: (1) changes in the long-term characteristics of economic change, (2) changes in methods of dealing with economic and social disintegration, (3) changes in ethnic, socioeconomic, and age characteristics of patients, (4) changes in social definitions of mental illness, (5) changes in methods of psychiatric therapy, and (6) changes in the capacity of mental hospitals to admit specific categories of patients. The implication is that, despite such changes, the fundamental mechanisms underlying our basic relation have probably continued to exist over the entire period under study.

This implies, in addition, that though such extrinsic social changes may occasionally be important in explaining the level of mental hospitalization, they probably exert their influence *in conjunction with* economic change. In fact, it is likely that such factors have some bearing on the relative magnitude of the impact of economic change on mental hospitalization. It is possible, for example, that the continued breakdown in the structure of ethnic kinship groups, and the consequent emergence of the nuclear family as the more prevalent family structure, has some bearing on the degree to which the mental disorders of older persons are tolerated in the family. If it is customary to maintain the older parents of the husband or wife in the family, then it might be less likely that older persons will be abandoned during periods of economic crisis.

There is some evidence to suggest that, in general, family structure may be moving in a long-term trend of decreased cohesion; note the rising trend in divorce rates, for example. Such a long-term decrease in family cohesion may have a pervasive effect on the degree to which economic stress will result in family disintegration, and may be related to an increasing trend of responsiveness of mental hospitalization to economic change.

It is interesting that for the period 1910–1960 more than two-thirds of the mentally hospitalized population in New York State were either foreign born or of foreign parentage. Several factors may underlie this finding. First, it is possible that the relatively large fraction of foreign born simply reflects a large fraction of foreign born in the New York State population. It is also possible that this finding results from a relatively high percentage of persons of relatively low socioeconomic status. In either case, however, it is possible that a substantial change in patterns of immigration may result in a dramatic change in the ethnic character of the patient population. Such a change may come about in a number of ways, including (1) change in the economic stability of the population, (2) change in the economic and social aspirations of the population, (3) change in the familiarity of the population with American institutions in general, or with psychiatric services in particular, and (4) change in the degree to which the population utilizes family and other kinship or ethnic-related methods of control and nurturance of the mentally ill.

Migrant populations are theoretically less economically stable than native populations. The reasons include difficulties in adapting economically to a new country of residence and the likelihood that the immigrants will be lower on the economic ladder than the native population.[7] Relatively low economic status places the immigrant in the position of being more expendable to a business enterprise during periods of economic decline. In addition, the immigrant population is to some extent likely to have different economic and social aspirations from the native population.

These differences in aspirations may be compounded by others that reflect low socioeconomic status. Depending on the group involved, the unusual aspirations may involve either increased or decreased concern for economic achievement or social advancement. Also, it is possible that low levels of cultural integration may be responsible for the discrepancies in patterns of values that relate to achievement. A relative lack of cultural integration may likewise have the effect of decreasing participation in the life of American institutions, including, perhaps, medicine and psychiatry. Possibly most important, however, is the degree to which the immigrant ethnic group depends upon alternative institutions of its own to deal with psychiatric illness, including particularly the family and the church.

Some of the same kinds of cultural change that are introduced to foreign ethnic populations may arise among native groups of different socioeconomic status. For example, changes in the occupational or social class structure of the population, such as have been continuously occurring with long-term increases in the average level of educational attainment, are likely to lead to changes in perspectives on, and understanding of, psychiatry. Thus, although the overall distribution of persons among different socioeconomic strata of the population may change slowly, the intellectual sophistication of each group may increase relatively rapidly owing to pressures for increased education brought about by technological change. Long-term changes in the structure of society may therefore lead to increased utilization of mental hospitals, for at least two reasons. On the one hand, contact with psychiatry might increase on account of sophistication of the population with regard to psychiatric methods; on the other hand, hospitalization may increase because persons with relatively low levels of education find it increasingly difficult to maintain a stable and integrated position in an economy of rapid technological advancement. The problem of the relatively poor economic integration of the poorly educated in a highly industrialized society is certainly not confined to young persons who never managed to complete professional or even formal education. It is perhaps just as serious for the older worker whose formal education and job training may lag many years behind modern educational requirements for an economically stable position.

Many retired persons, of course, are at present in an even more precarious economic situation because their fixed incomes shrink steadily with increasing inflation. Significant increases in the fraction of older workers or elderly persons in the population, as a result of the increasing life span in industrial societies, may therefore have the effect of increasing the utilization of psychiatric services because of the increasing vulnerability of the older person to economic stress.

Underlying the recent changes related to economic growth, a shift has occurred in the emphasis of intellectual discussion about the American economy in the last 25 years. The once dominant concept of cyclical change has been superseded by that of technological change. This shift in emphasis has been especially significant in labor economics and in disciplines that involve the measurement and prediction of fluctuation in economic indicators.

In econometrics, the concept of the business cycle has diminished in stylishness, and many of the techniques employed to measure short-term aggregate business fluctuations over the past 50 years are no longer used with much consistency. Techniques developed by the National Bureau of Economic Research,[8] which were once standard in the literature of economic measurement, seem now to be used infrequently. Similarly, the discussion of cyclical unemployment has changed to that of technological unemployment. These changes in emphasis probably reflect new problems arising from actual long-term changes in the structure of the economy and the pattern of economic growth.

Within the last 25 years, economic growth in the United States has appeared to be much smoother—that is, to consist of fewer severe upturns and downturns—than during the previous 50 years. This change may reflect a keener understanding on the part of business organizations of methods of controlling the demand for goods and services through market research and advertising. It may be that business concerns are also better able to capitalize on these more predictable demand factors. It is also possible that the Keynesian monetary and fiscal methods of manipulating the economy under governmental auspices have damped the amplitudes of the trade cycle.

Another long-term possibility is that the business cycle is still very much with us, but has become less important than longer-term economic growth because of changes in technology itself, perhaps particularly in the growth of computer-related industries. Another, but less optimistic, possibility is that the long-term economic growth pattern over the past 20 years in particular signifies a general lengthening of the business cycle.

It is clear, however, that the major concern of government and academic experts on the deleterious social consequences of economic change now seem to be focused on the problems of the unskilled, racial minorities, and older workers. Perhaps these groups are simply less able to adapt to the more rapid technological changes that are continually on the increase in the American economy. These people may present the most severe economic problems because the discrepancies between their incomes and those of other groups are reflected in more serious health and social problems. The problem is further complicated by the fact that such groups may suffer calamitously during periods of relatively mild fluctuation in business activity and employment. They are at times the only major groups that lose in terms of income and employment opportunities during periods when the economy generally exhibits dramatic evidence of long-term growth.

One of the more interesting and important sociological and economic features of an economy dominated by cyclical change is that relatively large fractions of the population gain or lose income and employment at approximately the same time, depending upon whether an economic upturn or a downturn is in progress. Very different social implications are probably in evidence during periods when significant components of the population gain or lose economic status at somewhat different times. The latter situation has apparently dominated economic activity during the last 25 years in the United States. This situation is characterized by overall economic growth with smaller cyclical movements superimposed. During such a period, most of the population is experiencing real economic advancement, while a minority absorbs the impact of economic instability.

When an individual loses economic status during a period of general economic advance, we may imagine that the psychosocial effect on him is far more extreme than when other persons, in a similar industry (and perhaps even a similar occupation), are also subject to economic loss. Data from the present study bear directly on this point. During the depression of the 1930's, for example, the increase in mental hospitalization was not as great as it has been during almost any other economic downturn since 1920. The reason for this curious finding may be that a very large number of persons lost income and employment at about the same time, particularly within similar industries and occupations. It may be generally true, then, that the more an individual feels that he is among a minority of the economically disadvantaged, or the closer he comes to feeling singled out by economic loss, the more likely he is to see the economic failure as a personal failure, one due to his own incompetence.

This may be a particularly acute problem for members of distinct ethnic groups who are rapidly becoming integrated into the economy. In the process of upward mobility, attitudes tend to change toward the belief that such movement is at least possible and perhaps even to be expected. Thus, a myth of total economic discrimination might be replaced by one of unlimited opportunity. It may be true that, under conditions of rapid upward mobility for members of a specific ethnic group, the group as a whole shows relative economic gains in comparison with the general population. Nevertheless, there will be some, and perhaps many, members of the same ethnic groups who lag substantially behind the economic progress of the group as a whole. During an economic downturn, those group members who actually regress in their economic and social position might feel under particularly severe stress, because now they are expected not only to achieve some gains in comparison with the population at large, but to achieve at least as much as other members of their own ethnic group. This argument need not be confined to ethnic groups per se, and may in fact extend to older workers, female workers, and workers in specific industries that have experienced extraordinarily rapid growth.

Changes in the structure of economic instability, from cyclical change to technologically based long-term change, are reflected in parallel changes in approach by economic and social welfare organizations that deal with problems of economic dislocation. A shift in emphasis has occurred from the approach of private charitable organizations that looked after the poor to substantial governmental efforts to provide security benefits for older persons and to distribute welfare funds to very poor families. Many of the large-scale efforts by federal, state, and local agencies to deal with unemployment and poverty were initiated during the Great Depression.[9] The distribution of welfare funds in particular reached massive proportions at that time and has continued to increase at moderate rates since then.

The data do not indicate that the relation between economic change and mental hospitalization has in any way diminished as a result of past efforts to deal with the economic problems of poverty. It should be pointed out, however, that this does not mean that these efforts have had no beneficial effects; the problem of mental hospitalization might have been far more severe had it not been for the effects of such programs as welfare, unemployment compensation, and social security. On the other hand, the efforts of public agencies to ameliorate economic adversity have become a general feature of American society during the last 30 years—a period during which the nation experienced sustained economic growth.

It is possible that merely the asking for and receiving of public funds during a period of general prosperity might bring feelings of unusual stigma and shame. For some, therefore, the procedure of becoming a recipient of public funds may be so severely stressful that it is sufficient to bring about significant family and personality disorganization, particularly after an earlier period of economic loss.

This is one of the ironic implications of governmental efforts to assist the person who suffers from severe economic problems while the overall culture places the highest premium on personal achievement and material success. In view of several competing hypotheses, it is difficult to know whether mechanisms of public compensation as a means of dealing with economic disorganization have either alleviated, or contributed to, the stresses that are generated by economic downturns.

Definitions of Mental Illness

Perhaps as potent for determining trends in mental hospitalization as changes in the structure of the economy, in methods of dealing with economic disintegration, or in the socioeconomic structure of the population are changes in the degree to which people are defined and treated as mentally ill. The decline in metaphysical and religious modes of identifying and treating mental disorder in the past century, and the concomitantly rapid growth of medical and psychological approaches to personality development and disorder, have led to long-term changes in the ways in which normal and abnormal behavior are perceived. Major changes in professional and popular thinking due to Freudian and more recent psychoanalytic conceptions have, possibly, had the overall effect of making us more sensitive to the presence of psychological disturbance.

On the one hand, the psychoanalytic school has attempted to make even the most bizarre psychosis somewhat intelligible, while on the other hand, the theme of psychopathology in everyday life has become a most persuasive framework for interpreting behavior. The psychoanalytic approach to the interpretation of behavior, on the basis of psychosexual development, has been employed in attempts to comprehend the behavior of criminals, mildly neurotic middle-aged housewives, political assassins, aggressive industrial managers, and youthful rebels.

Quite distinct from psychoanalytic conceptions of human motivation, psychiatry as a profession has come to assume the role of "healer of the unhappy." It is apparent that we have come to see unhappiness itself as something to be treated by psychotherapy or medicine. The enormous scope of modern-day psychiatry and clinical psychology even encompasses political disaffection (or "alienation" as it is sometimes called). Perhaps this has happened because a medical priesthood has replaced the religious priesthood that had been responsible for maintaining the values and order of a theocratic society. We now turn to the physician, the new healer of society, as one who is knowledgable in the ways of science, rather than in those of divine intervention, in the hope of dealing with every conceivable human affliction. This being the case, we might expect that, during periods of economic stress, ever-increasing numbers of persons would seek psychiatric help, and many of those would ultimately be found in hospitals.

This phenomenon of the physician coming to assume the major emotional burdens of society may have increased significantly within the last 15 years as a result of the mental-health movement.[10] In addition to frequent large-scale advertising campaigns to foster public understanding of mental disorder and ways of treating it, the mental-health movement may intentionally or unintentionally have contributed to the appearance of mental illness by helping people to identify disturbed behavior among their associates. In the last few years in particular, publicity given to epidemiological findings of astonishingly high levels of untreated mental disorder in the community[11] have probably led to increased efforts to bring psychiatry closer to the community, especially by way of the community mental-health center. The establishment of such centers and clinics has doubtless made psychiatry less awesome and more acceptable to a society that is perhaps more ready to call upon it during periods of even minor social stress.

Implications of Theoretical Interpretations

The inverse relation between economic change and mental hospitalization can be interpreted in at least two ways: (1) economic downturns bring about increases in psychiatric symptoms, and (2) economic downturns bring about increases in intolerance of mental illness.

From some perspectives, it appears impossible to distinguish the presence of mental illness from the intolerance of it. First, there would probably be little argument over the statement that mental illness exists to the extent that the society defines certain forms of behavior as due to mental illness. If, during economic downturns, certain types of deviance should be less well tolerated, the society may be more likely to perceive the presence of mental illness during those times. Conversely, if the mental disturbance is initially present without being defined as mental disorder, then it will be perceived and dealt with as another phenomenon—perhaps regarded as temporary aggression or melancholy, or even as a normal response to extraordinary stress.

Second, the kind of intolerance that implies rejection of, or aggression against, a member of the family or a close friend may itself be regarded as a symptom. It is not necessarily true[12] that the family member who is regarded as the most severely mentally ill will be the one who is eventually hospitalized. In fact, it is entirely possible that several members of the family have disturbed personality structures, and that the one who is most seriously disturbed may be instrumental in bringing about the hospitalization of another. Finally, there is the possibility that the *feeling* of being mentally ill, which might be taken to be a primary symptom, may be a result of relative intolerance of his own condition by the disturbed individual.

One of the major differences between the positions that economic change brings about either symptoms or intolerance is that, whereas the presence of symptoms is defined as an individual phenomenon, intolerance is usually thought of as taking place within a social context. The essential analytical difficulty in distinguishing development of symptoms from intolerance is that both of these concepts can be defined as either individual or social phenomena. As a matter of fact, mental illness itself can be defined as a breakdown in the norms of a social group. Mental illness is therefore both deviance for a group and, certainly, disturbance of an individual's personality. To complicate matters even further, the present study has demonstrated the likelihood that economic downturns bring about increases in both intolerance of mental illness and psychiatric symptoms. The use of different intellectual traditions in discussing this problem leads us to expand upon various types of implications that grow out of each interpretation.

If we discuss breakdown in the structure of social groups during economic downturns as individual behavior, we would perhaps be more likely to speculate whether other individual pathological behaviors are also likely to occur, such as suicide, homicide, and assault, or psychophysiological illness, such as asthma, ulcers, and colitis. In general, we are likely to think of political changes as relatively ordinary manifestation of disenchantment. However, in reality we find many types of "ordinary" disruptive behavior occurring in reaction to economic change—individualized reactions, social movements, and highly organized forms of political change, including changes of government and wars in which entire nations are mobilized.

It is instructive in this regard to compare the approaches taken by legal philosophers, clinicians, and social scientists to the problem of the collapse of democracy in Germany after the depression of the 1930's. From a moral-legal standpoint, the behavior of many members of the Nazi party is classifiable as crimes; one therefore imputes a predominance of rationality to these acts. The clinical approach, on the other hand, might discuss the leadership of the Nazi government, as well as a great part of the German masses, as psychoneurotic if not occasionally psychotic—in which case the legal mind would, logically, exonerate them of any criminal charges on grounds of nonresponsibility.

Finally, we have the morally relativistic position of the social scientist, who might take the value systems of different societies as sacred givens. Deviance is then understood as departure from societal norms at any particular time; for example, persons who were not sympathetic to the Nazi government were deviant. However, regardless of which intellectual discipline one subscribes to, the reality is that various types of bizarre behavior occurred in Nazi Germany, some more highly organized than others. Furthermore, there is little difficulty in identifying instances of both individually and socially bizarre behavior. Our moral position regarding these behaviors is an indication of our own judgment as to the deviant character of such acts.

A question raised by the findings of this study is whether such instances of deviance might have had anything to do with changes in the economic position of a large part of the German population as a result of the depression and subsequent economic changes. At this point, we can only speculate on the usefulness of making inferences from this type of study in order to shed light on a situation that involves a different cultural and political context. Such speculations do point to some of the logical implications of interpreting the relation between economic change and treated mental illness in accordance with a specified perspective. It was pointed out earlier that there are a group of scattered research reports indicating relations between economic change and suicide, homicide, and crime in general. These reports have yet to be corroborated by more highly refined research procedures, yet they would suggest many of the same general interpretations as do the findings of the present study.

If we take the point of view that persons who become mentally hospitalized, like those who commit various crimes against persons or property, are deviants with respect to behavior that is regarded as normal for the society, then we may find that research findings in the area of deviant behavior in general may provide us with additional insights into the relation between economic change and mental hospitalization. Probably the most consistent finding in the epidemiology of mental disorders is that the prevalence of treated and untreated psychopathology is inversely related to socioeconomic level.[13] It is also true that the prevalence of many forms of deviant and socially disintegrative behavior other than mental illness are inversely related to socioeconomic status, including criminal behavior generally, alcoholism, use of drugs, the breakup of families, and illegitimacy.[14]

Is it possible that the socially disruptive mechanisms which are involved in the relation between economic change and mental hospitalization are also implicated in many other types of deviant behavior? Earlier in this chapter, we speculated that the fact that mental hospitalization is inversely related to economic change might, to a significant degree, be responsible for the inverse relation between socioeconomic status and mental illness.

This same argument can be applied to other forms of deviant behavior. It may be that, in general, economic instability (a major producer of social disintegration) has its most damaging impact on the lowest socioeconomic strata. In that case, there would be an inverse relation between the stress of economic change, causing social disintegration, and socioeconomic status. At least four different mechanisms might underly this postulated inverse relation: (1) greater stability of high-level economic positions, (2) greater ability of persons at higher socioeconomic levels to acquire new positions in the event of economic crisis, (3) greater material resources of higher socioeconomic groups to withstand economic stress, and (4) greater emotional, or integrative, resources of higher socioeconomic groups in the event of economic stress.

One might, at first glance, imagine that persons at higher socioeconomic levels are to be found in economic positions of greater stability, that is, positions that are less sensitive to economic changes. This argument is usually stated in converse form, namely, that occupants of economic positions which require relatively low levels of skills, technical mastery or comprehension, or administrative responsibility are generally more expendable to an economic organization than persons in positions of higher status. Persons who enjoy positions of higher status not only are more valuable to the organizations that employ them, but would probably also be of greater value to other organizations in the same or in a similar industry. Thus, the person in a position of higher economic status is probably better able to acquire a new job during a decline in his organization's economic activities.

Second, there is strong evidence which indicates that persons in higher socioeconomic strata have more extensive informal social relations and belong to more formal and informal organizations apart from their primary economic positions.[15] It is therefore possible that the greater number of social contacts available to persons who occupy positions of higher socioeconomic rank may provide them with greater access to information about newly available economic opportunities. Third, as is true by definition, persons of higher socioeconomic status possess in greater measure the material resources necessary to cope with economic stress. Put simply, persons in higher socioeconomic positions can rely on a greater accumulation of wealth, which would allow for economic maintenance in times of crisis. Fourth, families in higher socioeconomic strata tend to be better integrated and more cohesive.[16] These families should therefore be more tolerant and nurturant of members who exhibit deviant behavior that might otherwise seriously strain family relations.

The reader, no doubt, will be able to suggest many more interpretations and implications of the basic inverse relation between economic change and mental hospitalization. This is partly because economic change, the central independent variable, is a feature of nearly all forms of either rapid or evolutionary social change. In view of the many studies that have shown inverse relations between socioeconomic status and mental illness, and in view of the great interest, if not concern, we have had with social change for some time, it may seem curious that prior to this study only scanty research has been done on the possible relation between economic change and mental hospitalization. Moreover, in view of the fact that the strong inverse relation between economic change and mental hospitalization has been with us for at least 127 years, one might ask why we have not had a large number of reports, perhaps from patients or clinicians, or even from hospital administrators, to the effect that such a relation might exist. One wonders, in sum, how the very close relations found in the present study could not have been revealed or even strongly suggested during the previous century and a quarter.

Recent Discovery of the Major Relation

Among the many possible reasons why the major relation reported in this study had not been suggested earlier, the following seem most important: (1) the complexity of the causal chain of events in the relation, (2) statistical problems in finding and measuring the relation, (3) the conception of mental hospitalization as an individual problem that is unrelated to social trends, and (4) the conception of economic success and failure as, similarly, an individual problem that can be understood without considering society-wide economic changes.

Complexity of the Causal Sequence

The complexity of the causal relation between economic change and mental hospitalization probably represents the most serious barrier to the understanding and intellectual credibility of the relation. The difficulty is initially raised by the fact that economic changes in the lives of individuals are not usually pointed to by clinicians as being of paramount significance either in their patients' illnesses or in their entry into treatment. Moreover, studies of the relation between life stresses and psychiatric disorder point to economic factors as only one of many different types of stress that might influence the course of psychiatric illness. Yet at the same time we find that in New York State, for over 127 years, economic changes are probably the single most important cause of mental hospitalization. What has been only partially understood, or even explored, however, is the relation between life stresses in general and economic changes in particular. Traditionally, it has been easier to understand the relation between economic status, on a static basis, and life stress. And there is indeed an extensive literature on the disproportionate distribution of health problems, family problems, and economic problems which is inverse to socioeconomic level.[17]

It is not an inordinate logical jump from the statistical relation between socioeconomic status and life stress to a dynamic model: as individuals move downward in socioeconomic status, their life stresses will increase. It should be pointed out that this extrapolation to a dynamic model from the static conception is made despite the finding of the Midtown Manhattan Study that the absolute number of individual life problems did not vary significantly among persons of different socioeconomic backgrounds.[18] This finding, however, appeared to contradict the most prominent group of findings reported by the same study: the prevalence and severity of mental disorder are (1) proportionately greater in lower socioeconomic strata and (2) directly related to the number of life problems experienced. Apart from the serious possibility of differential perception of the number of life stresses among different socioeconomic strata, and apart from the fact that the number of gratifications in life may be proportionately higher among the upper socioeconomic strata, groups with higher socioeconomic status are probably better able to cope with the stresses they experience than are lower socioeconomic groups.

The fact that higher socioeconomic groups possess greater material and emotional resources to deal with life problems may be one reason why we find indications that many types of social problems are more prevalent among lower socioeconomic groups. Perhaps an even more prominent factor in the greater instability of social life among lower socioeconomic strata is the greater instability of their economic life. This topic was discussed earlier in the present chapter and we need not repeat it here, except to point out that the dynamic model of the relation between economic and social instability has as yet been given little systematic study in the behavioral sciences.

The fact that economic change may bring about subsequent life stresses represents only one mechanism whereby economic stress might lead to mental hospitalization. Other mechanisms have been discussed in Chapter 9, including the possibility that economic stress may act as an additional "last-straw" factor, and that it may not act independently at all, but rather may aggravate many other life stresses. The absence of a well-understood model of the complex route by which economic stress may ultimately result in mental hospitalization is compounded by a traditional unicausal model of the historical process. In this model, either the most dramatic or the proximal precipitating factor is taken as the cause.

When, for example, a patient informs her clinician that *the* factor which precipitated her mental anguish was abandonment by her husband, neither the patient nor the clinician may be able to trace the cause of the ruptured marital relation to prior economic changes which may, in turn, have triggered the family breakdown. Or, even if both patient and clinician fully recognize the initiating impact of the economic stress, they still may view the ruptured relation as *the* precipitating factor. The problem here is that, by assuming a causal model that depends exclusively on a single cause, we exclude not only all other stress factors that may have occurred at the same time as the marital breakdown, but all factors that occurred prior to it and, most important, all factors that may have been basically responsible for the precipitating stresses. What this suggests, in addition, is that the clinical perspective may frequently overlook the relation among several interacting aspects of an individual's total social environment.

The various methodological and statistical problems that have traditionally haunted both trend analysis and psychiatric epidemiology have also been encountered in the present study. These problems involved: (1) the measurement of economic change, (2) the measurement of the relation between economic change and mental hospitalization, and (3) methods of controlling for many different long- and short-term social changes not intrinsically involved in the basic relation.

The Theme of Individualism

Perhaps the most important factors responsible for the relation between economic change and mental hospitalization that have not been reported earlier are those surrounding the theme of individualism in Western, and particularly American, intellectual and political life. The general cultural theme of individualism has had a pervasive impact on our understanding of both mental hospitalization and economic success and failure. Traditionally, it has been taken for granted that, since the mentally hospitalized patient is psychiatrically ill, mental hospitalization could be explained in accordance with prevailing theories of mental illness. These theories assumed that mental illness could be described within two broad categories, functional and organic. Until very recently, moreover, one or another unicausal model of mental illness was assumed to be operative. Under such models, mental disorder was thought to result from one specific agent of either a biochemical or a psychological nature. In both of these models, the broad social environment was largely ignored. Among the mental disorders that were attributed to organic (that is, nervous-system) damage, the proposed remedies were surgical or chemical, whereas among the functional illnesses efforts to alter personality structure were also used.

Even where psychotherapeutic methods of treatment were utilized, they usually relied upon theories of human behavior that were based on a perspective of individual psychology. Under the theme of individual psychology, even the major Freudian psychoanalytic writings came to be regarded as involving individual behavior as distinguished from what was thought of as social behavior. We need not dwell on the frequently unjustified critiques of Freudian psychology that base themselves on Freud's alleged disregard of the interpersonal foundations of personality development. The essential point is that there is a substantial intellectual tradition which has treated Freudian psychology as though it regarded the influences of cultures and social systems as irrelevant to the development of personality.[19] We may go so far as to say that since nearly all of the traditional psychotherapeutic techniques have as their aim the adjustment of the patient to the requirements and norms of society, the theories are individual-centered. By individual-centered we mean largely uninvolved with those changes that are initiated in the individual's social environment, which may have caused his failure to adjust to that environment.

The approach of individual psychology to the understanding of abnormal behavior is not peculiar to clinicians, but is probably the most prevalent viewpoint among the lay public (particularly within the United States). Among the general public, the occurrence of mental disorder is almost by definition an individual phenomenon which is unintelligible in social terms and is usually interpreted as irrational. Simply because mental illness connotes bizarreness to the general public, it must be viewed as an individual aberration.

The themes of individual psychology in clinical theory and mental disorder as individual abnormality may be closely related, however, to the theme of individualism that has been developed in Western, and especially American, culture. It is probably no accident, for example, that individual psychology has not predominated in the psychiatric practice of socialist countries.[20] For the general American public, the theme of individualism underlies concepts not only of just government but of an equitable legal system as well. Both the democratic process and much of the legal system are, to a great degree, founded on the philosophical concepts that include "free will." The free-will concept philosophically negates empirically based theories which argue that the behavior of an individual is strongly influenced by forces originating outside of himself.

Politically, free will has been used to justify the right of each individual to participate in the choice of his government on the ground that he exercises real choice—in other words, that he is free to exercise his choice. This freedom of choice is then distinguished from the procedures of dictatorial governments, in which the individual citizen submits blindly to those in authority. Similarly, the legal concept of criminality is grounded on the theological presupposition that individuals actually choose between right and wrong, and that it is not the society that influences them to choose one or the other, because, if society did provide the influences which determined that the individual should choose to engage in criminal behavior, then the society in general, and not the individual, would justifiedly be attacked. Thus, for any individual, the only alternative to the legal assumption of free will and implicit rationality is of course irrationality, and therefore insanity.

Elements of the same individualistic philosophy can early be seen in the thinking of many Americans about the economic success or failure of individuals. The assumption is that an individual succeeds or fails by his own talents, abilities, and efforts. Almost in the same conceptual terms of individual psychology, individual achievement is seen as the product of the personality. In other words, allegedly stable individual personality characteristics are deemed responsible for the individual's motivation and capability. But there is an equally important ideological element in the theme of individualism in economic life. The theme originates in the arguments that underlie the laissez-faire capitalism of such 19th-century political economists as John Stuart Mill.[21]

The theme was further developed under the influence of the social Darwinists who gave birth to notion of "rugged individualism."[22] This general philosophical theme of individualism in economic behavior has been somewhat attenuated by the introduction of social-welfare policies and governmental manipulation of the economy during the Great Depression and the post-Second World War periods. Despite the significant de-emphasis of individualism as a nationally proclaimed economic ideology, the theme of individual competence has not been replaced as the major perspective by which success or failure is judged.

The fact that ability to succeed in economic life is substantially determined by an individual's position in the social structure appears to contradict the American ideal of equality of opportunity. It is apparent that the clear and well-publicized fact that the social class (or socioeconomic position) of one's parents has an overwhelming influence on personality development and life chances in general has not been accepted. Instead, the ideology of the Protestant ethic continues to be perpetuated, even though the sense of urgency over achievement may have abated somewhat.[23]

Perhaps the heart of the problem is that, where large aggregations of individuals are not organized in common pursuit of an objective, the belief takes hold, buttressed by the individualistic perspective, that the behavior of these individuals is not subject to social influence. In other words, the conception of what is *social* tends to be defined as that which is *organized*. It is relatively easy to identify social movements, and frequently even riots, as social behavior, but the image of the individual working alone, or even within a small group, fails to take on a sociocultural appearance. What then remains is that there is little appreciation of the fact that human behavior is constantly influenced by the sociological characteristics of the individuals involved (such as their sex, age, occupation, education, ethnicity) and the social and cultural context in which the behavior takes place.

There may be certain gains for political democracy by a continuance of the ideology of individualism. However, it is difficult to imagine that there are long-range benefits to the political or legal systems of any modern nation in the illusion that individual personality and behavior are *not* intimately related to the culture and institutions of the overall society. In fact, as the present study has shown, it can be extremely harmful for the society not to recognize that instabilities in the economic system can have a substantially disruptive effect on many social institutions, including the family.

Finally, it is important that economic instability be understood not only in terms of major economic downturns such as depressions or recessions, but more generally as any departure from smooth economic development during which a significant number of people are excluded.

Appendixes
Notes
Index

Appendix I. Number of years during which specified levels of correlation occur between admissions to New York State civil state hospitals and the index of employment, New York State 1914–1960, by specific lags.

Trend Estimate used in Detrending	r (initial) = −0.85, r (nonautocorr.)[a] = −0.80					r (initial) = −0.80, r (nonautocorr.)[a] = −0.70					r (initial) = −0.70, r (nonautocorr.)[a] = −0.65				
	Lag = 0		Lag = 1		Combined[b]	Lag = 0		Lag = 1		Combined[b]	Lag = 0		Lag = 1		Combined[b]
	Yrs.	Spans	Yrs.	Spans	Yrs.	Yrs.	Spans	Yrs.	Spans	Yrs.	Yrs.	Spans	Yrs.	Spans	Yrs.
35–44 TFP[c] Female (47[d])															
None	39	(4)	23	(1)	42	39	(3)	26	(1)	44	43	(4)	35	(2)	44
Linear	21	(3)	15	(2)	30	29	(5)	19	(3)	34	38	(5)	24	(2)	40
Bestfit	19	(3)	13	(2)	30	28	(5)	18	(3)	30	35	(6)	28	(3)	42
Moving linear	0	(0)	0	(0)	16	28	(2)	0	(0)	34	35	(4)	23	(1)	37
45–54 TFP[c] Male (47[d])															
None	32	(2)	35	(4)	37	37	(3)	42	(4)	44	37	(3)	42	(5)	46
Linear	35	(4)	35	(3)	37	40	(4)	35	(3)	41	41	(1)	37	(3)	43
Bestfit	34	(2)	35	(4)	36	37	(4)	35	(3)	38	46	(3)	37	(3)	47
Moving linear	37	(1)	33	(3)	37	40	(1)	36	(1)	41	41	(1)	37	(1)	42
35–44 Female (47[d])															
None	35	(4)	25	(3)	41	45	(7)	29	(3)	47	46	(5)	31	(3)	47
Linear	35	(3)	21	(2)	35	35	(4)	28	(2)	36	38	(7)	41	(8)	41

	Col 1	Col 2	Col 3	Col 4	Col 5	Col 6	Col 7	Col 8
Linear	39 (4)	33 (3)	41 (3)	43 (5)	45 (5)	45 (3)	45 (4)	45 (3)
Bestfit	41 (4)	40 (5)	41 (5)	42 (6)	44 (6)	44 (3)	45 (6)	45 (3)
Moving linear	34 (2)	34 (1)	35 (1)	43 (2)	45 (2)	45 (3)	45 (3)	45 (3)
Marginal TFP[c] Male (40[d])								
None	38 (5)	37 (4)	38 (2)	40 (2)	39 (5)	40 (3)	40 (3)	40 (3)
Linear	36 (5)	28 (4)	36 (5)	40 (4)	34 (4)	40 (4)	39 (5)	40 (5)
Bestfit	36 (5)	28 (4)	36 (5)	40 (4)	34 (4)	40 (4)	39 (5)	40 (5)
Moving linear	31 (1)	25 (2)	35 (1)	39 (3)	31 (2)	39 (3)	35 (2)	40 (3)
Marginal TFP[c] Female (40[d])								
None	25 (1)	25 (2)	26 (2)	25 (1)	25 (1)	26 (1)	26 (1)	32 (1)
Linear	18 (2)	14 (2)	19 (3)	18 (4)	15 (3)	19 (3)	27 (3)	29 (3)
Bestfit	18 (2)	14 (2)	19 (3)	18 (4)	15 (3)	19 (3)	27 (4)	29 (3)
Moving linear	11 (1)	8 (1)	11 (1)	15 (2)	9 (1)	15 (1)	9 (3)	16 (1)
Marginal Male (40[d])								
None	38 (5)	32 (2)	38 (2)	38 (4)	37 (5)	38 (4)	40 (5)	40 (7)
Linear	38 (5)	35 (5)	38 (5)	40 (3)	38 (3)	40 (3)	40 (2)	40 (3)
Bestfit	32 (4)	27 (2)	32 (2)	34 (5)	31 (2)	35 (2)	35 (3)	37 (4)
Moving Linear	34 (2)	31 (1)	34 (1)	39 (2)	40 (2)	40 (2)	40 (2)	40 (2)
Marginal Female (40[d])								
None	25 (1)	26 (1)	26 (1)	25 (1)	26 (1)	26 (1)	26 (2)	26 (1)
Linear	17 (2)	19 (2)	20 (2)	19 (4)	21 (3)	21 (4)	30 (3)	30 (6)
Bestfit	17 (2)	19 (2)	20 (2)	19 (4)	21 (3)	21 (4)	30 (3)	30 (6)
Moving linear	0 (0)	11 (1)	11 (1)	6 (1)	11 (1)	16 (1)	13 (2)	16 (2)

Appendix I. (*continued*)

Trend Estimate used in Detrending	r (initial) = −0.85 r (nonautocorr.)[a] = −0.80					r (initial) = −0.80 r (nonautocorr.)[a] = −0.70					r (initial) = −0.70 r (nonautocorr.)[a] = −0.65				
	Lag = 0		Lag = 1		Combined[b]	Lag = 0		Lag = 1		Combined[b]	Lag = 0		Lag = 1		Combined[b]
	Yrs.	Spans	Yrs.	Spans	Yrs.	Yrs.	Spans	Yrs.	Spans	Yrs.	Yrs.	Spans	Yrs.	Spans	Yrs.
Negro TFP[c] Male (47[d])															
None	18	(1)	39	(3)	41	41	(2)	41	(3)	44	43	(4)	45	(3)	47
Linear	24	(2)	31	(3)	32	32	(2)	32	(2)	32	33	(3)	33	(3)	33
Bestfit	18	(1)	23	(2)	31	29	(2)	29	(3)	40	38	(4)	32	(4)	47
Moving linear	0	(0)	10	(1)	10	12	(1)	12	(1)	18	16	(1)	27	(3)	37
Negro TFP[c] Female (47[d])															
None	38	(2)	39	(2)	41	41	(2)	40	(3)	44	41	(2)	41	(2)	45
Linear	17	(1)	27	(3)	34	32	(2)	32	(3)	32	33	(3)	32	(2)	33
Bestfit	14	(1)	16	(1)	28	26	(2)	24	(3)	41	26	(5)	29	(2)	41
Moving linear	6	(1)	15	(1)	15	17	(2)	15	(1)	24	26	(2)	18	(2)	35
Jewish TFP[c] Male (41[d])															
None	22	(1)	35	(3)	35	27	(2)	37	(7)	38	27	(2)	39	(5)	41
Linear	18	(1)	35	(5)	35	23	(2)	36	(2)	36	37	(5)	39	(1)	39
Bestfit	18	(1)	35	(5)	35	23	(2)	36	(2)	36	37	(5)	39	(1)	39
Moving linear	0	(0)	29	(2)	29	0	(0)	34	(3)	34	27	(1)	39	(1)	39
Jewish TFP[c] Female (41[d])															
None	26	(2)	27	(2)	28	27	(2)	27	(1)	28	27	(2)	33	(3)	35
Linear	21	(3)	27	(3)	29	36	(5)	35	(4)	36	37	(2)	39	(2)	39

	A	B	C	D	E	F	G	H
Linear	33 (4)	18 (2)	33 (2)	35 (2)	32 (4)	40 (5)	38 (4)	41
Bestfit	33 (3)	18 (2)	33 (2)	34 (5)	32 (3)	40 (4)	33 (5)	40
Moving linear	32 (1)	7 (1)	33 (2)	35 (1)	19 (2)	39 (4)	33 (2)	40
Irish TFP[e] Female (41rᵈ)								
None	6 (1)	18 (2)	23 (2)	10 (1)	19 (2)	11 (1)	23 (2)	24
Linear	6 (1)	18 (2)	23 (2)	10 (1)	20 (2)	18 (2)	22 (3)	31
Bestfit	6 (1)	18 (2)	23 (2)	10 (1)	20 (2)	18 (2)	22 (3)	31
Moving linear	0 (0)	14 (2)	14 (2)	0 (0)	17 (2)	14 (3)	19 (2)	33
Italian TFP[e] Male (41rᵈ)								
None	26 (1)	28 (3)	38 (3)	32 (2)	37 (5)	34 (3)	39 (4)	41
Linear	25 (3)	26 (2)	27 (2)	35 (3)	33 (4)	40 (1)	36 (2)	41
Bestfit	18 (1)	30 (3)	30 (3)	28 (4)	31 (5)	29 (4)	34 (5)	34
Moving linear	6 (1)	0 (0)	6 (0)	34 (1)	7 (1)	40 (1)	36 (2)	41
Italian TFP[e] Female (41rᵈ)								
None	20 (2)	20 (1)	26 (1)	26 (2)	33 (2)	26 (1)	33 (2)	40
Linear	12 (1)	0 (0)	18 (0)	18 (2)	22 (2)	28 (3)	28 (3)	34
Bestfit	12 (1)	0 (0)	18 (0)	18 (2)	22 (2)	28 (3)	28 (3)	34
Moving linear	0 (0)	0 (1)	0 (1)	0 (0)	10 (1)	24 (1)	30 (2)	34
Spanish American TFP[e] Male (41rᵈ)								
None	0 (0)	0 (0)	0 (0)	10 (1)	9 (1)	11 (1)	11 (1)	20
Linear	12 (2)	0 (0)	15 (0)	15 (2)	6 (1)	23 (2)	23 (2)	25
Bestfit	6 (1)	0 (0)	11 (0)	10 (1)	8 (1)	11 (1)	11 (1)	20
Moving linear	7 (1)	0 (0)	13 (0)	7 (1)	0 (0)	17 (1)	0 (0)	24

Appendix I. (*continued*)

Trend Estimate used in Detrending	r (initial) = −0.85, r (nonautocorr.)[a] = −0.80					r (initial) = −0.80, r (nonautocorr.)[a] = −0.70					r (initial) = −0.70, r (nonautocorr.)[a] = −0.65				
	Lag = 0		Lag = 1		Combined[b]	Lag = 0		Lag = 1		Combined[b]	Lag = 0		Lag = 1		Combined[b]
	Yrs.	Spans	Yrs.	Spans	Yrs.	Yrs.	Spans	Yrs.	Spans	Yrs.	Yrs.	Spans	Yrs.	Spans	Yrs.
Grammar school TFP[c] Male (41[d])															
None	35	(2)	35	(3)	39	40	(4)	39	(3)	41	40	(2)	39	(3)	41
Linear	40	(2)	28	(5)	40	40	(1)	38	(3)	41	40	(1)	39	(4)	41
Bestfit	40	(6)	28	(5)	41	40	(2)	38	(4)	41	40	(3)	39	(4)	41
Moving linear	35	(2)	28	(2)	36	40	(1)	36	(2)	41	40	(1)	39	(3)	41
Grammar school TFP[c] Female (41[d])															
None	28	(2)	27	(2)	31	38	(4)	35	(2)	38	40	(3)	39	(3)	41
Linear	38	(3)	28	(3)	38	39	(1)	35	(2)	39	40	(1)	39	(3)	41
Bestfit	33	(2)	28	(2)	33	36	(1)	33	(1)	36	40	(1)	38	(1)	41
Moving linear	37	(1)	0	(0)	37	39	(1)	37	(2)	39	40	(1)	39	(1)	41
Grammar school Male (41[d])															
None	29	(3)	38	(4)	39	35	(5)	39	(5)	41	39	(5)	39	(6)	41
Linear	36	(5)	39	(3)	39	39	(5)	39	(1)	39	39	(5)	39	(1)	41

	c1	c2	c3	c4	c5	c6	c7	c8
None	29 (3)	22 (2)	32 (3)	29 (2)	28 (2)	38 (2)	35 (3)	39 (3)
Linear	25 (2)	33 (3)	34 (3)	33 (4)	35 (4)	36 (4)	37 (6)	37 (5)
Bestfit	18 (2)	33 (3)	33 (3)	32 (3)	33 (3)	34 (2)	36 (3)	36 (4)
Moving linear	6 (1)	25 (1)	25 (1)	6 (1)	28 (2)	28 (3)	31 (3)	35 (3)
Married TFP° Male (47[d])								
None	32 (2)	43 (3)	32 (2)	31 (3)	43 (3)	46 (6)	45 (6)	47 (3)
Linear	26 (2)	31 (3)	29 (2)	34 (4)	36 (4)	40 (5)	35 (5)	42 (6)
Bestfit	26 (2)	31 (3)	29 (2)	34 (4)	36 (4)	40 (5)	35 (5)	42 (6)
Moving linear	10 (1)	32 (1)	32 (1)	12 (1)	39 (1)	37 (3)	13 (3)	34 (1)
Married TFP° Female (47[d])								
None	21 (2)	38 (3)	27 (4)	22 (4)	42 (1)	43 (4)	24 (4)	45 (1)
Linear	7 (1)	14 (1)	14 (2)	14 (2)	20 (2)	20 (3)	14 (3)	30 (1)
Bestfit	7 (1)	14 (1)	14 (2)	14 (2)	20 (2)	20 (3)	14 (3)	30 (1)
Moving linear	0	8	10 (1)	0	10 (0)	19 (2)	14 (2)	23 (1)
Married Male (47[d])								
None	45 (4)	47 (3)	41 (4)	45 (3)	47 (3)	46 (4)	45 (4)	47 (5)
Linear	39 (6)	42 (5)	38 (5)	43 (4)	43 (4)	46 (5)	45 (5)	46 (4)
Bestfit	39 (6)	42 (5)	38 (5)	43 (4)	43 (4)	46 (5)	45 (5)	46 (4)
Moving linear	36 (1)	36 (2)	26 (1)	44 (4)	44 (4)	43 (3)	45 (4)	45 (4)
Married Female (47[d])								
None	22 (2)	25 (3)	34 (4)	22 (1)	42 (1)	39 (3)	28 (3)	44 (2)
Linear	6 (1)	17 (1)	6 (1)	16 (1)	22 (1)	21 (3)	23 (3)	29 (3)
Bestfit	6 (1)	17 (1)	6 (1)	16 (1)	22 (1)	21 (3)	23 (3)	29 (3)
Moving linear	0	0	0	0	0	18 (1)	18 (1)	18 (1)

Appendix I. (continued)

Trend Estimate used in Detrending	r (initial) = −0.85, r (nonautocorr.)[a] = −0.80					r (initial) = −0.80, r (nonautocorr.)[a] = −0.70					r (initial) = −0.70, r (nonautocorr.)[a] = −0.65				
	Lag = 0		Lag = 1		Combined[b]	Lag = 0		Lag = 1		Combined[b]	Lag = 0		Lag = 1		Combined[b]
	Yrs.	Spans	Yrs.	Spans	Yrs.	Yrs.	Spans	Yrs.	Spans	Yrs.	Yrs.	Spans	Yrs.	Spans	Yrs.
Spanish American TFP[c] Female (41[d])															
None	7	(1)	7	(1)	15	14	(3)	11	(1)	22	37	(2)	33	(4)	40
Linear	10	(1)	0	(0)	18	11	(1)	10	(1)	20	22	(3)	21	(3)	25
Bestfit	13	(2)	0	(0)	21	14	(2)	7	(1)	21	24	(4)	24	(3)	24
Moving linear	0	(0)	0	(0)	0	9	(1)	7	(1)	20	13	(1)	8	(1)	21
Urban TFP[c] Male (37[d])															
None	17	(2)	23	(4)	37	32	(3)	35	(4)	37	37	(5)	36	(6)	37
Linear	20	(1)	23	(5)	23	21	(1)	30	(5)	30	32	(3)	32	(5)	32
Bestfit	20	(1)	23	(5)	23	21	(1)	30	(5)	30	32	(3)	32	(5)	32
Moving linear	14	(1)	11	(2)	23	15	(1)	23	(2)	23	33	(3)	33	(3)	33
Urban TFP[c] Female (37[d])															
None	21	(2)	21	(2)	33	31	(3)	29	(3)	35	31	(3)	35	(4)	37
Linear	12	(2)	18	(2)	25	19	(2)	19	(3)	26	22	(4)	28	(2)	28

	1	2	3	4	5	6	7	8
Linear	23 (2)	29 (3)	30 (3)	32 (3)	31 (3)	32 (4)	33 (3)	33 (6)
Bestfit	23 (2)	29 (3)	30 (3)	32 (3)	31 (3)	32 (4)	33 (3)	33 (6)
Moving linear	0 (0)	9 (1)	9 (1)	0 (0)	11 (0)	11 (1)	31 (1)	31 (2)
Urban Female (37[d])								
None	21 (3)	22 (3)	23 (3)	28 (3)	22 (3)	30 (3)	30 (3)	33 (4)
Linear	8 (1)	12 (1)	12 (1)	9 (1)	14 (1)	14 (2)	17 (3)	24 (3)
Bestfit	12 (2)	16 (1)	16 (2)	14 (1)	16 (1)	16 (1)	17 (2)	23 (1)
Moving linear	6 (1)	9 (1)	15 (3)	6 (1)	9 (1)	15 (1)	18 (3)	19 (1)
Total admissions Male (46[d])								
None	36 (4)	32 (4)	44 (4)	37 (3)	44 (3)	46 (5)	44 (5)	46 (5)
Linear	25 (3)	32 (5)	33 (5)	40 (5)	38 (5)	40 (7)	39 (6)	41 (6)
Bestfit	25 (3)	32 (5)	33 (5)	40 (5)	38 (5)	40 (7)	39 (6)	41 (6)
Moving linear	6 (1)	29 (3)	29 (3)	23 (1)	32 (1)	32 (3)	41 (2)	41 (4)
Total admissions Female (46[d])								
None	36 (5)	18 (2)	39 (3)	38 (3)	22 (3)	43 (3)	38 (3)	43 (4)
Linear	17 (2)	10 (2)	19 (2)	20 (3)	15 (3)	24 (2)	16 (2)	25 (2)
Bestfit	20 (3)	16 (1)	22 (2)	20 (2)	16 (2)	22 (1)	17 (2)	24 (1)
Moving linear	0 (0)	0 (0)	0 (0)	0 (0)	0 (0)	0 (0)	18 (2)	28 (1)

[a] Residuals do not show positive or negative autocorrelation by estimate of the Durbin-Watson statistic. The present table relies on estimates that lie above the range of statistical doubt as indicated in the relevant Durbin-Watson distribution.

[b] The number of years at lag = 0 is added to the number at lag = 1; where identical years occur at both lags, these years are counted only once.

[c] Total Functional Psychosis: includes total admission with schizophrenia, manic-depressive psychosis, and involutional psychosis.

[d] Total number of years in series. In this study a stable relation is arbitrarily considered to involve a correlation of r (onautocorr.) $\leqq -0.65$ for at least 20 years at any one year's lag.

Appendix II.   Multiple inverse correlations between admissions to New York civil state hospitals and the index of employment, New York State 1914–1960, including possible relations from minus 1 to plus 3 years of lead or lag.

Trend estimate used in detrending		Total Period[a]	1922–1941	1941–1955	1941–1960
Married TFP[b]	Male (1914–1960)				
None		[c]	−0.91	−0.99	−0.75
Linear		−0.66	−0.93	−0.85	−0.66
Bestfit		−0.66	−0.93	−0.85	−0.74
Married TFP[b]	Female (1914–1960)				
None		[c]	−0.84	−0.58	−0.25
Linear		−0.38	−0.70	−0.60	−0.70
Bestfit		−0.40	−0.70	−0.61	−0.71
Married	Male (1914–1960)				
None		[c]	−0.89	−0.94	−0.67
Linear		−0.85	−0.90	−0.98	−0.92
Bestfit		−0.85	−0.90	−0.98	−0.92
Married	Female (1914–1960)				
None		[c]	−0.91	−0.73	−0.37
Linear		−0.45	−0.71	−0.71	−0.71
Bestfit		−0.46	−0.71	−0.71	−0.70
Negro TFP[b]	Male (1914–1960)				
None		[c]	−0.68	−0.96	−0.70
Linear		[d]	−0.48	−0.95	−0.57
Bestfit		−0.41	−0.50	−0.98	−0.56
Negro TFP[b]	Female (1914–1960)				
None		[c]	−0.80	−0.80	−0.54
Linear		[d]	−0.87	−0.82	−0.34
Bestfit		−0.36	−0.87	−0.82	−0.28
Jewish TFP[b]	Male (1914–1955)				
None		[c]	−0.97	−0.96	
Linear		−0.79	−0.78	−0.85	
Bestfit		−0.81	−0.78	−0.85	

Appendix II *(continued)*

Trend estimate used in detrending		Total Period[a]	1922–1941	1941–1955	1941–1960
Jewish TFP[b]	Female (1914–1955)				
None		°	−0.96	−0.79	
Linear		−0.77	−0.88	−0.79	
Bestfit		−0.78	−0.88	−0.81	
Irish TFP[b]	Male (1914–1955)				
None		°	−0.89	−0.90	
Linear		−0.77	−0.90	−0.66	
Bestfit		−0.78	−0.90	−0.80	
Irish TFP[b]	Female (1914–1955)				
None		°	−0.73	d	
Linear		−0.57	−0.64	−0.65	
Bestfit		−0.55	−0.56	−0.86	
Italian TFP[b]	Male (1914–1955)				
None		°	−0.93	−0.87	
Linear		−0.82	−0.85	−0.75	
Bestfit		−0.45	−0.92	−0.78	
Italian TFP[b]	Female (1914–1955)				
None		°	−0.96	−0.62	
Linear		−0.49	−0.94	−0.71	
Bestfit		−0.50	−0.95	−0.98	
Spanish American TFP[b]	Male (1914–1955)				
None		°	−0.70	−0.83	
Linear		−0.68	−0.61	−0.66	
Bestfit		°	−0.73	−0.44	
Spanish American TFP[b]	Female (1914–1955)				
None		°	−0.86	−0.86	
Linear		d	−0.78	−0.78	
Bestfit		d	−0.89	−0.46	
First admissions TFP[b]	Male (1914–1959)				
None		°	−0.92	−0.99	−0.77
Linear		−0.67	−0.87	−0.91	−0.80
Bestfit		−0.69	−0.87	−0.90	−0.78

Trend estimate used in detrending		Total Period[a]	1922–1941	1941–1955	1941–1960
First admissions TFP[b]	Female (1914–1959)				
None		[c]	−0.86	−0.81	−0.70
Linear		−0.47	−0.79	−0.81	−0.39
Bestfit		−0.47	−0.79	−0.80	−0.86
Total admissions	Male (1914–1959)				
None		[c]	−0.90	−0.99	−0.61
Linear		−0.76	−0.82	−0.98	−0.95
Bestfit		−0.75	−0.81	−0.98	−0.95
Total admissions	Female (1914–1959)				
None		[c]	−0.87	−0.83	−0.41
Linear		−0.71	−0.95	−0.85	−0.60
Bestfit		−0.60	−0.71	−0.95	−0.84

[a]Total number of years in series.

[b]Total Functional Psychosis: includes total admissions with schizophrenia, manic-depressive psychosis and involutional psychosis.

[c]For undetrended data, inverse correlations are absent for the total period (usually 46 years) because both admissions and employment usually show long-term upward trends which correlate positively.

[d]Inverse correlation was not found for this *full* period. The actual inverse relations may, therefore, vary considerably within this period or may only be present for a portion of it.

Notes

CHAPTER I

1. Two examples of many collections of literature reviews in this area are: Robert R. Merton and Robert A. Nisbet (eds.), *Contemporary Social Problems: An Introduction to the Sociology of Deviant Behavior and Social Disorganization* (New York: Harcourt, Brace and World, 1961); Mabel A. Elliott and Francis E. Merrill, *Social Disorganization* (New York: Harper, 1961).

2. See the reviews in George W. Baker and Dwight W. Chapman (eds.), *Man and Society in Disaster* (New York: Basic Books, 1962); Marc Fried, "Effects of Social Change on Mental Health," in Bernard J. Bergen and Claudwell S. Thomas (eds.), *Issues and Problems in Social Psychiatry* (Springfield, Ill.: Charles C. Thomas, 1966), pp 358–399; H. David Kirk, "The Impact of Drastic Change on Social Relations—A Model for the Identification and Specification of Stress," in George K. Zollschan and Walter Hirsch (eds.), *Explorations in Social Change* (New York: Houghton Mifflin, 1964), pp. 258–280.

3. Robert N. Wilson, "Disaster and Mental Health," in Baker and Chapman (eds.), *Disaster;* Fried, "Effects of Social Change," p. 375.

4. Max Weber, *The Theory of Social and Economic Organization* (New York: Oxford University Press, 1947).

5. Erik Lundberg, *Instability and Economic Growth* (New Haven: Yale University Press, 1968); H. G. Aitken, Jr. (ed.), *The State and Economic Growth* (New York: Social Science Research Counsel, 1959); B. F. Hoselitz and W. E. Moore (eds.), *Industrialization and Society* (Paris and The Hague: UNESCO and Mouton, 1963); B. F. Hoselitz, *Sociological Aspects of Economic Growth* (Glencoe, Ill.: Free Press, 1960); D. McClelland, *The Achieving Society* (Princeton, N. J.: Van Nostrand, 1961); G. M. Meier and R. E. Baldwin, *Economic Development: Theory, History, Policy* (New York: Wiley, 1957).

6. Gottfried von Haberler, *Prosperity and Depression* (Cambridge, Mass.: Harvard University Press, 1958).

7. W. F. Ogburn, *Social Change* (New York: Viking, 1936).

8. This is the classic Marxist position which has been modified, to some degree, by Thorstein Veblen. Karl Marx, *A Contribution to the Critique of Political Economy* (New York: International Library, 1904); T. Veblen, *The Vested Interests and the State of the Industrial Arts* (New York: Huebsch, 1919).

9. Lundberg, *Instability*, p. 7.

10. W. C. Mitchell, *What Happens During Business Cycles: A Progress Report* (New York: National Bureau of Economic Research, 1951); G. H. Moore (ed.), *Business Cycle Indicators* (Princeton, N. J.: Princeton University Press, 1961).

11. Mitchell, *What Happens During Business Cycles;* Moore, *Business Cycle Indicators.*

12. S. M. Lipset and R. Bendix, *Social Mobility in Industrial Society* (Berkeley: University of California Press, 1959), chap. VIII; Harold L. Wilensky, "Measures and Effects of Social Mobility," in N. J. Smelser and S. M. Lipset (eds.), *Social Structure and Mobility in Economic Development* (Chicago: Aldine, 1966).

13. Emile Durkheim, *Suicide: A Study in Sociology,* J. A. Spaulding and G. Simpson, eds. (Glencoe, Ill.: Free Press, 1951; originally published in Paris: F. Alcan, 1897); R. K. Merton, "Social Structure and Anomie," *American Sociological Review,* 3:672–682 (October 1938); Talcott Parsons, *The Structure of Social Action* (New York: McGraw-Hill, 1937).

14. Gerald Gurin, Joseph Veroff, and Sheila Feld, *Americans View Their Mental Health* (New York: Basic Books, 1960), pp. 25–29.

15. Thomas S. Langner and Stanley T. Michael, *Life Stress and Mental Health: The Midtown Manhattan Study* (New York: Free Press, 1963), II, 394.

16. The one apparent exception is: John A. Clausen and Melvin L. Kohn, "Relation of Schizophrenia to the Social Structure of a Small City," in Benjamin Pasamanick (ed.), *Epidemiology of Mental Disorder* (Washington, D. C.: Publication No. 60 of the American Association for the Advancement of Science, 1959), pp. 69–85. These authors, however, supply two alternative explanations for the lack of consistency between their findings and those of the studies listed below.

17. Robert E. L. Faris, "Cultural Isolation and the Schizophrenic Personality," *American Journal of Sociology,* 40:155–164 (September 1934); H. Warren Dunham, "The Ecology of the Functional Psychoses in Chicago," *American Sociological Review,* 2:467–479 (August 1937); Robert E. L. Faris, "Demography of Urban Psychosis with Special Reference to Schizophrenia," *American Sociological Review,* 3:203–209 (April 1938); Robert E. L. Faris and H. W. Dunham, *Mental Disorders in Urban Areas* (New York: Hafner, 1960); Stuart A. Queen, "The Ecological Study of Mental Disorders," *American Sociological Review,* 5:201–209 (April 1940); Clarence W. Schroeder, "Mental Disorders in Cities," *American Journal of Sociology,* 48:40–47 (July 1942); Ernest R. Mowrer, *Disorganization, Personal and Social* (Philadelphia: Lippincott, 1942); H. W. Dunham, "Current Status of Ecological Research in Mental Disorder," *Social Forces,* 25:321–326 (March 1947); William F. Roth, Jr. and Frank H. Luton, "The Mental Health Problem in Tennessee," *American Journal of Psychiatry,* 99:662–675 (March 1943); Robert E. Clark, "Psychoses, Income and Occupational Prestige," *American Journal of Sociology,* 54:433–440 (March 1949); Bert Kaplan, Robert B. Reed, and Wyman Richardson, "A Comparison of the Incidence of Hospitalized and Non-Hospitalized Cases of Psychosis in Two Communities," *American Sociological Review,* 21:472–479 (August 1956); Benjamin Malzberg, "Mental Disease in Relation to Economic Status," *Journal of Nervous and Mental Disease,* 123:257–261 (March 1956); Robert W. Hyde and Lowell V. Kingsley, "Studies in Medical Sociology I: The Relation of Mental Disorders to the Community Socioeconomic Level," *New England Journal of Medicine,* 231:543–548 (October 1944).

18. Sigmund Freud, *The Ego and the Id* (London: Hogarth, 1947); Freud, *The Problem of Anxiety* (New York: Norton, 1936); Erik H. Erikson, *Childhood and Society* (New York: Norton, 1950). See also the critique of this position in

D. H. Wrong, "The Oversocialized Conception of Man in Modern Sociology," *American Sociological Review,* 26:183–193 (1961).

19. E. Hess, "Ethology: An Approach Toward the Complete Analysis of Behavior," in R. Brown, E. Galanter, E. Hess, and G. Mandler (eds.) *New Directions in Psychology* (New York: Holt, Rinehart, and Winston, 1962); R. A. Hinde, "Some Recent Trends in Ethology," in S. Hoch (ed.), *Psychology: A Study of a Science* (New York: McGraw-Hill, 1959), vol. II; W. H. Thorpe, *Learning and Instinct in Animals* (London: Methuen, 1956) G. Allen "Genetic Aspects of Mental Disorder," in *The Nature and Transmission of the Genetic and Cultural Characteristics of Human Populations* (Proceedings of 1956 Annual Conference, New York: Milbank Memorial Fund, 1957); R. B. Cattell, D. B. Blewett, and J. R. Beloff, "The Inheritance of Personality," *American Journal of Human Genetics,* 7:122–146 C. J. Herrick, *The Evolution of Human Nature* (Austin: University of Texas Press, 1956); F. J. Kallmann, "The Genetics of Mental Illness," in Silvano Arieti (ed.), *American Handbook of Psychiatry* (New York: Basic Books, 1959), I, 175–196; F. J. Kallmann, "The Genetic Theory of Schizophrenia," *American Journal of Psychiatry,* 103:309–322 (1946); D. J. Merrill, "Inheritance of Manic-Depressive Psychosis," *Archives of Neurology and Psychiatry,* 66:272–279 (1951).

20. Robert K. Merton, "Bureaucratic Structure and Personality," *Social Forces,* 17:560–568 (1940); William H. Whyte, Jr., *The Organization Man* (New York: Doubleday, 1957).

CHAPTER 2

1. Marc Fried, "Effects of Social Change on Mental Health," in Bernard J. Bergen and Claudwell S. Thomas (eds.), *Issues and Problems in Social Psychiatry* (Springfield, Ill.: Charles C Thomas, 1966), pp. 358–399.

2. *Ibid*, pp. 374–375.

3. Paul O. Komora and Mary A. Clark, "Mental Disease in the Crisis," *Mental Hygiene,* 19:289–301 (April 1935).

4. *Ibid.,* p. 301.

5. *Ibid.,* p. 293.

6. *Ibid.,* pp 295–296.

7. Horatio M. Pollock, "The Depression and Mental Disease in New York State," *American Journal of Psychiatry,* 91:736–771 (January 1935).

8. *Ibid.,* p. 767.

9. *Ibid.*

10. *Ibid.,* p. 771.

11. *Ibid.,* emphasis supplied.

12. Komora and Clark, "Mental Disease," pp. 296–297.

13. *Ibid.,* p. 297, emphasis supplied.

14. Pollock, "Depression and Mental Disease."

15. Komora and Clark, "Mental Disease," p. 299, emphasis supplied.

16. Ernest R. Mowrer, "A Study of Personal Disorganization," *American Sociological Review,* 4:475–487 (August 1939).

17. *Ibid.,* p. 477.

18. *Ibid.,* p. 479.

19. Neil A. Dayton, *New Facts on Mental Disorders* (Springfield, Ill.: Charles C Thomas, 1940).

20. *Ibid.,* p. 23.

21. *Ibid.*

22. *Ibid.*, pp. 23–27.

23. Benjamin Malzberg, *Social and Biological Aspects of Mental Disease* (New York: State Hospitals Press, 1940), chap. XI.

24. *Ibid.*, p. 278.

25. H. Warren Dunham, *Sociological Theory and Mental Disorder* (Detroit, Mich.: Wayne State University Press, 1959), chap. VI.

26. *Ibid.*, p. 98.

27. *Ibid.*, p. 100.

28. *Ibid.*, p. 98, emphasis supplied.

29. Thomas F. Pugh and Brian MacMahon, *Epidemiologic Findings in United States Mental Hospital Data* (Boston: Little, Brown, 1962), p. 70.

30. *Ibid.*, p. 72.

31. *Ibid.*

32. National Institute of Mental Health, *Patients in Mental Institutions, 1950 and 1951* (Washington, D. C.: U. S. Government Printing Office, 1954), p. 7.

33. Ellen Winston, "The Assumed Increase of Mental Disease," *American Journal of Sociology*, 40:427–439 (January 1935).

34. Charles K. Bush, "Growth of General Hospital Care of Psychiatric Patients," *American Journal of Psychiatry*, 113:1059–1062 (June 1957).

35. J. S. Tyhurst, "Psychological and Social Aspects of Civilian Disaster," *Canadian Medical Association Journal*, 76:385 (1957).

36. J. S. Tyhurst, "The Role of Transition States—Including Disasters—in Mental Illness," in Walter Reed Army Institute of Research and the National Research Council (sponsors), *Symposium on Preventive and Social Psychiatry* (Washington, D. C.: Walter Reed Army Institute of Research, 1957), pp. 149–169.

37. Tyhurst, "Transition States," pp. 150–151.

38. *Ibid.*, p. 151, emphasis supplied.

39. *Ibid.*, p. 150.

40. Muriel Hammer, "The Influence of Small Social Networks as Factors of Mental Hospital Admission," *Human Organization*, 22:243–251 (Winter 1963–64).

41. Elliott G. Mishler and Nancy E. Waxler, "Decision Process in Psychiatric Hospitalization," *American Sociological Review*, 28:576–587 (August 1963).

42. Wesley C. Mitchell, *What Happens During Business Cycles: A Progress Report* (New York: National Bureau of Economic Research, 1951); Geoffrey H. Moore (ed.), *Business Cycle Indicators*, 2 vols. (Princeton, N. J.: Princeton University Press, 1961); Horst Menderhausen, *Changes in Income Distribution During the Great Depression* (New York: National Bureau of Economic Research, 1946); Paul F. Lazarsfeld and Samuel A. Stouffer, *Research Memorandum on the Family in the Depression* (New York: Social Science Research Council, Bull. 29, 1937).

43. New York State Department of Mental Hygiene, *Annual Reports*.

44. Gottfried von Haberler, *Prosperity and Depression* (Cambridge, Mass.: Harvard University Press, 1958), p. 259.

45. Mitchell, *Business Cycles;* Moore, *Indicators*.

46. New York State Department of Labor, Division of Research and Statistics, "Adjusted Indexes of Manufacturing Production Worker Employment and Payrolls by Principal Industrial Areas in New York State, Monthly, 1914–1948," *Handbook of Labor Statistics, 1948* (New York: Special Bulletin, No. 226, November 1959, p. 16.

47. New York State Department of Labor, Division of Research and Statistics, "Employment Tables (Manufacturing Industries)," unpub., prepared for the Division of Employment and Manpower Statistics of the Bureau of Labor Statistics, U. S. Department of Labor.

48. Herbert H. Hyman, *Survey Design and Analysis: Principles, Cases and Procedures* (Glencoe, Ill.: Free Press, 1955).

49. Frederick E. Croxton and Dudley J. Cowden, *Applied General Statistics* (New York: Prentice-Hall, 1955).

50. W. A. Wallis and H. V. Roberts, *Statistics: A New Approach* (Glencoe, Ill.: Free Press, 1956); Croxton and Cowden, *Applied General Statistics*, pp. 577–578; D. Cochrane and G. H. Orcutt, "Application of Least Squares Regressions to Relationships Containing Autocorrelated Error Terms," *Journal of the American Statistical Association*, 44:32–61 (1949); J. Johnston, *Econometric Methods* (New York: McGraw-Hill, 1963), chap. VIII.

51. J. Durbin and G. S. Watson, "Testing for Serial Correlation in Least-Squares Regression," pts. I and II, *Biometrika*, 1950, 1951; Johnston, *Econometric Methods*.

52. J. Durbin, "Estimation of Parameters in Time-Series Regression Models," *Journal of the Royal Statistical Society*, ser. B., 22:139–153 (1960); Johnston, *Econometric Methods*, chap. VIII.

53. M. Ezekiel and K. A. Fox, *Methods of Correlation and Regression Analysis* (New York: Wiley, 1959).

54. R. L. Anderson, "Distribution of the Serial Coefficient," *Annals of Mathematical Statistics*, 13:1 (1942); M. S. Bartlett, "Some Aspects of the Time Correlation Problem in Regard to Tests of Significance," *Journal of the Royal Statistical Society*, 98:536 (1935); M. S. Bartlett, "On the Theoretical Specifications and Sampling Properties of Auto Correlated Time Series," *Journal of the Royal Statistical Society*, 8:27, Supplement (1946).

55. Ezekiel and Fox, *Methods*.

CHAPTER 3

1. J. Durbin and G. S. Watson, "Testing for Serial Correlation in Least-Squares Regression," pts. I and II, *Biometrika*, 1950, 1951.

2. Fourier analysis is a technique frequently used in electrical engineering and geophysics to determine the components of a complex trend. It is the first time, to this writer's knowledge, that these procedures have been used in the analysis of hospitalization data. For general references, the reader is directed to M. J. Lighthill, *An Introduction to Fourier Analysis and Generalized Functions* (Cambridge: Cambridge University Press, 1959); A. Papoulis, *The Fourier Integral and Its Applications* (New York: McGraw-Hill, 1962). General treatments of the application of techniques of spectral analysis to economic data are found in G. S. Fishman, *Spectral Methods in Econometrics* (Cambridge, Mass.: Harvard University Press, 1969); C. W. J. Granger, *Spectral Analysis of Economic Time Series* (Princeton, N. J.: Princeton University Press, 1964); G. Tintner, *Econometrics* (New York: Wiley, 1952), pp. 216–238.

3. Wesley C. Mitchell, *What Happens During Business Cycles: A Progress Report* (New York: National Bureau of Economic Research, 1951); Geoffrey H. Moore (ed.), *Business Cycle Indicators* (Princeton, N. J.: Princeton University Press, 1961), 2 vols.

4. Utica State Hospital, *Annual Reports*, 1841–1915.

5. American Psychiatric Association, *Diagnostic and Statistical Manual of Mental Disorders [DSM I]* (Washington, D. C.: American Psychiatric Association, 1952), p. 5; see also the *Diagnostic and Statistical Manual*, 2nd ed. *[DSM II]* (Washington, D. C.: American Psychiatric Association, 1968), p. 32.

6. American Psychiatric Association, *DSM I*, pp. 12–13.

7. Silvano Arieti (ed.), *American Handbook of Psychiatry* (New York: Basic Books, 1959), vol. I, part III.

8. American Psychiatric Association, *DSM I*, pp. 40–42.

9. *Ibid.*, p. 24.

10. E. Y. Deykin, Shirley Jacobson, Gerald L. Klerman, and Maida Solomon, "The Empty Nest: Psycho-Social Aspects of Conflict Between Depressed Women and Their Grown Children," *American Journal of Psychiatry*, 122:1422–1426 (June 1966).

CHAPTER 4

1. Wesley C. Mitchell, *What Happens During Business Cycles: A Progress Report* (New York: National Bureau of Economic Research, 1951); Geoffrey H. Moore (ed.), *Business Cycle Indicators*, 2 vols., (Princeton, N. J.: Princeton University Press, 1961).

2. Andrew F. Henry and James F. Short, *Suicide and Homicide* (Glencoe, Ill.: Free Press, 1954).

3. Charles I. Schottland, *The Social Security Program in the United States* (New York: Appleton Century Crofts, 1963).

4. B. F. Hoselitz, "The Role of Urbanization in Economic Development: Some International Comparisons," in R. Lurner (ed.), *India's Urban Future* (Berkeley: University of California Press, 1962), pp. 157–181; L. Schnore, "The Statistical Measurement of Urbanization and Economic Development," *Land Economics,* 37:229–245 (1961); T. L. Smith, *The Sociology of Rural Life,* rev. ed. (New York: Harper, 1947).

5. The base population data for Jews were obtained from the *Annual Jewish Yearbook* (New York: Jewish Publication Society of America, 1907–1960). Estimates of the New York State Negro population are taken from National Office of Vital Statistics, *Vital Statistics—Special Reports,* 1900–1960.

6. William J. Goode, *World Revolution and Family Patterns* (New York: Free Press, 1963); Ferdinand Toennies, *Community and Society—Gemeinschaft und Gesellschaft,* trans. and ed. by Charles P. Loomis (East Lansing, Mich.: Michigan State University, 1957).

7. T. W. Adorno, "Neutralized Religion and Its Functions," in Norman Birnbaum and Gertrud Lenzer (eds.), *Sociology and Religion* (Englewood Cliffs, N. J.: Prentice-Hall, 1969); originally published in T. W. Adorno, Else Frenkel-Brunswick, Daniel J. Levinson, and R. Nevitt Sanford, *The Authoritarian Personality* (New York: Harper, 1950), pp. 728–738; W. Seward Salisbury, *Religion In American Culture: A Sociological Interpretation* (Homewood, Ill.: Dorsey Press, 1964), pp. 280–289.

8. Clarence D. Long, *The Labor Force Under Changing Income and Employment,* (Princeton, N. J.: Princeton University Press, 1958), chap. VI.

9. Long, *The Labor Force*, pp. 133–140.

10. Nathan Glazer and Daniel P. Moynihan, *Beyond the Melting Pot: The Negroes, Puerto Ricans, Jews, Italians and Irish of New York City* (Cambridge, Mass.: M.I.T. Press, 1963), pp. 25–75, 186–216.

11. Thomas Scheff, "Users and Non-Users of a Student Psychiatric Clinic," *Journal of Health and Human Behavior,* 7:114–121 (1966); Glazer and Moynihan, *Beyond the Melting Pot,* p. 175; L. Srole, T. S. Langner, S. T. Mitchell, M. K. Opler, and T. A. C. Rennie, *Mental Health in the Metropolis: Midtown Manhattan Study,* vol. I (New York: McGraw-Hill, 1962), p. 317.

12. Lawrence F. Pisani, *The Italian in America, A Social Study and History* (New

York: Exposition Press, 1957), chap. XI; Glazer and Moynihan, *Beyond the Melting Pot,* pp. 194–204; Herbert J. Gans, *The Urban Villagers* (New York: Free Press, 1962), pp. 136–162.

13. Julius A. Roth, "The Treatment of the Sick," in John Kosa, Aaron Antonovsky, and I. K. Zola (eds.), *Poverty and Health, A Sociological Analysis* (Cambridge, Mass.: Harvard University Press, 1969), pp. 214–244; Benjamin Malzberg, *Social and Biological Aspects of Mental Disease* (New York: State Hospitals Press, 1940), p. 226; Thomas F. Pugh and Brian MacMahon, *Epidemiological Findings in United States Mental Hospital Data* (Boston: Little, Brown, 1962); D. G. Wilson and E. M. Lance, "The Effects of Cultural Change on the Negro Race in Virginia," *American Journal of Psychiatry,* 114:25–32 (1957).

14. U. S. Bureau of the Census, *Historical Statistics of the U. S., Colonial Times to 1962 and Revisions* (Washington, D. C.: U. S. Government Printing Office, 1965), series H223–233; Donald J. Bogue, *The Population of the United States* (Glencoe, Ill.: Free Press, 1959), pp. 340–349.

15. Thus, for example, since 1956, the statistical tables in the *Annual Reports* of the New York State Department of Mental Hygiene have given an aggregated figure that includes all patients who have had eight or fewer grades of school (without a more refined breakdown).

16. David Mechanic, *Medical Sociology, A Selective View* (New York: Free Press, 1968), p. 383.

CHAPTER 5

1. Robert N. Wilson, "Disaster and Mental Health," in George W. Baker and Dwight W. Chapman (eds.), *Man and Society in Disaster* (New York: Basic Books, 1963), p. 148.

2. Hubert M. Blalock, Jr., *Social Statistics* (New York: McGraw-Hill, 1960), p. 345.

3. *Ibid.,* pp. 302–305.

4. J. Durbin, "Estimation of Parameters in Time-Series Regression Models," *Journal of the Royal Statistical Society,* ser. B., 22:139–153 (1960).

5. J. Durbin and G. S. Watson, "Testing for Serial Correlation in Least Squares Regression," pts. I and II, *Biometrika,* 1950, 1951.

6. New York State Department of Mental Hygiene, *Statistical Guide* (Albany, N. Y.: State Hospitals Press, 1934).

7. *Ibid.,* p. 45.

CHAPTER 6

1. In addition to the documentation of socioeconomic differences among ethnic groups discussed in Chapter 7, a specific evaluation of Jewish-Italian differences is found in Fred L. Strodtbeck, Margaret R. McDonald and Bernard C. Rosen, "Evaluation of Occupations: A Reflection of Jewish and Italian Mobility Differences," *American Sociological Review,* 22:546–552 (October 1957).

2. Milton L. Barron, "The Incidence of Jewish Intermarriage in Europe and America," *American Sociological Review,* 11:6–12 (February 1946); Robert R. Bell, *Marriage and Family Interaction,* rev. ed. (Homewood, Ill.: Dorsey Press, 1967), pp. 154–155; Thomas P. Monihan and William Kephart, "Divorce and Desertion by Religious and Mixed Religious Groups," *American Journal of Sociology,* 59:454–465 (March 1954); Marvin Bressler, "Selected Family Patterns in W. I. Thomas' Unfinished Study of the Bintl Brief," *American Sociological Review,* 17:563–571

(October 1952); Eric Rosenthal, "Acculturation Without Assimilation," *American Journal of Sociology,* 66:285 (November 1960); Nathan Glazer and Daniel P. Moynihan, *Beyond the Melting Pot* (Cambridge, Mass.: M.I.T. Press, 1936), p. 165.

3. Herbert J. Gans, *The Urban Villagers: Group and Class in the Life of Italian Americans* (New York: Free Press, 1962), pp. 27, 35, 36–39, 207; Lawrence F. Pisani, *The Italian in America* (New York: Exposition Press, 1957), pp. 131, 161–162; R. H. Schermerhorn, *These Our People: Minorities in American Culture* (Boston: D. C. Heath, 1949), pp. 237–241, 255–258; Glazier and Moynihan, *Beyond the Melting Pot,* pp. 189–205.

4. Andrew F. Henry and James F. Short, *Suicide and Homicide* (Glencoe, Ill.: Free Press, 1954).

CHAPTER 7

1. Horst Menderhausen, *Changes in Income Distribution During the Great Depression* (New York: National Bureau, 1946).

2. U. S. Bureau of the Census, "Hours and Earnings for Production Workers in 25 Manufacturing Industries by Sex and Degree of Skill: 1914 to 1948," *Historical Statistics of the United States, Colonial Times to 1957* (Washington, D. C.: U. S. Government Printing Office, 1957), p. 94.

3. Menderhausen, *Changes in Income Distribution,* Table 37, p. 109.

4. *Ibid.*, pp. 107, 71, 110, 70.

5. *Ibid.*, p. 71, n. 41.

6. *Ibid.*, p. 75, n. 43; p. 74, Table 26; J. C. Baker, *Executive Salaries and Bonus Plans* (New York: McGraw-Hill, 1938), p. 27.

7. U. S. Bureau of Labor Statistics, *Unemployment: Terminology, Measurement, and Analysis* (Washington, D. C.: U. S. Government Printing Office, 1961), pp. 63–64.

8. Patricia C. Sexton, *Education and Income* (New York: Viking Press, 1961). The name of the city surveyed was not revealed; it is referred to as "Big City."

9. *Ibid.*, pp. 12–13.

10. Daniel Creamer, *Personal Income During Business Cycles* (New York: National Bureau of Economic Research, 1956).

11. Detailed descriptions of this technique are found in, for example, Arthur F. Burns and Wesley C. Mitchell, *Measuring Business Cycles* (New York: National Bureau of Economic Research, 1946); Wesley C. Mitchell, *What Happens During Business Cycles: A Progress Report* (New York: National Bureau of Economic Research, 1951).

12. Compiled mainly by NBER researchers; see Creamer, *Personal Income,* pp. 118–119; Chart 8, p. 30; Table 6, pp. 31–33; Table A-1, pp. 116–119; Table 13, p. 53; Table 18, p. 59; Table 12, p. 49; Charts 11 and 12; pp. 43, 45.

13. *Ibid.*, Chart 8, p. 30; Table 6, pp. 31–33; Table A-1, pp. 116–119; and Table 21, p. 68.

14. *Ibid.*, Table 37, p. 109.

15. For this relation during 1926–1927, see, for example, Everett W. Lord, *The Relation of Education and Income* (Indianapolis, Ind.: Alpha Kappa Psi Fraternity, 1928); for 1939–1949, Herman P. Miller, *Income of the American People* (New York: Wiley, 1955), p. 67.

16. "Elementary and Secondary Schools, Enrollment and Attendance, and High School Graduates: 1870–1956," U. S. Bureau of the Census, *Historical Statistics of the United States, Colonial Times to 1957* (Washington, D. C.: U. S. Government Printing Office, 1957), p. 207. (1) Percentage of the population 5 to 17 years old who

were enrolled in public day schools: 1910, 73.5; 1920, 77.8; 1940, 85.3; 1956, 83.6. (2) Percentage of the population at least 17 years old who are high-school graduates: 1910, 8.8; 1920, 16.8; 1930, 29.0; 1940, 50.8; 1956, 62.3. (3) Percentage of the population 18 to 21 years old who were enrolled in institutions of higher learning: 1910, 5.12; 1920, 8.09; 1930, 12.42; 1940, 15.68; 1954, 29.90.

17. J. Tizard, B. Litt, and N. O'Connor, "The Employability of High-Grade Mental Defectives," *American Journal of Mental Deficiency*, 54:563:576 (April 1950); 55:144–157 (July 1950).

18. R. E. Fairbank, "The Subnormal Child—17 Years After," *Mental Hygiene*, 17:177–208 (1933); W. R. Baller, "A Study of the Present Social Status of a Group of Adults Who, When They were in Elementary Schools, were Classified as Mentally Deficient," *Genetic Psychological Monographs*, 18:165–244 (1936).

19. Tizard *et al.*, "Mental Defectives," p. 154.

20. August B. Hollingshead and Frederick C. Redlich, *Social Class and Mental Illness* (New York: Wiley, 1958), pp. 187–188.

21. *U. S. Census of Population: 1950,* Special Reports, "Nativity and Parentage," Tables 10 and 23.

22. Donald J. Bogue, *The Population of the United States* (Glencoe, Ill.: Free Press, 1959), pp. 636–637.

23. Miller, *Income,* p. 47.

24. Andrew F. Henry and James F. Short, *Suicide and Homicide* (Glencoe, Ill.: Free Press, 1954), p. 57.

25. U. S. Bureau of Labor Statistics, *Unemployment: Terminology, Measurement, and Analysis* (Washington, D. C.: U. S. Government Printing Office, 1961).

26. Bogue, *Population,* p. 637.

27. Henry and Short, *Suicide and Homicide,* pp. 49–51.

28. Bogue, *Population,* p. 74.

29. W. Lloyd Warner and Leo Srole, *The Social Life of a Modern Community* (New Haven, Conn.: Yale University Press, 1941).

30. M. Vartan Malcolm, *The Armenians in America* (Boston: Pilgrim Press, 1919).

31. Bernard Berelson and Gary A. Steiner, *Human Behavior: An Inventory of Scientific Findings* (New York: Harcourt, Brace and World, 1964), p. 465.

32. Bernard C. Rosen, "Race, Ethnicity, and the Achievement Syndrome," *American Sociological Review*, 24:47–60 (February 1959).

33. Herbert H. Hyman, "The Value Systems of Different Classes: A Social Psychological Contribution to the Analysis of Stratification," in Reinhard Bendix and Seymour M. Lipset (eds.), *Class, Status, and Power: A Reader in Social Stratification* (Glencoe, Ill.: Free Press, 1953), pp. 426–442.

34. Jerome K. Meyers and Bertram H. Roberts, *Family and Class Dynamics In Mental Illness* (New York: Wiley, 1959).

35. It is interesting that the histories of two of the three high-status groups, the Armenians and Jews, show a traditional image of persecution and despised minority status; see, for example, Arnold Rose and Caroline Rose, *America Divided: Minority Group Relations in the United States* (New York: Knopf, 1948), pp. 180–199; Robin Williams, *Strangers Next Door* (Englewood Cliffs, N. J.: Prentice-Hall, 1964), p. 253; Benjamin Ginsberg, "Anti-Semitism," *Encyclopedia of the Social Sciences,* vol. 1 (New York: Macmillan, 1930), pp. 119–125; Rouben Gavoor, "Armenian Americans," in Francis T. Brown and Joseph S. Poucek (eds.), *Our Racial and National Minorities* (New York: Prentice-Hall, 1937), pp. 436–450; M. C. Gabrielian, *The Armenians or the People of Ararat,* Philadelphia, Pa.: Allen, Lane and Scott, 1892: "Owing to the calamitous wars, merciless persecutions, voluntary and involuntary exiles, and emigrations into different countries, they have been often justly compared to

the Jews," p. 79; Works Progress Administration, *The Armenians in Massachusetts* (Boston: Armenian Historical Society, 1937); Vahan M. Kurjian, *A History of Armenia* (New York: Armenian General Benevolent Union, 1958), esp. chap. 47, "The Armenians Outside of Armenia," pp. 460–473. Several writers find that such despised status leads to feelings of self-hate on the part of members of these groups—mitigated only by the advancement of social status. At the same time, the high social mobility achieved by them would make for a self-image of pronounced status inconsistency. Status inconsistency would, in turn, lead to an unusual concern to fill the "status gap"; see Seymour Martin Lipset and Reinhard Bendix, *Social Mobility in Industrial Society* (Berkeley: University of California Press, 1959), pp. 64–54; Robert E. Park, "Human Migration and the Marginal Man," *American Journal of Sociology* (May 1928), p. 893; Allison Davis, "Acculturation in Schools," in Milton L. Barron (eds.), *American Minorities* (New York: Knopf, 1957), p. 447. The German ethnic group is also reported to have been traditionally concerned with socioeconomic status (especially as this is associated with "authoritarian" socialization patterns) since feudal times; Theodore Abel, "Is a Psychiatric Interpretation of the German Enigma Necessary?" *American Sociological Review,* 8:525–530 (October 1943); Knut Pipping, Rudolph Abshagen, and Anne-Eva Brauneck, *Gesprache mit der Deutschen Jugend: Ein Betrag zum Autoritatsproblem,* I (Helsingfors, Centraltryckeriet: Societas Scientiarum Fennica, Commentationes Humanarum Litterarum XX, 1954); David Rodnick, "On Authoritarianism in Germany," *American Sociological Review,* 23:679 (December 1958).

36. W. Lloyd Warner and Leo Srole, *The Social Systems of American Ethnic Groups* (New Haven, Conn.: Yale University Press, 1945); Donald J. Bogue, *The Population of the United States* (Glencoe, Ill.: Free Press, 1959), pp. 366–374.

37. Marcus Lee Hanson, *The Immigrant in American History* (Cambridge, Mass.: Harvard University Press, 1940); Oscar Handlin, *The Uprooted* (Boston: Little, Brown, 1951).

38. U. S. Census of Population, 1950, Special Reports, *Nativity and Parentage,* Tables 10 and 23.

39. Gerhard Lenski, "Status Crystallization: A Non-Vertical Dimension of Social Status," *American Sociological Review,* 19:405–413 (August 1954);———"Social Participation and Status Crystallization," *American Sociological Review,* 21:458–464 (August 1956); William F. Kenkel, "The Relationship Between Status Consistency and Politico-Economic Attitudes," *American Sociological Review,* 21:365–368 (June 1956); Gerhard Lenski, "Comment on Kenkel's Communication," *American Sociological Review,* 21:368–369 (June 1956); Handlin, *The Uprooted;* Maldwyn Allen Jones, *American Immigration* (Chicago: University of Chicago Press, 1960); Robert E. Part and Herbert A. Miller, *Old World Traits Transplanted* (New York: Harper, 1921); William Foote Whyte, *Street Corner Society* (Chicago: University of Chicago Press, 1943).

CHAPTER 8

1. Donald J. Bogue, *The Population of the United States* (Glencoe, Ill.: Free Press, 1959).

2. "Years of high unemployment (high in relation to the postwar average) were defined as years in which the average annual unemployment rate was more than 4.0 percent. Years of low unemployment were defined as those years in which the average annual rate was less than 3.0 percent, and years of medium unemployment were defined as years in which the rate was between 3.0 and 4.0 percent. An index of age

differential was computed by summing the rates for the years in each of these three groups by age groups, and dividing the sum for each age group by the sum for all ages"; Bogue, *Population,* p. 634, no. 6.

3. Bogue, *Population.*

4. U. S. Bureau of Labor Statistics, *Unemployment: Terminology, Measurement and Analysis* (Washington, D. C.: U. S. Government Printing Office, 1961), pp. 61–63.

5. W. S. Woytinsky, "Income Cycle in the Life of Families and Individuals," *Social Security Bulletin* (January–June 1943), pp. 11–67.

6. U. S. Bureau of the Census, *U. S. Census of Population: 1950,* Series P-E, No. 2-A, Table 22.

7. U. S. Bureau of the Census, U. S. Census of Population, *Characteristics of the Population: 1950* (Washington, D. C.: Government Printing Office, 1950), vol. II, part 1, U. S. Summary, Table 139.

8. Woytinsky, "Income Cycle," Table 2, p. 11.

9. S. M. Eisenstadt, *From Generation to Generation: Age Groups and Social Structure* (New York: Free Press of Glencoe, 1956); Margaret Mead, "On the Concept of Plot in Culture," *Transactions of the New York Academy of Science,* II, 2:24–28 (I, 1939); Ruth Benedict, *The Chrysanthemum and the Sword* (Boston: Houghton Mifflin, 1945); A. Van Gennep, *The Rites of Passage,* trans. M. B. Vizedom and G. L. Caffee (Chicago: University of Chicago Press, 1960); Talcott Parsons, "Age and Sex in the Social Structure of the United States," *American Sociological Review,* 7:589–603 (October 1942); D. C. Miller and W. Form, *Industrial Sociology: An Introduction to the Sociology of Work Relations* (New York: Harper, 1951); Charlotte Buhler, "The Curve of Life as Studied in Biographies," *Journal of Applied Psychology,* 19:405–409 (August 1935); ———"Meanful Living in the Mature Years," in R. Kleemeier (ed.), *Aging and Leisure* (New York: Oxford University Press, 1961); pp. 345–387; Erik H. Erikson, *Childhood and Society* (New York: Norton, 1950); ———"Identity and the Life Cycle," *Psychological Issues,* 1:18–171 (1959); Maurice E. Linden and Douglas Courtney, "The Human Life Cycle and its Interruptions," *American Journal of Psychiatry,* 109:906–915 (June 1953).

10. Sigmund Freud, *The Ego and the Id* (London: Hogarth, 1947; first published in 1923); H. Hartmann, *Ego Psychology and the Problem of Adaptation* (New York: International Universities Press, 1958; first published in 1939); ———and E. Kris, "The Genetic Approach in Psychoanalysis," *The Psychoanalytic Study of the Child* (New York: International Universities Press, 1945), I, 11–30; R. M. Loewenstein, "Conflict and Autonomous Ego Development During the Phallic Phase," *The Psychoanalytic Study of the Child* (New York: International Universities Press, 1950), V, 47–52); E. Kris, "Neutralization and Sublimation: Observations on Young Children," *Psychoanalytic Study of the Child* (New York: International Universities Press, 1955), X, 30–46.

11. Buhler, "The Curve of Life," p. 408, author's italics.

12. Erikson, "Identity and the Life Cycle," pp. 98–99.

13. Linden and Courtney, "The Human Life Cycle," p. 911.

14. H. J. Friedsam, "Older Persons in Disaster," in George W. Baker and Dwight W. Chapman (eds.), *Man and Society in Disaster* (New York: Basic Books, 1962), pp. 151–182.

15. E. S. Marks and C. E. Fritz, "Human Reactions in Disaster Situations (3 vols.), unpub. report, National Opinion Research Center, 1954, pp. 143–145; Friedsam, "Disaster," p. 169.

16. The age categories showing the very highest birth and marriage rates are respectively 18–22 and 20–24 for the United States, 1910–1960; see Bogue, *Population,* pp. 321–324.

17. R. H. Hooker, "Correlation of the Marriage-Rate with Trade," *Journal of the Royal Statistical Society,* 64:485–592 (September 1901); Lucien March, "Comparison numérique de courbes statistiques," *Journal de la Société de Statistique de Paris,* 46:255–277, 306–311 (1905); G. Udny Yule, "On the Changes in the Marriage- and Birth-Rates in England and Wales During the Past Half Century; with an Inquiry as to their Probable Causes," *Journal of the Royal Statistical Society,* 69:122 (March 1906); William F. Ogburn and Dorothy S. Thomas, "The Influence of the Business Cycle on Certain Conditions," *Journal of the American Statistical Association,* 18:205–340 (September 1922); Dorothy S. Thomas, *Social Aspects of the Business Cycle* (New York: Knopf, 1927); G. Udny Yule, "The Growth of Population and the Factors which Control It," *Journal of the Royal Statistical Society,* 88:1–58 (January 1925); Samuel A. Stouffer and Lyle M. Spencer, "Marriage and Divorce in Recent Years," *Annals of the American Academy of Political and Social Sciences,* 188:56–59 (November 1936); ———"Recent Increases in Marriage and Divorce," *American Journal of Sociology,* 44:551–554 (January 1939); Alfred J. Lotka and Mortimer Spiegelman, "The Trend of the Birth Rate by Age of Mother and Order of Birth," *Journal of the American Statistical Association,* 35:595–601 (June 1940); Dudley Kirk, "The Relation of Employment to the Level of Births in Germany," *Milbank Memorial Fund Quarterly,* 20:126–138 (1942); H. Leibenstein and W. Galenson, "Investment Criteria, Productivity, and Economic Development," *Quarterly Journal of Economics,* 69:343–370 (August 1955); Virginia L. Galbraith and Dorothy S. Thomas, "Birth Rates and the Interwar Business Cycles," *Journal of the American Statistical Association,* 36:465–484 (December 1941); Joseph J. Spengler, "Economics and Demography," in Phillip M. Houser and Otis D. Dunkin (eds.), *The Study of Population* (Chicago: University of Chicago Press, 1959).

18. Friedsam, "Disaster," p. 176.

19. Seymour Martin Lipset and Reinhard Bendix, *Social Mobility in Industrial Society* (Berkeley: University of California Press, 1959).

20. Samuel A. Stouffer and Paul F. Lazarsfeld, *Research Memorandum on the Family in the Depression* (New York: Social Science Research Council, Bull. 29, 1937).

21. The research, in general, indicates that the higher a person's income and class status, the greater his participation in voluntary associations, and therefore the lower his proportionate interaction in family social life; see William J. Goode, "Family and Mobility," in Reinhard Bendix and Seymour Lipset (eds.), *Class, Status and Power,* 2nd ed. (New York: Free Press, 1966), p. 598; Floyd Dotson, "Patterns of Voluntary Association Among Urban Working-Class Families," *American Sociological Review,* 16:687–693 (October 1951); Mirra Komarovsky, "The Voluntary Association of Urban Dwellers," *American Sociological Review,* 11:686–698 (December 1946); Frederick A. Bushee, "Social Organizations in a Small City," *American Journal of Sociology,* 51:217–226 (November 1945); William C. Mather, "Income and Social Participation," *American Sociological Review,* 6:380–384 (June 1941); W. Lloyd Warner and Paul S. Lunt, *The Social Life of a Modern Community* (New Haven, Conn.: Yale University Press, 1941); Robert S. Lynd and Helen M. Lynd, *Middletown* (New York: Harcourt, Brace, 1929); August B. Hollingshead, *Elmtown's Youth* (New York: Wiley, 1949); E. Wight Bakke, *Citizens Without Work* (New Haven, Conn.: Yale University Press, 1940).

22. Peter M. Blau, "Social Mobility and Interpersonal Relations," *American Sociological Review,* 21:290–294 (June 1956); Lipset and Bendix, *Social Mobility,* p. 65; Eugene Litwak, "Occupational Mobility and Family Cohesion," *American Sociological Review,* 25:15 (February 1960); Talcott Parsons, "The Social Structure of the Family," in Ruth N. Anshen (ed.), *The Family: Its Functions and Destiny* (New York: Harper, 1949); ———"Revised Analytical Approach to the Theory of

Social Stratification," in R. Bendix and S. M. Lipset (eds.), *Class, Status and Power: A Reader in Social Stratification* (Glencoe, Ill.: Free Press, 1953), p. 116.

23. Linden and Courtney, "The Human Life Cycle," pp. 912–915; Marjorie F. Lowenthal, "Social Isolation and Mental Illness in Old Age," *American Sociological Review*, 29:54–70 (February 1946).

24. John A. Clausen and Marion Yarrow, "Paths to the Mental Hospital," *Journal of Social Issues*, 11:25–32 (November 1955); John Cumming and Elaine Cumming, *Closed Ranks: An Experiment in Mental Health Education* (Cambridge, Mass.: Harvard University Press, 1957); Bruce P. Dohrenwend, Viola W. Bernard, and Lawrence C. Kolb, "The Orientations of Leaders in an Urban Area Toward Problems of Mental Illness," *American Journal of Psychiatry*, 118:683–691 (February 1962); Howard E. Freeman and Ozzie G. Simmons, "Mental Patients in the Community," *American Sociological Review*, 23:147–154 (April 1958); Gerald Gurin, Joseph Veroff, and Sheila Feld, *Americans View Their Mental Health* (New York: Basic Books, 1960); Paul V. Lemkau and Guido M. Crocetti, "An Urban Population's Opinion and Knowledge about Mental Illness," *American Journal of Psychiatry*, 118:692–700 (February 1962); Jum C. Nunally, Jr., *Popular Conceptions of Mental Health* (New York: Holt, Rinehart, and Winston, 1961); Glen V. Ramsey and Melita Seipp, "Public Opinions and Information Concerning Mental Health," *Journal of Clinical Psychology*, 4:397–406 (October 1948); Charlotte G. Schwartz, "Perspectives on Deviance—Wives' Definitions of their Husbands' Mental Illness," *Psychiatry*, 20:275–291 (August 1957); Julian L. Woodward, "Changing Ideas on Mental Illness and its Treatment," *American Sociological Review*, 16:443–454 (August 1951); Derek L. Phillips, "Rejection: A Possible Consequence of Seeking Help for Mental Disorders," *American Sociological Review*, 28:963–972 (December 1963).

25. Howard E. Freeman and Ozzie G. Simmons, *The Mental Patient Comes Home* (New York: Wiley, 1963), pp. 48–55.

26. *Ibid*, pp. 52, 54

27. Gerald Gordon, *Role Theory and Illness: A Sociological Perspective* (New Haven, Conn.: College and University Press, 1966); Talcott Parsons, *The Social System* (Glencoe, Ill.: Free Press, 1951), pp. 436–437.

28. Percentages of females in the civilian female labor force, 16 years old and older: 1940—single, 54.2; widowed and divorced, 36.2; married, 14.7; 1950—single, 58.1; widowed and divorced, 37.8; married, 23.8. See Clarence D. Long, *The Labor Force Under Changing Income and Employment* (Princeton, N. J.: Princeton University Press, 1958), p. 115.

29. Stouffer and Lazarsfeld, *Family in the Depression*, pp. 28–34.

30. *Ibid*, pp. 627–639.

31. U. S. Bureau of Labor Statistics, "Unemployment," Table 6, p. 61.

CHAPTER 9

1. Thomas S. Langner and Stanley T. Michael, *Life Stress and Mental Health: The Midtown Manhattan Study*, vol. II (New York: Free Press, 1963); Lloyd H. Rogler and August B. Hollingshead, *Trapped: Families and Schizophrenia* (New York: Wiley, 1965); Milbank Memorial Fund (Annual Conference), *The Biology of Mental Health and Disease* (New York: Harper, 1952); American Psychiatric Association, *Diagnostic and Statistical Manual: Mental Disorders* (Washington, D. C.; American Psychiatric Association, 1952).

2. Langner and Michael, *Life Stress;* Rogler and Hollingshead, *Trapped*

3. Langner and Michael, *Life Stress;* Rogler and Hollingshead, *Trapped;* Gerald Gurin, Joseph Veroff, and Sheila Feld, *Americans View Their Mental Health* (New

York: Basic Books, 1960); August B. Hollingshead and Fredrick C. Redlich, *Social Class and Mental Illness* (New York: Wiley, 1958).

4. Karen Horney, *The Neurotic Personality of Our Time* (New York: Macmillan, 1933); Abram Kardiner and Lionel Ovesey, *The Mark of Oppression: A Psychosocial Study of the American Negro* (New York: Norton, 1951); Robert K. Merton, *Social Theory and Social Structure,* rev. ed. (Glencoe, Ill.: Free Press, 1957), chap. IV; Kurt Lewin, Tamara Dembo, Leon Festinger, and Pauline Sears, "Level of Aspiration," in J. McV. Hunt (ed.), *Personality and the Behavior Disorders* (New York: Ronald Press, 1944), I, 333–378; Robert J. Kleiner and Seymour Parker, "Goal-Striving, Social Status and Mental Disorder: A Research Review," *American Sociological Review,* 28:189–202 (April 1963).

5. August B. Hollingshead, "Some Issues in the Epidemiology of Schizophrenia," *American Sociological Review,* 26:5–14 (February 1961); Gurin *et al., Americans View.*

6. Elton F. Jackson, "Status Consistency and Symptoms of Stress," *American Sociological Review,* 27:469–480 (August 1962).

7. Jacob Tuckman and Robert J. Kleiner, "Discrepancy Between Aspiration and Achievement as a Predictor of Schizophrenia," *Behavioral Science,* 7:443–447 (October 1962); H. Warren Dunham, Patricia Phillips, and Barbara Srinivasan, "A Research Note on Diagnosed Mental Illness and Social Class," *American Sociological Review,* 31:223–226 (April 1966).

8. Mary H. Lystad, "Social Mobility Among Selected Groups of Schizophrenic Patients," *American Sociological Review,* 22:288–292 (June 1957); Leo Srole, Thomas S. Langner, Stanley T. Michael, and Thomas A. C. Rennie, *Mental Health in the Metropolis: The Midtown Manhattan Study* (New York: McGraw-Hill, 1962); E. Gartley Jaco, "Social Stress and Mental Illness in the Community," in Marvin B. Sussman (ed.), *Community Structure and Analysis* (New York: Crowell, 1959), pp. 388–409; J. N. Morris, "Health and Social Class," *Lancet,* 1:303–305 (February 1959).

9. Rema Lapouse, Mary A. Monk and Milton Terris, "The Drift Hypothesis and Socio-Economic Differentials and Schizophrenia," *American Journal of Public Health,* 46:978–986 (August 1956); Hollingshead and Redlich, *Social Class.*

10. M. B. Owen, "Alternative Hypotheses for the Evaluation of Faris and Dunham's Results," *American Journal of Sociology,* 47:48–51 (July 1941); H. Warren Dunham, *Sociological Theory and Mental Disorder* (Detroit, Mich.: Wayne State University Press, 1959), chap. IV; Morris, "Health and Social Class"; Bruce P. Dohrenwend, "Social Status and Psychological Disorder: An Issue of Substance and an Issue of Method," *American Sociological Review,* 31:14–24 (February 1966); Dunham, *et al.,* "Research Note."

11. Hollingshead and Redlich, *Social Class;* Srole *et al., Midtown Manhattan Study;* Rogler and Hollingshead, *Trapped.*

12. Pitirim Sorokin, *Social Mobility,* New York: Harper, 1927; Lloyd W. Warner, "The Society, The Individual, and His Mental Disorders," *American Journal of Psychiatry,* 94:274–284 (September 1937); Jurgen Ruesch, *Chronic Disease and Psychological Invalidism: A Psychosomatic Study,* New York: American Society for Research in Psychosomatic Problems, 1946, pp. 104–124; ———Annemarie Jacobson, and Martin B. Loeb, "Acculturation and Illness," *Psychological Monographs: General and Applied,* vol. 62, no. 5, whole no. 292, Washington, D. C.: The American Psychological Association, 1948; ———"Social Technique, Social Status, and Social Change in Illness," in Clyde Kluckhohn, Henry A. Murray, and David M. Schneider (eds.), *Personality in Nature, Society, and Culture* (New York: Knopf, 1956), pp. 123–136.

13. M. Sims, "Comparative Study of Disease Incidence in Admissions to Base Psychiatric Hospital in Middle East," *Journal of Mental Science,* 92:118–127 (January 1946); M. Ekblad, "Psychiatric and Sociological Study of Series of Swedish Naval Conscripts," *Acta psychiatrica et neurologica,* supplement no. 49:1–201 (1948); O. Odegaard, "The Incidence of Psychoses in Various Occupations," *International Journal of Social Psychiatry,* 2:85–104 (Autumn 1956).

14. Robert E. L. Faris "Cultural Isolation and Schizophrenic Personality," *American Journal of Sociology,* 40:155–164 (September 1934); Edwin Lemert, "An Exploratory Study of Mental Disorders in a Rural Problem Area," *Rural Sociology,* 13:48–64 (March 1948); E. Gartley Jaco, "Social Factors in Mental Disorders in Texas," *Social Problems,* 4:322–328 (April 1957); ———"Incidence of Psychoses in Texas, 1951–1952," *Texas State Journal of Medicine,* 33:85–91 (February 1951); E. M. Gruenberg, "Community Conditions and Psychoses of Elderly," *American Journal of Psychiatry,* 110:888–895 (June 1954); Melvin L. Kohn and John A. Clausen, "Social Isolation and Schizophrenia," *American Sociological Review,* 20:265–273 (June 1955).

15. Leta McKinney Adler, "The Relationship of Marital Status to Incidence of Recovery from Mental Illness," *Social Forces,* 32:185–194 (December 1953); B. Malzberg, "Marital Status and Mental Disease Among Negroes in New York State," *Journal of Nervous and Mental Disease,* 123:457–465 (1956); Amerigo Farina, Norman Germezy, and Herbert Barry, "Relationship of Marital Status to Incidence and Prognosis of Schizophrenia," *Journal of Abnormal and Social Psychology,* 67:624–630 (December 1963).

16. O. Odegaard, "Emigration and Mental Health," *Mental Hygiene,* 20:546:553 (October 1936); Chistopher Tietze, Paul Lemkau, and Marcia Cooper, "Personality Disorder and Spatial Mobility," *American Journal of Sociology,* 48:29–39 (July 1942); Abraham A. Weinberg, "Problems of Adjustment of New Immigrants to Israel," Part I, *World Mental Health,* 5:57–63 (May 1953), Part II, 5:129–135 (August 1953); ———"Mental Health Aspects of Voluntary Migration," *Mental Hygiene,* 39:450–464 (July 1955); J. M. Last, "The Health of Immigrants: Some Observations from General Practice," *Medical Journal of Australia,* 1:158–162 (January 1960).

17. W. S. Robinson, "Ecological Correlations and the Behavior of Individuals," *American Sociological Review,* 15:351–357 (June 1950). A major difficulty with the ecological correlations is that they often invite a wide range of competing explanations, including another type of questionable causation, namely spuriousness, see, for example, Herbert Hyman, *Survey Design and Analysis: Principles, Cases and Procedures* (Glencoe, Ill.: Free Press, 1955); Hubert M. Blalock, Jr., *Social Statistics* (New York: McGraw-Hill, 1960).

18. Gottfried von Haberler, *Prosperity and Depression* (Cambridge, Mass.: Harvard University Press, 1958).

19. J. A. Schumpeter, *Business Cycles,* vol. 1, New York: McGraw-Hill, 1936, p. 161.

20. N. D. Kondratieff, "The Long Waves in Economic Life," *Review of Economic Statistics,* 17:105 (1935).

21. Clement Juglar, *Des Crises Commerciales* (Paris: Guillaumin, 1st ed., 1860; 2nd ed., 1889).

22. Joseph Kitchin, "Cycles and Trends in Economic Factors," *Review of Economic Statistics,* 5:10–16 (January 1923).

23. Schumpeter, *Business Cycles.*

24. von Haberler, *Prosperity and Depression;* J. M. Keynes, *General Theory of Employment, Interest and Money* (New York: Harcourt Brace, 1936), chap. 3.

25. R. G. Hawtrey, *Capital and Employment* (New York: Longmans, Green, 1937), p. 176.

26. Frederick Hayek, *Profits, Interest and Investment* (London: Routledge and Sons, 1939).

27. John A. Hobson, *The Economics of Unemployment* (London: Allen and Unwin, 1922).

28. W. T. Foster and W. Katchings, *Profits* (Boston: Houghton Mifflin, 1925).

29. Edwin Lemert, *Social Pathology* (New York: McGraw-Hill, 1951); Jerome K. Myers and Leslie Schaffer, "Social Stratification and Psychiatric Practice: A Study of an Out-Patient Clinic," *American Sociological Review*, 19:307–310 (January 1954); John A. Clausen and Marian Yarrow, "Paths to the Mental Hospital," *Journal of Social Issues*, 11:25–32 (November 1955).

30. M. B. Owen, "Alternative Hypotheses for the Evaluation of Faris and Dunham's Results," *American Journal of Sociology* 47:48–51 (July 1941).

31. J. S. Tyhurst, "The Role of Transition States—Including Disasters—in Mental Illness," in Walter Reed Army Institute of Research and the National Research Council, Sponsors, *Symposium on Preventive and Social Psychiatry* (Washington, D. C.: Walter Reed Army Institute of Research, 1957), p. 164.

32. Joint Commission on Mental Illness and Health, *Action for Mental Health* (New York: Basic Books, 1961), p. 84, emphasis in original. Three other excellent examples of the effects of social interaction on mental patient recovery and mentally ill behavior generally are Otto von Mering and Stanley H. King, *Remotivating the Mental Patient* (New York: Russell Sage Foundation, 1957); Morris S. Schwartz and Emmy Lanning Shockley, *The Nurse and the Mental Patient* (New York: Russell Sage Foundation, 1956); M. Greenblatt, R. H. York, and Esther L. Brown, *From Custodial to Therapeutic Patient Care in Mental Hospitals* (New York: Russell Sage Foundation, 1955).

33. The literature on negative public attitudes toward the mentally ill is voluminous; see, for example, Jum C. Nunnally, Jr., *Popular Conceptions of Mental Health* (New York: Holt, Rinehart, and Winston, 1961); Derek L. Phillips, "Rejection: A Possible Consequence of Seeking Help for Mental Disorders," *American Sociological Review*, 28:963–972 (December 1963); Allan Gregg, "A Critique of Psychiatry," *American Journal of Psychiatry*, 101:285 (March 1944); August B. Hollingshead and Fredrich C. Redlich, "Social Mobility and Mental Illness," *American Journal of Psychiatry*, 112:342 (September 1955); Stanley H. King, *Perceptions of Illness and Medical Practice* (New York: Russell Sage Foundation, 1962), p. 140.

34. R. S. de Ropp, *Drugs and the Mind* (New York: St. Martin's, 1957), pp. 167–168.

35. Joint Commission, *Action for Mental Health*, p. 58, emphasis in original.

36. The possible relation between attitudes and perception (cognitive organization) has been the source of much theory and empirical study in social psychology; for example, Theodore M. Newcomb, "The Prediction of Interpersonal Attraction," *American Psychologist*, 11:575–586 (November 1956); ———"The Study of Consensus," in R. K. Merton, Leonard Broom, and L. S. Cottrell, Jr. (eds.), *Sociology Today: Problems and Prospects* (New York: Basic Books, Inc., 1959), pp. 277–292; G. H. Mead, *Mind, Self and Society* (ed. C. H. Morris) (Chicago: University of Chicago Press, 1934); F. Heider, "Attitudes and Cognitive Organization," *Journal of Psychology*, 21:107–112 (January 1946); D. Cartwright and F. Harary, "Structural Balance: A Generalization of Heider's Theory," *Psychological Review*, 63:277–293 (March 1956); Theodore M. Newcomb, "An Approach to the Study of Communicative Acts," *Psychological Review*, 60:393–404 (May 1964).

A central assumption in the work of Heider, for example, is that "when an individual has attitudes toward two objects, cognitive imbalance exists for him if the two objects belong together (by any of several criteria) while his cathectic orientations toward them are opposed—*e.g.,* if he 'likes' one of the two related objects and dislikes the other... If *A* likes both *B* and *C* but believes that *B* dislikes *C*, this constellation is one of imbalance. Or if *A* likes some of *B*'s traits and dislikes others (all of them obviously belonging together in *B*), the situation is, again, one of imbalance" (Newcomb "Study of Consensus," p. 281). When imbalance exists, there is a situation of strain, and the individual under this strain reacts by attempting to align his attitudes and cognitive organization.

As to possible application to the case of the perception of "mental illness," for example, *A*'s perception of *B*, her husband, entails a situation of attitudinal cognitive imbalance for *A:* her husband, whose role, as husband, invokes positive affect, appears mentally ill, a role which invokes severely negative affect. *A* can resolve this imbalance by changing either attitudes or perceptions. Let us say that in the initially balanced outcome *B* continues to be perceived positively, and therefore not as mentally ill. Then suppose, however, that *B*'s behavior becomes stressful for *A;* for example, *B*, being mentally ill, is unable to support *A*. *A* is now in a new situation of imbalance. *B* is perceived both positively, as loved husband, and negatively, as unable to support *A*. The newly added negative perception might well tip the imbalance in favor of a balanced negative perception. Thus, the negative perception of *B*'s deviant behavior may no longer be withheld.

37. John Dollard, Leonard W. Doob, Neal E. Miller, O. H. Mowrer, and Robert R. Sears, *Frustration and Aggression* (New Haven, Conn.: Yale University Press, 1939), p. 11.

38. John A. Clausen, "The Sociology of Mental Illness," in Merton *et al., Sociology Today,* p. 495, my italics.

39. Muriel Hammer, "Influence of Small Social Networks as Factors on Mental Hospital Admissions," *Human Organization,* 22:243–251 (Winter 1963–64).

40. Bernard Berelson and Garry A. Steiner, *Human Behavior: An Inventory of Scientific Findings* (New York: Harcourt, Brace and World, 1964); Bernard Barber, *Social Stratification: A Comparable Analysis of Structure and Process* (New York: Harcourt, Brace and World, 1957); August B. Hollingshead, *Elmtown's Youth* (New York: Wiley, 1949).

41. As we have seen in Chapter 7, both high cohesiveness and high sensitivity are also characteristic of the Armenian group. Even stronger evidence of family cohesion would be evidenced for minority groups generally, and especially for the foreign stock; Charles F. Marden and Gladys Meyer, *Minorities in American Society* (New York: American Book Co., 1962). Here again, however, it is well-established for the United States that the foreign stock show much higher rates of mental hospitalization than the native population; Jack P. Gibbs, "Rates of Mental Hospitalization: A Study of Societal Reaction to Deviant Behavior," *American Sociological Review,* 27:782–792 (December 1962); Arnold M. Rose and Holger R. Stub, "Summary of Studies on the Incidence of Mental Disorders," in Arnold M. Rose (ed.), *Mental Health and Mental Disorder* (London: Routledge and Kegan Paul, 1956), pp. 87–116.

42. Emile Durkheim, *Suicide,* trans. by John A. Spaulding and George Simpson (New York: Free Press, 1951); Stanley R. Brav, *Jewish Family Solidarity: Myth or Fact?* (Vicksburg, Miss.: Nogales Press, 1940); Fred L. Strodtbeck, "Family Interaction, Values, and Achievement," in Marshall Sklare, *The Jews: Social Patterns of an American Group* (Glencoe, Ill.: Free Press, 1958), p. 147.

43. Howard E. Freeman and Ozzie G. Simmons, *The Mental Patient Comes Home* (New York: Wiley, 1963).

44. Richard T. La Pierre, *A Theory of Social Control* (New York: McGraw-Hill, 1954).

45. Hammer, "Influence of Small Social Networks."

46. Gibbs, "Rates of Mental Hospitalization."

47. Paul F. Lazarsfeld, "Problems in Methodology," in Merton *et al.*, *Sociology Today*, pp. 39–80.

48. Andrew F. Henry and James F. Short, *Suicide and Homicide* (Glencoe, Ill.: Free Press, 1954), p. 24.

49. Talcott Parsons, "Revised Analytical Approach to the Theory of Social Stratification," in R. Bendix and S. M. Lipset (eds.), *Class, Status and Power: A Reader in Social Stratification* (Glencoe, Ill.: Free Press, 1953), pp. 92–128.

50. *Ibid*, pp. 24–25.

51. *Ibid*, p. 52.

52. Arnold M. Rose and Holger R. Stub, "Incidence of Mental Disorders"; Robert M. Frumkin, "Occupation and Major Mental Disorders," in Rose, *Mental Health*, pp. 135–160; August B. Hollingshead and Frederick C. Redlich, *Social Class and Mental Illness* (New York: Wiley, 1958).

53. Louis I. Dublin and Bessie Bunzel, *To Be or Not To Be* (New York: Harrison Smith and Robert Haas, 1933); Henry and Short, *Suicide and Homicide*.

54. Robert E. L. Faris and H. W. Dunham, *Mental Disorders in Urban Areas* (New York: Hafner, 1960; first ed., 1939); Rose and Stub, "Incidence of Mental Disorders"; Frumkin, "Major Mental Disorders"; Hollingshead and Redlich, *Social Class.*

55. Seymour Martin Lipset and Reinhard Bendix, *Social Mobility in Industrial Society* (Berkeley: University of California Press, 1959).

56. Samuel A. Stouffer and Paul F. Lazarsfeld, *Research Memorandum on the Family in the Depression* (New York: Social Science Research Council, Bull. 29, 1937).

57. H. Schelsky, *Wandlungen in der Deutschen Familien in der Gegenwart* (Stuttgart: Enke-Verlag, 1954); C. E. Fritz and J. H. Mathewson, *Convergence Behavior in Disasters: A Problem in Social Control* (Disaster Study Number 9; Washington: National Academy of Sciences—National Research Council, 1957); S. Z. Klausner and H. V. Kincaid, *Social Problems of Sheltering Flood Evacuees* (New York: Columbia University Bureau of Applied Social Research, 1956); A. F. C. Wallace, *Tornado in Worcester: An Exploratory Study of Individual and Community Behavior in an Extreme Situation* (Disaster Study Number 3; Washington: National Academy of Sciences—National Research Council, 1956); M. Young, "The Role of the Extended Family in a Disaster," *Human Relations*, 7:383–391 (August 1954); H. J. Friedsam, "Older Persons in Disaster," in George W. Baker and Dwight W. Chapman (eds.), *Man and Society in Disaster* (New York: Basic Books, 1962), pp. 151–184; Leopold Rosenmayer and Eva Kockeis, "Propositions for a Sociological Theory of Aging and the Family," *International Social Science Journal*, 15:410–426 (1963).

58. F. C. Redlich, "The Concept of Health in Psychiatry," in John A. Clausen and Robert N. Wilson (eds.), *Explorations in Social Psychiatry* (New York: Basic Books, 1957), p. 158.

59. Henry J. Wegrocki, "A Critique of Cultural and Statistical Concepts of Abnormality," in Kluckhohn, Murray, and Schneider (eds.), *Personality in Nature, Society, and Culture*, pp. 699–700.

60. See, for example, Wegrocki, "Concepts of Abnormality." Redlich, *Health in Psychiatry;* Marie Jahoda, *Current Concepts of Popular Mental Health* (New York: Basic Books, 1958).

61. Lawrence S. Kubie, "Social Forces and the Neurotic Process," in Alexander H. Leighton, John A. Clausen and Robert N. Wilson, *Explorations in Social Psychiatry* (New York: Basic Books, 1957), pp. 77–104.

62. Wegrocki, "Concepts of Abnormality," pp. 698–700.

63. John A. Clausen, "The Sociology of Mental Illness," in Merton *et al., Sociology Today,* p. 495.

64. Ruth Benedict, "Anthopology and the Abnormal," *Journal of General Psychology,* 10:59–82 (January 1934).

65. H. W. Dunham, *Sociological Theory and Mental Disorder* (Detroit, Mich.: Wayne State University Press, 1959), chap. VI, p. 234.

66. Redlich, "Health in Psychiatry."

67. *Ibid,* p. 155.

68. Jahoda, *Positive Mental Health.*

69. Leo Srole, *et al., Midtown Manhattan Study,* p. 61.

70. *Ibid,* p. 63–64.

71. Dorothea C. Leighton, John S. Harding, David B. Macklin, Allister B. Macmillan, and Alexander H. Leighton, *The Character of Danger, Psychiatric Symptoms in Selected Communities, The Stirling County Study of Psychiatric Disorder and Sociocultural Environment* (New York: Basic Books, 1963), III, 52.

72. Clausen, "The Sociology of Mental Illness," p. 493.

73. Anita K. Bahn, "The Development of an Effective Statistical System in Mental Illness," *American Journal of Psychiatry,* 116:798–800 (March 1960); August B. Hollingshead, "Some Issues in the Epidemiology of Schizophrenia," *American Sociological Review,* 26:5–14 (February 1961).

74. John A. Clausen, "The Sociology of Mental Illness," in Merton *et al., Sociology Today,* p. 493.

75. G. H. Mead, *Mind, Self and Society,* ed. by C. H. Morris (Chicago: University of Chicago Press, 1934), part III.

76. Enid Mills, *Living with Mental Illness* (London: Routledge and Kegan Paul, 1962), p. 13. See also John Cumming and Elaine Cumming, "Mental Health Education in a Canadian Community," in Benjamin D. Paul (ed.), *Health, Culture, and Community* (New York: Russell Sage Foundation, 1955), pp. 43–69; Shirley Star, "The Public's Idea About Mental Illness," presented to the Annual Meeting of the National Association for Mental Health, Indianapolis, Ind., November 5, 1955; "The Place of Psychiatry in Popular Thinking," presented to the Annual Meeting of the American Association for Public Opinion Research, Washington, May 9, 1957; George Warren Brown School of Social Work, "Summary of Thesis Research, 1949–1950," Washington University, St. Louis, 1951; "Summary of Thesis Research, 1950–1951," Washington University, St. Louis, 1952. The last two unpublished studies were not reviewed by this writer; reviews are given in Stanley H. King, *Perceptions of Illness and Medical Practice* (New York: Russell Sage Foundation, 1962), chap. V.

CHAPTER 10

1. A classic statement is given in Max Shane and Milton S. Roemer, "Hospital Costs Relate to the Supply of Beds," *Modern Hospital,* 92:71–73, 168 (April 1959).

2. This is especially true for Paul O. Komra and Mary A. Clark, "Mental Disease in the Crisis," *Mental Hygiene,* 19:289–301 (April 1935); see also the discussion in Robert E. Patton and Abbott S. Weinstein, "First Admissions to New York Civil State Hospitals, 1911–1958," *Psychiatric Quarterly,* 34:245–274 (1960, part II).

3. Patton and Weinstein, "First Admissions," p. 16.

4. Erving Goffman, *Asylums* (New York: Doubleday-Anchor, 1961); John K. Wing, "Institutionalism in Mental Hospitals," *British Journal of Social and Clinical Psychology,* 1:38–51 (1962).

5. Howard E. Freeman and Ozzie G. Simmons, *The Mental Patient Comes Home* (New York: Wiley, 1963).

6. Goffman, *Asylums.*

7. Wing, *Institutionalism.*

8. W. Caudill and E. Stainbrook, "Some Covert Effects of Communication Difficulties in a Psychiatric Hospital," *Journal of Psychiatry,* 17:27–40 (1964); Charles Perrow, "Hospitals, Technology, Structure, and Goals," in J. March (ed.), *Handbook of Organizations* (Chicago: Rand McNally, 1965); A. H. Stanton and M. S. Schwartz, *The Mental Hospital* (New York: Basic Books, 1954).

9. American Psychiatric Association, *Diagnostic and Statistical Manual of Mental Disorders* (Washington, D. C.: American Psychiatric Association, 1952), pp. 15, 18.

10. *Ibid.,* p. 24.

11. Freeman and Simmons, *The Mental Patient Comes Home;* J. K. Myers and L. Bean, *A Decade Later: A Follow-Up of Social Class and Mental Illness* (New York: Wiley, 1968).

12. L. Srole, T. S. Langner, S. T. Mitchell, M. H. Opler, and T. A. C. Rennie, *Mental Health in the Metropolis: The Midtown Manhattan Study,* vol. I, (New York: McGraw-Hill, 1962).

13. Robert H. Connery *et al, The Politics of Mental Health: Organizing Community Health in Metropolitan Areas* (New York: Columbia University Press, 1968).

14. American Psychiatric Association, *Diagnostic and Statistical Manual Of Mental Disorders,* 2nd ed. (Washington, D. C.: American Psychiatric Association, 1968), pp. 46–47.

CHAPTER 11

1. Gregory Bateson, Don D. Jackson, Jay Hayley and John Weakland, "Toward a Theory of Schizophrenia," *Behavioral Science,* 1:251–264 (1956); Theodore H. Lidz, Steven Fleck, and Alice R. Cornelison, *Schizophrenia and the Family* (New York: International Universities Press, 1965); Howard E. Freeman and Ozzie G. Simmons, "Mental Patients in the Community: Family Settings and Performance Levels," *American Sociological Review,* 23:147–154 (1958).

2. H. E. Freeman and O. G. Simmons, *The Mental Patient Comes Home* (New York: Wiley, 1963); J. B. Myers and L. Bean, *A Decade Later: A Follow-up of Social Class and Mental Illness* (New York: Wiley, 1968).

3. Harold Phelps, "Cycles of Crime," *Journal of Criminal Law and Criminology,* 20:107–121 (May–June 1929); Ray Mars Simpson, "Unemployment and Prison Commitments," *Journal of Criminal Law and Criminology,* 23:404–414 (September–October 1932); Andrew F. Henry and James F. Short, *Suicide and Homicide* (Glencoe, Ill.: Free Press, 1954).

4. Henry and Short, *Suicide and Homicide.* B. McMahon, S. Johnson and T. F. Pugh, "Relation of Suicide Rates to Social Conditions, Evidence From U. S. Vital Statistics," *Public Health Reports,* 78:285–293 (1963).

5. H. Warren Dunham, "Social Structures and Mental Disorders: Competing Hypothesis of Explanation," in *Causes and Mental Disorder: In Review of Epidemiological Knowledge* (New York: Milbank Memorial Fund 1959), pp. 227–265.

6. *Ibid.*

7. Donald L. Bogue, *The Population of the United States* (Glencoe, Ill.: Free Press, 1959), p. 74; Edward P. Hutchinson, *Immigrants and Their Children* (New York: Wiley, 1956).

8. The basic statistical procedures are evaluated in Arthur F. Burns and Wesley C. Mitchell, *Measuring Business Cycles* (New York: National Bureau of Economic Research, 1946).

9. Charles I. Schottland, *The Social Security Program in the United States* (New York: Appleton Century Crofts, 1963), pp. 29–39; Russell E. Smith and Dorothy Zietz, *American Social Welfare Institutions* (New York: Wiley, 1970).

10. David Mechanic, *Mental Health and Social Policy* (Englewood Cliffs, N. J.: Prentice-Hall, 1969); Robert H. Connery (ed.), *The Politics of Mental Health: Organizing Mental Health in Metropolitan Areas* (New York: Columbia University Press, 1968).

11. The Midtown Manhattan Study, for example, found among a sample of 1020 men and women between the ages of 20 and 59, in the authors' lowest classification of socioeconomic status, 47.3 percent to be "impaired," 23.1 percent with "moderate symptom formation," 25.0 percent with "mild symptom formation," and 4.6 percent "well." See L. Srole, T. S. Langner, S. T. Mitchell, M. K. Opler and T. A. C. Rennie, *Mental Health in the Metropolis: The Midtown Manhattan Study,* vol. I (New York: McGraw-Hill, 1962), p. 230.

12. Muriel Hammer, "Influence of Small Social Networks as Factors in Mental Hospital Admissions," *Human Organizations,* 22:243–251 (Winter 1963–64).

13. An extensive review is found in Paul M. Roman and Harrison M. Trice, *Schizophrenia and the Poor* (Ithaca, New York: Cornell University School of Industrial and Labor Relations, 1967).

14. M. M. Gordon, *Social Class in American Sociology* (Durham, N. C.: Duke University Press, 1958); Bernard Barber, *Social Stratification: A Comparative Analysis. of Structure and Process* (New York: Harcourt Brace, 1957); K. Mayer, *Class and Society* (New York: Random House, 1955).

15. See the reviews of the literature in Gordon, *Social Class;* Barber, *Social Stratification;* and Mayer, *Class and Society.*

16. William J. Goode, "Family Disorganization," in Robert K. Merton and Robert A. Nisbet, *Contemporary Social Problems: An Introduction to the Sociology of Deviant Behavior and Social Disorganization* (New York: Hartcourt Brace, 1961), pp. 415–421.

17. See the reviews of the literature in Goode, "Family Disorganization"; Gordon, *Social Class;* Barber, *Social Stratification;* Mayer, *Class and Society.*

18. Thomas S. Langner and Stanley T. Michael, *Life Stress and Mental Health: The Midtown Manhattan Study,* vol. II (Glencoe, Ill.: Free Press, 1963), p. 151.

19. See the literature in Herbert Marcuse, *Eros and Civilization: A Philosophical Inquiry into Freud* (New York: Random House, 1955), pp. 217–251.

20. Ari Kiev, *Psychiatry in the Communist World* (New York: Science House, 1968).

21. J. S. Mill, *Principles of Political Economy* (Toronto: University of Toronto Press, 1965; first published in 1848).

22. Richard Hofstadter, *Social Darwinism in American Thought* (Philadelphia: University of Pennsylvania Press, 1944).

23. David Reismann, Nathan Glazer, and Reuel Denney, *The Lonely Crowd* (New Haven, Conn: Yale University Press, 1961); W. W. Rostow, *The Stages of Economic Growth: A Non-Communist Manifesto* (Cambridge, England: Cambridge University Press, 1957).

Index

Admissions, mental-hospital, *see* Mental hospitalization

Age: relation between economic change and mental hospitalization by illness according to sex and, 37–41; relation between economic change and mental hospitalization according to (19th century), 48; long-term changes in relation between economic fluctuations and mental-hospital admissions by (1915–1967), 58, 64–67, 69; impact of economic change on mental-hospital admissions by, 112–118; effects of economic loss and role failure resulting in sensitivity to economic change by, 157–167

Alcoholism: sensitivity to economic change for hospital admissions with, 39–40, 42, 44; discharges of patients with, 215, 217–219; increases in hospitalization of, during economic downturns, 225

American Psychiatric Association, 219

Analyses, statistical and graphic: detrending of secular (or long-term) trends, 26–27; detrending of intermediate-sized trends, 27–28; correlation procedure, 28; procedure for dealing with dispersed stress reactions, 29–30; ecological character of relations and problem of intercorrelating data on different levels of analysis, 30–31

Armenians, high socioeconomic status of, 149–150, 151, 152

Ayres' Index of Industrial Production in the United States, 24, 36, 47, 190

"Balance Theory," and intolerance of the mentally ill, 183

Benedict, Ruth, 196

Bogue, Donald J., 148–149, 151–152, 157–158, 171

Buhler, Charlotte, 164

Bureau of Labor Statistics, 158–159, 171

Burns-Mitchell technique, 134

Cerebral arteriosclerosis (CER), psychosis with: sensitivity to economic change for hospital admissions with, 40–41, 43, 44, 140; discharges of patients having, 220–221

Civil War, relation between mental-hospital admissions and, 35, 36

Clark, Mary A., 13–15, 16, 17

Clausen, John A., 184

Courtney, Douglas, 164, 165

Creamer, Daniel, 134–135

Criminals, treatment versus punishment of, 223–224

Darwinists, 247

Dayton, Neil A., 18

Department of Labor (New York), index of employment for manufacturing industries, 25

Department of Mental Hygiene (New York), 206; *Annual Reports* of, 24, 25

Depression, Great: studies of effects of, on mental-hospital admissions, 13–26, 35, 204, 208; changes in income distribution during, 130–133; relation between income changes during 1929–1933 and 1910–1960, 133–135; patient discharges during, 209; mental hospitalization during, compared with other economic downturns, 236; unemployment, poverty, and welfare during, 237

Deviance, implications of economic change for institutions dealing with, 223–225

Discharges: impact of economic change on, 214–221; inverse relation of, to economic change, 216–217; of patients with functional versus certain organic disorders, 217–219; of senile patients versus those having psychosis with cerebral arteriosclerosis, 220–221; relation of, to family economic status, 221–222

Drugs, tranquilizing, effect of increased use of, on readmission rates, 73

Dunham, H. Warren, 18–19, 196

Dunlop, John T., 132–133

Duration of illness prior to admission, relation to economic change and mental hospitalization according to (19th century), 55–57

Durbin, J., 28, 80

Durbin-Watson Test, 28, 80

Dutch and Flemish, response to economic stress by socioeconomic status of, 151, 153

Economic change(s): social mobility, individual role performance, and, 4–7; and mental illness, 7–11; impact of, on hospital capacity, 204–213; impact of, on patient care, 213–214; impact of, on discharges, 214–221; implications of, for institutions dealing with deviance, 223–225; social and personality disorganization during, 226–231
relation between mental hospitalization and: strength of, in 20th century, 32–35; in 19th century, 35–36, 47–57; in post-1960 period, 36–37; for specific mental disorders, 37–46; by age and sex, 37–41, 48, 58, 64–67, 69, 112–118, 157–167, 170–172; by level of educational attainment, 41–44, 51–55, 71–72, 126–129, 136–140; by marital status, 48, 58, 64–67, 69, 118–120, 172–174, 187; by occupation, 48–51; by duration of illness prior to admission, 55–57; long-term trends in (1915–1967), 57–73; for selected ethnic groups, 62–64, 69–71, 84–85, 120–123, 143–156; sensitivity of, 64–71, 135–143; and readmissions, 73; relative importance of, 77–82; relative importance of large and small (economic changes), 82–83; differences in reactions to (economic change) among different populations, 84–95; by country of birth, 85–91; by country of parents' birth, 93–95; tests of stability of, 74–109; by county (New York) of residence, 99–106; by economic status, 106, 123–126; in

private licensed mental hospitals, 106–108; by emergency admissions, 108; by socioeconomic status, 144–153; direction of, 175–178; question of spuriousness in, 178–182; sequence of causation in, 199–201; implications of empirial relation, 231–243; recent discovery of major relation, 243–248. *See also* Depression, Great; Mental hospitalization; Mental illness

Economic loss: extent of (a primary predictive model), 130–135, 174; model and sensitivity of mental hospitalization to economic change, 135–143; model, predictions based on, 157–160

Economic status: effect of economic change on mental-hospital admissions by, 106, 123–126; of family, relation of discharge to, 221–222

Educational attainment, relation between economic change and mental hospitalization according to, 71–72, 126–129, 136–140; by illness, 41–44; in 19th century, 51–55

Eisenstadt, S. M., 160–164

Employment: and unemployment, rates of as indicators of general economic fluctuations, 6; relation between intermediate-size and short-term trends in mental-hospital admissions and, 32–35; levels, impact of changes in, 201–203. *See also* Economic change

English: mental-hospital admission rates for, 62; impact of economic change on mental-hospital admissions for, 122–123; relation of socioeconomic status of, to economic change of mental-hospital admissions, 151, 153

Epilepsy: sensitivity to economic change for hospital admissions with, 41, 43, 44; discharges of patients with, 215, 217–219

Erikson, Erik H., 164–165

Ethnic background, impact of economic change on mental hospitalization by, 62–64, 69–71, 84–85, 120–123; by country of birth, 85–91; by country of parents' birth, 93–95; for low socioeconomic status groups, 144–149; for high socioeconomic status groups, 149–150; overall relation between ethnicity and socioeconomic status, 150–153; sensitivity to economic downturn by duration of residence of foreign born in United States, 153–156; hospitalization of native versus foreign born, 233–234

Family: impact of, on personality development, 176; relation of discharge to economic status of, 221–222; and development of psychotic patterns of behavior, 227–228

Finnish, response to economic stress by socioeconomic status of, 151, 153

Foreign born, *see* Ethnic background

Fourier analysis, use of, in this study, 27, 35, 47, 64, 205

Freeman, Howard E., 168–170, 188–189

French: mental-hospital admission rates for, 62; response to economic stress by socioeconomic status of, 150, 151, 152–153

Freud, Sigmund, 164, 245–246

Friedsam, H. J., 167

Fritz, C. E., 166

"Frustration-aggression" hypothesis, and intolerance of the mentally ill, 183

Functional psychosis: sensitivity to economic change for hospital admissions with, 42, 44–46, 140; rates of mental-hospital admission by ethnic group for, 62–64; discharges of patients with, 215, 217–219. *See also* Involutional psychosis; Manic-depressive psychosis; Schizophrenia

Germans: mental-hospital admission rates for, 62; impact of economic change on mental-hospital admissions for, 122–123; response to economic stress by socioeconomic status of, 149–151

Gibbs, Jack P., 189–190

Goffmann, Erving, 214

Greeks, response to economic stress by socioeconomic status of, 150, 151

Hartmann, H., 164

Health Opinion Survey, 197

Henry, Andrew F.: on loss of socioeconomic status during economic downturns, 53, 128, 148, 150; on relation of homicide to business cycles, 149; study of suicide by, 190–191, 192

Hollingshead, August B., 142–143, 150, 192

Hospital capacity, impact of economic change on, 204–213; and assumption of overcrowding, 205, 206; and assumption of policy restrictions on number of admissions, 205–210; and assumption of relation between admissions and number of patients, 206, 210–213; and assumption that capacity increases are needed for new admissions, 206, 213

Hyman, Herbert H., 150

Individualism, theme of, and relation between economic change and mental hospitalization, 245–248

Institutions, social, defined, 3

Integrity versus despair, as alternatives for an individual seeking ego identity, 164–165

Involutional psychosis: sensitivity to economic change for hospital admissions with, 38, 42, 44–46, 140; discharges of patients with, 215

Irish: mental-hospital admission rates for, 62; impact of economic change on mental-hospital admissions for, 122–123; response to economic stress by socioeconomic status of, 150, 151, 153; sensitivity of hospitalization of, to economic changes, 182

Italians: mental-hospital admission rates for, 62, 69–70; impact of economic change on mental-hospital admissions for, 122–123; response to economic stress by socioeconomic status of, 150, 151, 153; sensitivity of hospitalization of, to economic changes, 182

Jahoda, Marie, 196, 197

Jews: mental-hospital admission rates for, 62, 70; impact of economic change on mental-hospital admissions for, 122–123; response to economic stress by socioeconomic status of, 149–150, 151, 152; sensitivity of hospitalization of, to economic changes, 182, 187

Keynes, John Maynard, 235

Komora, Paul O., 13–15, 16, 17

Korean War, relation between mental-hospital admissions and, 35, 36

Kris, E., 164

Kubie, Lawrence S., 195

La Pierre, Richard T., 189

Lazarsfeld, Paul F., 171

Lemert, Edwin M., 189

Linden, Maurice E., 164, 165

Liquor legislation, effects of, on mental-hospital admissions, 15, 16

Lowenstein, R. M., 164

MacMahon, Brian, 19–20

Magyars (Hungarians), response to economic stress by socioeconomic status of, 151

Malzberg, Benjamin, 18–19

Manic-depressive psychosis: sensitivity to economic change for hospital admissions with, 37–38, 42, 44–46, 140; discharges of patients with, 215

Marital status: relation between economic change and mental hospitalization according to age and (19th century), 48; long-term changes in relation between economic fluctuations and mental-hospital admissions by (1915–1967), 58, 64–67, 69; impact of economic change on mental-hospital admissions by, 118–120; sensitivity to economic downturn by, 172–174, 187

Marks, E. S., 166

Menderhausen, Horst, study by, on changes in income distribution during Great Depression, 130–134, 135, 136, 139, 157

Mental deficiency: sensitivity to economic change for hospital admissions with, 41, 43–44; correlation between employment and mental-hospital admissions for mentally normal and, 140–141; discharges of patients with, 215, 217–219

Mental-hospital admissions, *see* Mental hospitalization

Mental hospitalization: studies of the effect of Great Depression on, 13–26, 35; for specific mental disorders, 37–46; private, 106–108; emergency, 108; voluntary and court-committed, 142–143. *See also* Economic change, relation between mental hospitalization and; Mental illness

Mental illness: and economic changes, 7–11; economic stress among persons perceived and treated as having, 167–170; predisposition toward or symptoms of, 175–177; definitions of, 194–200, 237–240; and social class, 231–232, 241–242
  intolerance of, 199–200, 239–240; passive and overt, 182–184; test of, to explain differential sensitivity to economic change, 184–187; possible effects of, and mental disorder on different populations of patients, 187–188; evidence of independent studies on, 188–192; possible decrease of, during economic downturns, 193–194; place of, as component in indicator of mental illness, 194–199

Mental Illness and Health, Joint Commission on, 183

Midtown Manhattan Study, 9, 197, 243–244

Mill, John Stuart, 247

Mills, Enid, 199

Mowrer, Ernest R., 17–18

Myers, Jerome K., 150

National Bureau of Economic Research, 6, 24–25, 134–135, 235

Nazis, interpretations of behavior of, 240

Negroes: mental-hospital admission rates for, 62, 69–70; impact of economic change on mental-hospital admissions for, 122–123; response to economic stress by socioeconomic status of, 145–149, 151, 153

Occupation, relation between economic change and mental hospitalization according to (19th century), 48–51

Paresis: sensitivity to economic change for hospital admissions with, 41, 43, 140; discharges of patients with, 215, 217–219

Parsons, Talcott, 190

Pathology, versus social disintegration, 229–230

Patient care, impact of economic change on, 213–214

Patton, Robert E., 206–208

Pearsonian correlation coefficient, 27, 28, 29, 77

Pollock, Horatio M., 15–16

Psychiatric symptoms, 175–177, 199–200; and economic downturns, 239–240

Psychiatry, historical role of, 226–228, 238–239

Psychopathic Hospital of Cook County (Chicago, Ill.), 17–18

Pugh, Thomas F., 19–20

Readmission rates to mental hospitals, 73

Redlich, Frederick C.: study by, of prevalence of treated mental illness, 142–143, 192; on concept of mental illness, 195, 196–197

Roberts, Bertram H., 150

Role failure: predictions based on effects of, 160–167; extent of, 174; during economic downturns, 193

Rosen, Bernard C., 150

Russians, occupational status of, 150

Scandinavians: impact of economic change on mental-hospital admissions for, 122–123; response to economic stress by socioeconomic status of, 151, 153

Schizophrenia: sensitivity to economic change for hospital admissions with, 37, 41–42, 44–46, 140; discharges of patients with, 215, 218; development of patterns of, through familial interaction, 227

Schwartz, Morris S., 182

Scotch: response to economic stress by socioeconomic status of, 151, 152; sensitivity of hospitalization of, to economic change, 182

Senility: sensitivity to economic change for hospital admissions with, 40, 42–43, 44–45, 140; discharges of patients with, 215–216, 220–221

Sex: relation between economic change and mental hospitalization by illness according to age and, 37–41; sensitivity to economic downturn according to, 170–172; discharges of seniles by, 220

Short, James F.: on loss of socioeconomic status during economic downturns, 53, 128, 148, 150; on relation of homicide to business cycles, 149; study of suicide by, 190–191, 192

Simmons, Ozzie G., 168–170, 188–189

Slavic group: impact of economic change on mental-hospital admissions for, 122–123; response to economic stress by socioeconomic status of, 150, 151, 153

Social class, and mental illness, 231–232, 241–242

Social disintegration, 6–7; versus pathology, 229–231

Social mobility, economic change, and individual role performance, 4–7

Social and personality disorganization during economic change, 226–231

Socioeconomic status: effect of economic change on mental-hospital admissions by, 106, 123–126; relation between sensitivity to economic change and mental-hospital admissions of ethnic groups by, 144–153; of family, relation of discharge to, 221–222

Spanish Americans, response to economic stress by socioeconomic status of, 145, 151, 153

Srole, Leo, 149–150, 151

Stirling County Survey, 197–198

Stouffer, Samuel A., 171

Stress situations: three-phase model of reactions to, 21–23; procedure for dealing with dispersed reactions to, 29–30; reactions of total population to, 75–76

Suicide: patterns of, and mental-hospital admissions, 190–192; inverse relation between economic change and, 230

Swallow, Richard (patient), 199

Tizard, J., 140

Tyhurst, J. S., 21–22, 182

Unemployment rates, by age group, and correlation between mental hospitalization and economic indicator, 157–160. *See also* Employment

United States Family Composition Study (1935–1936), 159

Utica State Mental Hospital, 49

Warner, W. Lloyd, 149–150, 151

Wegrocki, Henry J., 195

Weinstein, Abbott S., 206–208

Welsh, response to economic stress by socioeconomic status of, 153

Wilson, Robert N., 75

Wing, John K., 214

World Wars, First and Second, relation between mental-hospital admissions and, 35, 36, 178–179

Woytinsky, W. S., 159

Date